THE WHOLE WORLD IS MY NEIGHBOR

THE WHOLE WORLD IS MY NEIGHBOR

by Bernard F. Meyer, M.M.

With an introduction by Richard Cardinal Cushing

FIDES PUBLISHERS, INC.

NOTRE DAME, INDIANA

Cum Permissu Superiorum: MARYKNOLL

NIHIL OBSTAT:
Louis J. Putz, C.S.C.
University of Notre Dame

IMPRIMATUR:
Leo A. Pursley, D.D.
Bishop of Fort Wayne-South Bend

The Whole World Is My Neighbor is a rewritten and enlarged version of *Your Life to Share,* St. Paul Publications, Bombay, India, 1962.

LIBRARY OF CONGRESS CATALOG CARD NUMBER: 64-22893

TO MARY

MOTHER OF MANKIND

Glory and Exemplar of the royal priesthood conferred on all the People of God, who shared totally with us, not counting the cost, the Life that had been placed in her keeping.

FOREWORD

These reflections on the lay apostolate around the world are the result of four years spent in a study tour which began in 1958. The trip took me to 30 countries of Asia, Africa and Latin America, as also several in Europe. From 1918 to 1950 I had been a missionary in South China, so was already familiar with that field.

The original purpose of the tour was to compare successful apostolic methods used in various areas of the world with a view of their adaptation elsewhere. It became quickly evident, however, that the role of the Christian must be carried out today in a very different context from even one generation ago. Rapid social change tends to modify all of life in the modern world, including the response to religion. In the traditional cultures of the past, religion was always taken to be an essential part of life, even basic to it. Today there is an obviously growing dichotomy between religion and life, accompanied by increasing secularization of culture.

Modern man sees life in a far more dynamic way than did his forebears, and if religion is to have real relevance for him it must be presented as our contact with the infinite Trinitarian Source of all dynamism. This contact, moreover, is not for man in his spiritual nature only, but for him as a unique composite of spirit and matter which can achieve its true development only as an integrated whole. The complete Christian, therefore, must concern himself with building a social structure in which the dynamism of the Holy Trinity will be most fully operative, not with his personal sanctification alone. His being in society is part of God's creative purpose for him. He must try to understand the meaning of God's plan and cooperate to carry it out. The missionary who seeks only to bring as many as possible to Christ accomplishes only part of his work. He must train them to live as "whole" Christians, which involves forming them to be leaders of a new society inspired by Christian principles.

Except for some personal experiences and observations, this book lays little claim to originality. I have tried to bring together material from many sources to illustrate various aspects of the situation faced by the Christian today in trying to fulfill his dynamic vocation. I wish here to express grateful acknowledgment for it all. Perhaps readers and discussion groups can find here a starting point to pursue further the deeper meaning of man's vocation in God's world. God made man in His own image to help carry out on earth the creating, redeeming and sanctifying work of the Holy Trinity. Man's vocation is the perfecting of both men and things, so that on the last day God may gather them all to Himself for a new heaven and a new earth.

BERNARD F. MEYER, M.M.
Maryknoll, New York

INTRODUCTION

When the lawyer, "wishing to justify himself," asked our Divine Lord, "And who is my neighbor?", he heard in answer the beautiful, instructive parable of the good Samaritan. The parable, of course, was meant for Christians of all ages, but its application must change with the changing times. In this book, Father Meyer sets out to examine how the people of God of this age—an age different even from that of a generation ago—can integrate their daily human lives with their religion; how they, like the good Samaritan, can bring their beliefs to practical action; how they can be "neighbors" to the people of the world.

He points out the necessity of immediate action by rather alarming statistics. Christians of all beliefs represented about half of humanity in 1900; they formed a third in 1950; by the year 2000 they will be less than a fourth. Latin America, alone, for example, needs more priests and lay apostles than there are at present in the entire Church of North America and Europe. Obviously, then, a great share of the burden must be carried by the laity who are so much more numerous.

Nor does the author minimize the problem involved. Because Catholics, at work in business and in the professions, are out of contact with their neighbors and fellow-parishioners the greater part of the time, there is danger that they take an impersonal view of life in their parish and fail to realize the full potential of the lay apostolate. This potential does not consist in 5% of the parish spending its time for the 95%; it consists in their inspiring the other 95% to make Christ known among their fellow-men.

To his task, Father Meyer brings an imposing background. He spent thirty-two years in the mission fields of South China where he saw, first hand, what the enemies of the Church can do. He saw them send ordinary men of conviction out among other ordinary men, and saw them, by their conviction and zeal, win thousands to the false and disastrous philosophy of communism. With this background, the author then travelled the world for four years to observe and compare apostolic methods for use and application in the lay apostolate. In this masterful book he gives us the results of his years of experience and observation. He gives a practical handbook for those of us who appreciate our responsibilities as Christians. It is a complete hand-book, for it discusses every aspect of the lay apostolate. His treatment of education, charity in action, the roles of bishop, priests, nuns, and brothers, the apostolate in parish and community is most complete and informative. He discusses lay movements with which we are most familiar and others about which we have heard and know little. Above all, he enlivens his treatment of the subject with inspiring examples, interesting anecdotes, and forceful quotations from responsible and recognized authorities.

Father Meyer has written a book for our times, and points out an age-old lesson, so often forgotten, when he warns us that we would be missing the point of our being created in God's image if we looked upon the Christian life simply as a kind of passive fidelity, the avoidance of sin, and the enduring of present difficulties in view of a better life to come. On the contrary, we have a duty, as Pope Pius XII so strongly put it, "of bringing about the return of modern society to the sources rendered sacred by the Word of God made flesh." And the Pope added sternly: "If ever Christians neglect this duty . . . they will be committing treason against the God-Man."

For reminding us of this duty, for showing us in detail how we can fulfill it in our day and age, I am most grateful to Father Meyer and heartily endorse his book.

RICHARD CARDINAL CUSHING
Archbishop of Boston

TABLE OF CONTENTS

1. THE PEOPLE OF GOD IN THE WORLD

Pope Pius XII, in the customary address to new Cardinals at the first consistory of his pontificate, told them: "The faithful —the laity, to be more precise—find themselves today in the front ranks of the Church. Through them the Church is the vital principle of human society." In those few words the Holy Father stated God's plan for the Catholic laity in the world: it is they alone, who are in society, that can make it a Christian society.

The word "laity" comes from the Greek *laikos,* member of the *laos,* the People. When God promised offspring to the childless Abraham, He declared that He would make them His chosen people that they might be the people of His Son and progenitors of a new race whose heritage was heaven. The Jewish leaders rejected that exalted vocation and so God raised up new children to Abraham by spiritual birth from Christ to be His new chosen people, heirs of His kingdom and called to bring all men to share it. A kingdom is not constituted simply by having a king. It requires also a People, a people who have a sense of solidarity and act as one in all that concerns their welfare and common destiny. They are proud of their citizenship in the kingdom and have a dynamic desire to speak of it everywhere. God's People are, moreover, under a command from their King to spread His kingdom to all men.

When we speak of a "people" the idea of men engaged in action comes at once to mind. The farmer, the worker, the shopkeeper, the housewife, soldier, official, teacher, young people and old, all show this human characteristic to express themselves in action according to their state of life. Now the great modern religious discovery, or re-discovery, is that the People of God desire and need to express their religion in the concrete actions of daily life. Pope Leo XIII said that man is made to work, to act, as the bird to fly. God created man a composite of soul and body, and his soul can express itself only through bodily action. If, however, God's People get the idea that a part of their life of action as a people is not connected with their relationship to their King, that religion is manifested chiefly by individual and internal action, then they will find it difficult to share the common life of the kingdom with others by their action as a People. In reality, God Himself become Man preached a kingdom of love and justice, social as well as spiritual. He assigned to His People as a corporate task the bringing of all men into that kingdom. It can never be established by a few priests and specialized apostles; every citizen must spiritually beget new citizens.

A. Bearing Witness as a People of God

In a very thoughtful book, *The People of God,* Abbot Vonier writes, "This appellation is not only frequent in Christian literature, it is directly scriptural. In the New Testament it is used as often as the word 'Church,' while it fills every page of the Old Testament . . . We know that the Church means a plentitude of supernatural graces, an entirely divine institution, a creation of the Holy Spirit, a fullness of *charismata;* such features are not commonly associated with the word 'People.' On the other hand, the acts of divine providence, the deeds of God's mercy and justice, the varieties of human powers and merits, the tribulations and successes of life, the external works of religion, and many other things of which we shall speak, denote more directly the ways of a People."

Abbot Vonier points out how this conception of Catholics

as a People helps to integrate our daily human lives with religion. He writes, "Much can be learned from this proclamation by God's messengers, and there can be a certain narrowness of treatment in the doctrines of the Church which is not an uncommon danger even for the theologian; his concept of the Church may tend to be too mystical and too internal. This narrowness is corrected if we associate considerations concerning the People of God with the dogmas of the Church of Christ . . . A 'people' is not defined by spiritual categories, but whether it is defined or not . . . the concept of a People adds to the Church the permanent and irrefragable character of externalness. If we look at the Church as a People, we are saved from those tendencies which would make of the Church an invisible society of saints and elect."

Such tendencies, warns the Abbot, might even lead to paralysis of the Church's social action by playing into the hands of those who seek to deny her such a role. "My most ardent wish," he states, "is to make Catholics understand how manifold and rich is their life in Christ; how they constitute in the world a new society, of whose existence the powers of evil are extremely jealous. . . . the movements to which we give the generic name of 'modern revolution' have made it their task to deprive Christianity of being a People in this world. There may be individual Christians, says the revolutionary, but they must not form a Christian society—a policy which takes its cue from the Gospel; he does not want a People of God; nationhood must be entirely secularized."

What would be the life of a People under God their King? It is sketched for us in a few words. "A People of God would be one for whom God is the supreme interest, the ultimate value, the beginning and end of all undertakings, the final arbiter of all issues; so that men would live for Him without any reservation. . . . Such a people, then, would sing the praises of God whether employed in ploughing the fields on this earth or contemplating the Divinity in heaven. Its men and women would beget children in this life with as much holiness of intention as they would associate with the pure spirits. They would praise God with the gifts of the material world as joyfully as with the intellectual comprehension of the mysteries of eternity. Both great and small would praise Him . . ."

Finally, we are shown how the concept of themselves as a People enables the laity to fulfill the function assigned to them by Pope Pius XII of making the Church the vital principle of human society. "Not only prayer," Abbot Vonier tells us in conclusion, "action also is intimately associated with this undying title. One might suggest that theology of the people of God would be most helpful towards a deeper understanding of the claims of 'Catholic Action.' . . . It is positively wrong to restrict the service of God to ritual or sacramental functions; all God's people must serve Him with the unlimited variety of their endowments. If the Church is not only a supernatural institution but—as we have tried to show in this book —a People of God, it ought to be evident that no one need remain outside the scheme of active cooperation in the realization of God's plan. . . . To take away from the Christian people the idea and sentiment of universal consecration would be a disastrous procedure; on the other hand, to speak of them in terms of a People of God is not merely a high compliment, but also a most practical form of encouragement. A divine people is never inactive; it has a holy ambition, it unceasingly aspires to the establishment of the Kingdom of God" *(Collected Works,* Newman Press, 1952).

B. Today's Challenge to God's People

The Church is faced today with an apostolic crisis, and the ideas of Abbot Vonier suggest how it may be met—by the united strength of a great People. We are a People of more than 500,000,000, and just as a nation is mobilized when faced with some great danger, so the apostolic situation of the Church today calls for a universal spiritual mobilization. If, for example, we consider the world missionary effort in relation to the "population explosion" now taking place, a most serious situation is revealed. During the last 25 years, while the earth's population increased by 700 million, the increase of Catholics by birth or conversion did not surpass 13 million. For one non-Christian who is converted each year, there are more than 40 new ones born into paganism. Catholics formed 19.1 per cent of the world's people in 1954; today, 1964, we are scarcely 18.0 per cent. Christians of all beliefs represented about half of humanity in 1900; they formed a third in 1950; by the year 2000 they will be less than a fourth.

At present almost half the annual conversions of the Church are in Africa, but the Catholics there have reached only 20 million, or 4 per cent of the world total. The Moslems are advancing in Africa twice as fast as we are. A French authority states that between 1931 and 1951 the number of Moslems in Africa rose from 40 million to 80 million (*Le Monde,* Paris, January 16, 1957). By now there would be 100 million. Judging from today's trends, Africa by the year 2000 may well have 400 million people: Moslems 220 million, Catholics 60 million, Protestants 40 million, pagans or no religion 80 million. In Latin America the nearly 200,000,000 people are 85 per cent baptized and form one-third of the People of God. Before the end of the century Latin America will have over 500 million people, but how many will be Catholics? From gradual loss of confidence in the social role of God's People great numbers seem to be at the crisis point where they may easily turn to other leaders. In Asia we may expect all present figures to approximately double by the year 2000. Asia would have about 3.0 billion people, of whom 80 million Catholics, but more than half of these in the Philippines.

If the Church goes on becoming more and more a minority in the total of mankind, how can she fulfill her mission to convert the world? The prospect of a world where the Church embraces a constantly shrinking sector that scarcely counts at national and world levels should stir us out of any complacency about certain particular successes apart from the full picture. In spite of the greatly increased world appeal of the Holy Father, for example, secularist humanism continues its forward march. The world may bestow great praise on his social encyclicals yet draw no closer to the Church. Only the People of God can demonstrate how the encyclicals are to be lived out in life and provide a social climate that others will desire to enjoy. This requires concerted action by all the People of God, in the words of Abbot Vonier, ". . . no one need remain outside the scheme of active co-operation in the realization of God's plan." No piecemeal action, whether in terms of area covered or actionists involved, can solve the problem. The People of God must act as one to make the dynamism of the Holy Spirit penetrate human society everywhere in the world.

The entire 500 million People of God must be mobilized as a single apostolic force. Latin America alone, for example, needs more priests and lay apostles than there are at present in the entire Church of North America and Europe. The Church would not and could not attempt to do their apostolic work for the Catholics of any part, but they must be helped to develop their own resources. When a people mobilize, all personal and particular considerations become secondary to the needs of the emergency. Some 5 per cent are given special training and sent to the front lines wherever there is need of added strength. The others work long hours to supply them, form groups and committees to embrace all in the community of effort. Even children are caught up in the common purpose. A surge of dynamism is generated which surprises even those taking part and they wonder why it could not be always operative.

The Communists are doing just that. We leave the work of the apostolate to a few, while every Communist tries to influence five people. It makes one shiver to think on the end result of such multiplication, called "geometric progression" by mathematicians. Our own convert work is chiefly by "arithmetic progression," that is, by addition. It is told that when Pope Pius XI was preparing his encyclical, *On Atheistic Communism,* he sent a young priest through Europe to study the Communists' method of penetration. It was found to be by a "person to person" program. The Communists set up "cells" everywhere, in factories, schools, offices, government departments. All discussions in the cells were "polarized" towards action, setting up other cells to win more people. The average Catholic priest spends his time year in and year out ministering to the same lay Catholics of his parish. The perhaps 5 per cent of lay apostles occupy themselves chiefly with the other 95 per cent. But the Communists pass on what they receive. Extension is for them an almost automatic process because they train for it. They are fully mobilized and with the goal to "win the world in this generation."

In less than 50 years the Communists have already won more than one-third of the world's people. Let us not deceive ourselves that it was always achieved by the use of force, which is forbidden to us. France and Italy, free Catholic countries, have the largest Communist parties in Europe outside of Russia. During 1948-1949 I saw the Communist take-over of China, which we had told ourselves would never accept a philosophy that negated the human values of its culture, especially in family life. But Communism did not present itself as a philosophy in the traditional sense. It appealed to the people as a practical doctrine by which they could enjoy the human dignity that is every man's right. "Is that bad?" people would ask us. A most important factor favoring the Communists was a wide disaffection towards the nationalist government because of the economic situation. In 1918, when I arrived in China, there was sufficient food, but by 1948 the population had risen from 250 million to 450 million and little had been done to increase food production. Imagine what would happen if our own food supply were cut in half!

During this mission study trip I have visited underdeveloped countries with a total of almost 1.0 billion people. Inquiry brought out that, except in Africa with its lower population density, landless peasants who live by casual work formed all the way from 40 to 80 per cent of the population. Thirty years ago their average daily wage for the 200-250 days a year they had work would buy 8-10 pounds of rice. Today it will buy 3-4 pounds, sometimes even less! The free world must act fast with specific programs for increasing food production to ease this burden which daily grows more intolerable for the great masses who exist on the edge of destitution in the villages and slums of these countries. The main Communist strategy is simple. It is to keep the free world off balance by alternately threatening and peaceful gestures to prevent our acting effectively in the underdeveloped countries. Meanwhile, as the struggle for livelihood becomes daily more hopeless from the pressure of population growth on the still primitive farming methods, those countries will fall easily to Communist propaganda.

When Lenin said the road to Communist world victory led through Peking, he made China the symbol of all the underdeveloped countries of Asia, Africa and Latin America where day by day the rich grow richer and the poor grow poorer. The Communist plan for take-over of these countries is apparently aimed at some point before their new and inexperienced governments can solve the problems of food and the adequate use of human resources. In countries where food is relatively plentiful, they resort to bribery and armed terrorism. In the others they have only to mount their propaganda and wait for the fruit to ripen. One notes, incidentally, that Communist aid to needy countries rarely takes the form of experimental farms or fertilizer factories to help increase the food supply. Japan, with 100 million people, produces and uses more artificial fertilizer than over one billion people of the underdeveloped countries. An exception is little Taiwan (Formosa), for fifty years under the Japanese, which has a per acre rice crop second to that of Japan. If India used the Japanese rice-growing methods, she would have plenty of food for her 400 million people and a surplus for export! Why send her grain, made far more costly by shipping and handling expenses, instead of helping her produce her own?

Let it not be thought that we are here confusing the spiritual and social apostolates. For the People of God they are part of the one life, as Abbot Vonier has so abundantly made clear. The vocation of the Catholic layman is precisely to make the unity of the Mystical Body a reality in a social as well as a spiritual way. True human progress according to God's design consists in developing the complete human nature composed of a spiritual soul and a material body united in a way that is unique in all creation. It is wrong to think of Catholic social action as concerned only or even chiefly with material things. Only animals have material action alone and only spirits have spiritual action alone. Men in society are meant to reflect the image of the Holy Trinity in all their mutual relationships of daily life, in work and similar activities as well as in prayer. The spiritual is, of course, primary, and sad experience keeps constantly reminding us that social action unaccompanied by spiritual witness as well is barren, for man does not live by bread alone.

C. In a Massive Crisis, Massive Action

If up to now we have not mobilized the People of God in combined spiritual and social action from a sense of dedication to Christ our King, perhaps our present confrontation by the Communist world vision and global campaign may convince us to do so. Certainly we can no longer feel that we do our part by forming little groups of lay apostles here and there whose contacts may be counted on their fingers and are themselves so little successful in multiplying contacts through others. A student of organization methods wrote me: "The successful penetration of the Communists everywhere is based on a tremendous multiplication of contacts plus a good disciplinary organization." We have no program comparable to theirs among the vast masses who are the bearers of life in the world and who by our failure to "reach" them accept Marxism by default as the only social system they have heard of that claims to meet modern needs. Whether the social teachings of Christ or Marx are to become better known among mankind depends on the whole-heartedness with which we undertake to make the full teaching of Christ known by men everywhere. That is where the technique of multiplied contacts must operate. We do not believe that souls are converted by techniques, but the grace of conversion can enter the picture only after Christ has been made known through all the communication means.

To develop the full potential of the lay apostolate most surely does not consist in having perhaps 5 per cent of a parish as apostles who spend most of their time working for the other 95 per cent, going around in a circle of the baptized. In the mobilization of God's People, the role of the 5 per cent is to inspire the other 95 per cent in their parish, their school, to make Christ known among their fellow men. If the 95 per cent are helped to become apostles they will thereby themselves acquire an active and dynamic approach to their Faith instead of the relatively passive and formal one so common. Beginning with the visible, tangible apostolic field of their own area, the circle would expand gradually to include the city, the state, the country, the world. Surely a parish of 1000 faithful, a college with 1000 students, could send and maintain an average of 20 apostles in other areas besides a much larger number working at home. They would not go merely as individuals, but as teams sent by their community and backed with its support. That would mean the whole Church sending out a really world-conquering force of 10,000,000 apostles. Do we have the vision, the conviction, the faith to accept the challenge?

In general, the apostolic teams would acquire experience

working nearby before going to more distant fields. Some would go during holidays from school or work, but as many as possible for longer periods. Every young Mormon gives two years of his life to missionary work away from home. The Legion of Mary among the three million Catholics of Ireland sends nearly 2000 members to England each year during their vacations from school or work. They take even menial positions to support themselves, then spend evenings and weekends in an intensive apostolate. Some strong student teams might transfer to schools threatened by Communist domination to provide a rallying point for non-communist students. Every year in the United States, apostles by the tens of thousands should go from the North and East to the South and West, or to the Latin American front which is in such need, some even further afield. European Catholics might go to Africa, as well as to needy areas of their own continent. Indeed, with modern travel facilities, lay apostles can go anywhere in the world that they are needed. In Asia, many thousands should go from the South to the North of India and from the Philippines other thousands should penetrate all Southeast Asia with the Good News.

These would be no "fly-by-night" apostles leaving behind them little of permanence. Teams from each parish or school should return every year to the same area until at least a nucleus has been established among the people there. It is also essential to go with the correct notion of the apostolate, which is not that they do certain work "for" others but that they encourage and train people of the area to act. They would combine the spiritual and social apostolates as a twofold expression of God's goodness towards mankind. Infinite Goodness created us because "goodness desires to share itself." God desires them not only to know Him as a Father but also to share His created gifts. It was not part of His creative plan that any man should lack the opportunity to gain a decent livelihood for his family. Not all the hunger and degradation suffered by so many is simply the fault of those who directly exploit them, too often that is possible because we have not made God's plan for mankind known to them.

Who shall be responsible for creating and forming this apostolic force throughout the world? Clearly, it must be first of all the leaders whom God has appointed. The bishop by his office is not only priest and teacher, he is also the leader of his people and with him are associated all his priests, as well as brothers and nuns in their own vocations. At present their time is chiefly occupied with caring for Catholics in the parishes and schools, "saving the saved." Even in the mission field, when a priest's converts reach beyond a thousand they absorb so much of his time that the number of new converts tends to fall off. In Latin America a missionary observed: "We devote ourselves to our first duty, parishes and schools, but I keep asking myself if that is enough. We are developing a good program of religious formation but have done very little to train our people for action in the social institutions that have so strong an influence on their lives. Is that not one of the chief reasons why in reality the society around us is becoming daily more secular, even leftist, and we lose so many of our young people?" This same reflection troubled the missionaries who had seen the Communist take over in China and those I met elsewhere who were aware of Marxism spreading around them. "What should we have done?"

It is not something that a few missionaries lost among millions can do as individuals. There must be concerted action so that many become involved in the work of Christ. To have really mass movements of men towards the Church, or at least become sympathetic towards the Church, there must first be a mass apostolic movement towards them by the Church. The conversion of three thousand at Pentecost was not by Peter alone, but by the whole group of about 120 apostles and disciples who carried his message out among the crowd. Then those three thousand themselves became apostles in all the districts from which they came, as far away as Antioch and even Rome. Antioch became a strong center of the faith. It was there that the term "Christians" was first applied to the believers and there Peter established his see for some years before going to Rome. Yet the first converts were made by laymen and only later did the apostles in Jerusalem send them Barnabas as pastor.

Obviously, the burden of the apostolate must be carried by the laity, who are so much more numerous and through whom, in the words of the Holy Father, "the Church is the vital principle of human society," because they are society. But the basic responsibility belongs to those in authority, the bishops and priests, as well as brothers and nuns in their schools and other institutions. Here is the primary reason why they should all bring in lay people to handle much of the routine work of their office, so that they themselves may be more free to organize the Church's apostolate at every level. If they could all free themselves to devote 20 per cent of their working time to planning and organizing the lay apostolate, what a change would appear. Even in the missions, it is now possible to have lay volunteers take much routine work off their hands and some could help with organizing the apostolate itself. For it is only by Holy Orders that bishop and priest stand apart. Their other powers can be delegated to the laity and must be to provide an adequate number of leaders and teachers to carry out the command of Christ.

It has been said that the battles of the world have been won, in the last resort, by average men without special qualifications. The great struggle now already joined for men's minds and hearts will also be won by average men, with all the strength and weakness of average men. The Communists base their entire method on the concept that an ordinary man of conviction who goes out among other ordinary men with one basic idea that they do not have is bound to win. Let no one say, "Our people do not have that kind of zeal." Try them, by showing your own. To demand sacrifices for the faith often awakens people to its value more than direct instruction. We give too little attention to changing the direction of our people's lives towards fulfillment through self-sacrifice rather than through self-satisfaction. We require of them certain religious practices, but fail to arouse their deeper capacity for giving themselves. It constitutes a problem in religious as well as lay vocations, as is evident from the special attraction of the missionary vocation.

The problem is brought more clearly into focus by this taunt printed in 1957 by a French Communist newspaper: "The gospel is a much more powerful weapon for the renovation of society than our Marxist view of the world. Yet it is we who shall conquer you in the end. Of our salaries and wages we keep only what is absolutely necessary and the rest we give up for propaganda purposes. To this same propaganda we also devote our leisure time and part of our vacation. You, however, give only a little time and scarcely any money for the spreading of Christ's gospel. How can anyone believe in the all-surpassing value of this gospel if you do not practice it, if you do not spread it, if you sacrifice neither your time nor your money for that purpose?" May it not be said that one of the chief reasons why so many young Catholics today fail to appreciate their religion is because it does not challenge them? We do not appeal to the natural idealism of their age, offer them a cause to work and suffer for that would give them the sense of worthwhile achievement, of self-value, that youth need in their formative years to acquire a true concept of what man can do and be. That is left to the Communists.

D. Christ's Fishers of Men Used Nets

As we reflect on the certainty that when our Lord told the Apostles to "make disciples of all peoples," He would not have commanded His Church to undertake an impossible task, our minds go back over the Gospel story to seek a clue. We are told that when He stood by the Sea of Galilee and promised to make Peter and Andrew, James and John fishers of men, they at once "left their nets." It seems clear that those progenitors of the Church's long missionary line who were used to large-scale fishing with nets would be most unlikely to think of their vocation to be fishers of men in terms of one-by-one conversions with hook and line methods. Indeed, they were to more than once hear from the Master's own lips, "Launch out into the deep and let down the nets." May we not see here a sign that was afterwards fulfilled in their missionary careers right from Pentecost with its 3000 conversions? Indeed, our Lord seemed to be taking this idea for granted when He said, "Again, the kingdom of heaven is like a net cast into the sea that gathered in fish of every kind" (Matt. 13:47).

It is a curious commentary on the present Christian mind that it tends to consider large-scale conversions as somehow lacking in sincerity, yet few of us would be Catholics today if our ancestors had not come into the Church by vast movements. Might it be an example of the "arrived" being ashamed of their origins, or is it due simply to a deficient sense of history? The Lombards in Italy, the Visigoths in Spain (first Arians but later won over), the Germans and Saxons in central Europe, the Scandinavians to the North, the Slavs, Magyars and Russians in the East, became Catholics as entire peoples within relatively short periods of time. Rheims cathedral is the memorial of the mass conversion of the Franks (French) under Clovis and Clotilda. St. Patrick before his death had converted all Ireland. The very terms of the commission by which Pope Gregory sent St. Augustine the monk to England implied mass conversions: "Do not destroy the pagan temples, but baptize them with holy water, put up altars there and holy relics." Quite obviously that could not be done unless the entire community to whom a temple belonged were agreed to give up worship of the pagan gods.

The plan followed in the Christian formation of all these

peoples was very much like that used by the Apostles for mass conversions. Such large numbers could not receive a great deal of instruction before baptism and chief reliance was placed on their formation in the faith by the community. This was above all necessary with the illiterate tribes of Europe. The instructions of Pope Gregory to St. Augustine are a clear guide: "Where now exists the custom of offering sacrifices to their diabolical idols, permit them to celebrate on the same date Christian festivities under another form. For example, on the day of the feast of the Holy Martyrs, have the faithful erect shelters of branches and organize *agapes.* By permitting them such external joys, the internal joys will be the more easily acquired. One cannot eliminate all the past from stubborn customs at one time. A mountain is not climbed by jumping, but by slow steps."

The pioneers who planted the Faith in South America, Mexico and the Philippines were few and assigned "prayer leaders" in each village who took the people through the prayers and small catechism by rote. Yet in a relatively short time whole peoples were Christian. Whatever may be the present situation as regards religious practice, the faith is in their blood and many have given witness with their lives as in the 1910 persecution in Mexico. The chief problem has been lack of clergy since the independence movements drove out the friars; as late as 1910 half the priests of Yucatan State in Mexico were expelled. The number forced out of the Philippines even after the American occupation following the war with Spain is said to be nearly a thousand and scarcely ten came then from the U.S. to replace them.

While Filipino Catholics number 30 millions, India has little more than 5 million out of 400 million people, nearly 90 per cent of them among the half of the population living in the southern part of the country. Most are descendants of mass converts. Within a period of one month St. Francis Xavier baptized 10,000 Malabar Coast fishermen and in two years about 25,000 in all, not to mention those baptized by others there. Today in those parishes it is common to have 90 per cent adult Communions every Sunday. Long before the time of St. Francis there had been the "Thomas Christian" communities, which today still form a good proportion of the Catholics in India. The famous Father Lievens north of Calcutta baptized 10,000 during August, 1886; in October, 20,000; in January, 1887, another 25,000. When ill-health forced him to leave India the movement continued, though at a slower pace.

A study made several years ago in India showed that the mass converts with less instruction had persevered better than smaller groups with much more instruction. A missionary of India writes: "An isolated Christian village cannot survive in a pagan region. It would be impossible to find Catholic husbands for the girls, all the neighboring villages being non-Christians. It is only when groups are converted, as in the mass conversion movements, that villages and families can persevere" (E. de Meulder, S.J., *Christ to the World,* 1962). In 1961 I met a missionary from west India who told me that in his area it had been decided not to baptize anyone until several thousand were ready in order to insure mutual support in the faith and they found the catechumens zealous to bring more so they themselves could be baptized. It would appear that both the original tradition and practical considerations favor large-scale conversions, whether by directly mass movements or intense multiplication of individual contacts. Today neither of these receives the emphasis it deserves.

Let us not think of large-scale conversions only as an incident of history that is past. Its day returns again and again, though the pattern keeps changing according to circumstances. The Apostles had mass movements, but the method of multiplied personal contacts perhaps accounted for most converts in the early Church. Europe again saw mass movements, similarly Latin America, because of political circumstances. St. Francis Xavier and Father Lievens won the gratitude of the people by rescuing them from debt slavery to the money lenders, but they also knew how to relate their social action to God's love for His human children, which many engaged in social action have failed to do. In the early Church it was especially the Christian spirit of mutual love in a selfish "dog-eat-dog" society. Some missionaries have estimated that there should now be 30 million Catholics in India instead of 5 million, if people's searching and readiness had been recognized in the past. Africa should have an additional 20 millions. Father De Meulder calls North India, with 500,000 Catholics in among 200 million pagans, "a huge empty cradle waiting for the Babe of Bethlehem. The tragedy does not consist in secondary questions; it lies in the emptiness of the cradle" (*Christ to the World*, 1962).

Today vast millions of emerging peoples are searching for a new identity among the nations. They seek a new political identity in self-government, a new social identity in education and economic progress. By the same token, they seek a new religious identity in keeping with man's new knowledge of himself. It is clear also that the new identities will be accepted as peoples, following a more or less common pattern, not as individuals. Their new religious identity, moreover, will not develop in isolation from the others but will form with them a unified culture. For the Church's religious mission among them to succeed, it must be presented as inspiring a new culture. The mass movements of all those peoples in search of a new identity represents a great turning-point in world history comparable to Europe's search of 1500 years ago. Can we devise a large-scale method of showing them God's plan for man's development appropriate to today's circumstances, when building a new society is again uppermost in men's minds?

In Japan, the results from several religious surveys reveal a state of flux, with only about 30 per cent of younger people professing a personal religion as compared with 70 per cent among their parents. Yet 56 per cent thought that people should be more concerned with religion and 94.4 per cent considered that each one has responsibility for his own acts. One reason for our relatively few converts in Japan may be the fact that in its close-knit society there is great hesitancy to take such a step alone. Another is the common tendency among the Japanese to look on religion as a matter of personal sentiment. Few of them are aware of the Church's deep social interest. Certain "native religions," which are having a tremendous growth, make it a point to saturate whole areas with their presentation and to get their converts undertaking action as close-knit groups. It is interesting to note that they emphasize a monotheistic concept of God, which makes them appear suited to provide a more modern religious identity.

Apparently a new missionary approach is needed, a new spirit of ecumenism based on the unity of all men under the fatherhood of God. This may involve having certain groups occupy for some time an intermediate stage on their way to the Church. A missionary in the Archdiocese of Dakar, West Africa, Henri Gravand, C.S.Sp., describes an example of this in *Christ to the World* (1963, No. 2). In his mission district of 50,000 pagans many young people became catechumens. One day a group of adults from a village asked for baptism and not long after a similar group from another village. Seeing their children on the eve of baptism, they desired not to be separated from them in the next world. They were told the requirements for baptism, including monogamous marriage. A number were polygamists and all said that they could not learn a new way of life at their age, though they were happy to see the children become Christians. Before long, many in both villages and in others were enrolled as Moslems. The first even built a mosque beside the chapel. They explained, "The Catholic religion is the most beautiful, but only the young can take it. We have built the mosque beside the chapel hut of our children who are Christians so we can pray to the same God side by side."

The missionaries discussed the problem in their district meetings and finally one proposed the idea of a special group, a fellowship of the "God-fearing" as Moses decreed for Gentiles who lived among the Jews. An African priest suggested a name with proper African Christian coloring, "Relatives of the Christians." For the African there is no bond more powerful than that of relationship, even a distant one. Enrollment was at a public ceremony where various speakers stressed the "one Christian family" idea and its twofold basis: God one Father of all and Christ through whom alone man can come to the Father. Each person publicly declared his support of the Christian faith and his desire to die in it. He received a membership card with his old name and a new Christian name. The author explains that "giving one's name" is a symbol for giving one's entire person, and "accepting a name" means recognition of another's authority. The practice of the early Church allowed adults to bear a Christian name and support Christianity without having received baptism. The Emperor Constantine himself was apparently of that category. A French theologian, Father A. M. Henry, O.P., told the missionaries that "there is reason to rejoice at this rediscovery of an institution that is more and more necessary in the Church today."

Father Gravand states that the chief danger to avoid would be making the pledge a purely secular one by stressing its secondary aspects, such as mutual assistance or the membership card. The essential point is the desire of faith in Christ and desire of the sacraments, at least before death, and that should be made clear in the ceremony itself by a special prayer and a sign. These might consist of the first step towards baptism which the early Church called the "catechumens' sacrament." The prayer would be the exorcism in the native language and the sign the giving of blessed salt, with an explanation of both. The members should also be initiated into simple Christian prayer, with some plan for them to sanctify the day of the Lord and have them hear the Word of God several times a year. They would also be urged to practice charity for love of God, as giving their natural helpfulness an eternal value. In a letter written later Father Gravand stated that of more than 4,000 pagans enrolled in one area, over 300 later entered the baptism course and more than 100 went on to baptism. Moreover, some 8,000 young people had already been baptized. The whole area is becoming oriented towards the Church and the spread of Moslemism there has practically stopped.

2. GOD'S PEOPLE IN A CHANGING WORLD

When Rip van Winkle of Washington Irving's famous story returned to his village after a sleep of twenty years in the mountains, he found life going on pretty much as before. The most noticeable changes were in the people themselves. But a modern Rip van Winkle would find the way of life itself unfamiliar. Greater social changes have occurred during the past 50 years, and the last 20 at a much accelerated pace, than in the previous 1500 years.

Cardinal Suhard of Paris in his eloquent pastoral letter on the Church in the modern world, *Growth or Decline?*, calls today's world changes *a crisis of unification.* He writes, "The stages by which it has come about are well known: the great discoveries of science engendered movement and speed; space has changed its dimensions; the airplane has welded continents and linked up the Antipodes. Communications have multiplied. Everything–production, consumption, distribution, economics and finance–all is now done on an international scale. The humblest object of daily life comes from the ends of the earth. Each of us depends on the rest of mankind for the bare fact of survival. And it is the same in the spheres of feeling and thought. The press is everywhere, and with it the film; for the cinema everywhere reproduces the same cosmopolitan features upon the screen. And the ether, which knows no frontiers, takes the music, the news and the thought of all to all indiscriminately. Radio and television are the brain and the nerve force which, for the first time in its history, have made the pulses of the planet beat with the same rhythm at the same moment in time."

The Cardinal states that a common civilization is coming into being, not simply in language, law and commerce as with the Roman empire, but a uniform way of life and a uniform type of man, a "world humanism." He observes, "The modern man who is coming into existence seems in truth to proceed from an organic unity and an inner principle of life; and it is the same with the City he is preparing for his use. The most obvious feature of that new humanism is its technical character. Born of scientific discovery and the machine, to them it owes the style it has everywhere assumed, it is based on them, it relies on them to bring the coming order into being. The scientific outlook is daily ousting classical culture and taking its place. The object of thought has changed; the world of pure ideas has been abandoned for efficient action.

"This effort man is making is not individual. Henceforth, each has need of all. The unit of work is no longer the artisan but the team. Bonds are being knit which stretch far beyond the frontiers of province and nation, and reach, on a world-wide scale, a communitarian humanism, a universalist civilization" *(The Church Today,* Fides, 1953).

A. Today's Problem of Depersonalization

This very unity of which Cardinal Suhard speaks is, however, a product of the machine and not of humanity. The "crisis of unification" tends itself to bring about a crisis of human depersonalization. The very extension of communications, so well described by the Cardinal, has acted to break down the old natural human communities with their close-knit solidarity which assured mutual sharing of human values. Within those natural communities the same people were in personal contact at many points: in the neighborhood, the parish, in business, recreation, local government. At the local store, for example, one met those whom he knew also in other relationships. But today a man goes into a supermarket, is duly served by another man, then walks right out of the circle of the other's life. This is not to imply that we should try to turn back the clock, but the role of the Christian to bring men together as "member of member in Christ" takes on a new meaning and a new urgency. He must consider his role very carefully in the context of what is happening in modern life so that he may be able to fulfill it in that context.

The unification that the Cardinal speaks of is taking place outside ourselves, as it were, without a personal involvement. It is not a free union of men but one imposed by a tyrant technology. This union functions admirably to promote "production, consumption, distribution, economics and finance," but not the "I" and "Thou" relationships of persons, which in fact it tends to weaken. It becomes rather a union of faceless men who are but pawns dependent on the machine, numbered hands in a factory, anonymous individuals in a crowd, strangers on the street. The very title of David Riesman's book, *The Lonely Crowd,* depicts so clearly the state of modern man. This is the dilemma that challenges the People of God even in their own existence as a people as well as in their vocation to make mankind a single People. The technology that is able to "weld the continents" tends also to weld men together into an amorphous monolith in which the person becomes lost.

The primary bond of union among men should be that which arises from their sense of being valued by one another for themselves as persons rather than for their technical skills. Canon Brien of France, at the Eichstatt Mission Catechetical Week in 1960, described the effect of technology on this bond as a second cause of depersonalization. He said, "The technological process imposes an impersonal attitude on both persons and societies. To obtain better material results, all efforts must be rationalized to place an almost exclusive emphasis on formulas, schemes and plans in which there is no place for considering the human person and the activity of God in the world" (*Asia,*

Hong Kong, December 1960). Dietrich von Hildebrand, in *The New Tower of Babel,* tells the effect on social relations. He writes, "When a man judges himself to be worth only as much as his performance is worth, social disparities necessarily become unbridgeable abysses" (Kenedy, 1953). This may even apply to the apostolate, if we think of it in the sense of working "on" people as if we were in some sense superior to them.

Canon Cardijn, founder of the Young Christian Workers, has many times declared that the young worker today experiences a deep sense of isolation and loneliness. In the factory he is valued only in terms of profit and in his leisure time he finds few relationships where he is valued for himself. Even social relations tend to be measured by technological standards of what the other can contribute to me, what I can get out of the relationship. Thus thrown back upon himself instead of being welcomed by others as a fellow human, the young worker tends to seek release of psychological tensions in pleasures of the body instead of the human spirit, in drink, gambling, sex. When human relationships become depersonalized, the standards of human values become depreciated, the right order and pattern of life obscured. The baneful influence penetrates even into the basic human relationships. It separates youth from their parents and elders, invades the mutual confidence of friends, even touches the intimate union of spouses with the blight of self-seeking. This has become the age of universal "status-seeking," of being concerned with what one has rather than with what one is. It is above all the young generation that suffer from such subordination of men to things. That has become the social matrix within which they are formed and the social climate in which they grow to adulthood.

"Aloneness and doubt" are, according to Erich Fromm, "the worst of all pains, even the pains of hunger." Modern man suffers this pain from his earliest years and during all his life. It saddens his declining years with neglect by his children. Emotionally exhausted from the depersonalizing conditions of life today, he joins the anonymous crowd of those who seek to forget themselves in new sensual titillations. Literature, the graphic arts, amusements, become debased from pandering to the lower part of man. Even husband and wife are often caught up in the "lonely crowd" and fail to find peace with each other and their children. Sex for many has become common, promiscuous, without real meaning as between human persons, this reaching even into the sanctuary of the family. As values dissolve for lack of being rooted in true community and mutual regard, even the young may practice sex in a precocious imitation of an adult life that is itself deformed. The depersonalization of man tends to dehumanize him in all aspects of life at every level. This is the great tragedy of our time.

One is tempted to believe that, unless the People of God can meet this challenge of modern society in the way and on the scale that it demands, faithful Catholics may themselves eventually be reduced to a comparative remnant. Owing to man's becoming subjected to technology, and the machine has no morality, no standards of moral values are any longer held up as absolute. Catholics not part of a strong community find themselves hard put to maintain Christian values, for example, in marriage. A letter published in *America* stated that of 3100 Catholics married during 1955 in Vancouver, Canada, 1600 were married outside the Church ("The Laity Speaks," May 18, 1957). As Father John L. Thomas, S.J. has pointed out ". . . the impulse to conform and the desire for the security which comes from doing as others do are bound to place a strain upon the individual Catholic." Father Thomas emphasizes that it is important to strengthen solidarity among Catholics and observes that then ". . . the strain towards conformity will operate to support group ideas, and the security of the individual will be rooted in Christian solidarity" (*The Catholic Family*, America Press, 1956).

B. Social Change and the Christian

How are the Catholic laity to fulfill the role assigned to them by the Holy Father to make the Church the vital principle of a human society which becomes daily more depersonalized in the very process of its unification? How can they bring together these two great streams of human development, the technological and the human? The rushing stream of scientific knowledge is absolutely necessary at the very least to feed, clothe and house the constantly increasing millions of men. Atomic energy, for example, though the product of war, becomes a peacetime necessity to produce power in view of the rapid depletion of fossil fuels, such as oil and gas. The other stream, development of the person in human relationships, has been neglected because its gentle flow cannot be used to turn the wheels of industry. Yet in that stream is the "living water" of human life.

Catholics today often have more frequent contacts in work or business with others at a distance than with their neighbors and fellow parishioners. There is even danger that they will take an impersonal view of their life in the parish. The parish church may come to be regarded as a sort of "sacramental service station" where they can secure religious instruction and sacrament ministration as needed. In modern life it can become difficult to see the parish as a community of persons who have the responsibility to help one another develop as Catholics. If the spirit of charity grows weak from decay of community relationships during six weekdays, a short period of Mass participation on Sunday cannot restore it. The mission of bringing all men into one fold, one body, may tend to be viewed in terms of propaganda rather than of bearing person to person witness. Indeed, unless the priest himself understands the changes taking place in society, he may tend to view the parish in terms of so many families and individuals to whom he gives his best in professional service like a "spiritual doctor" rather than the dynamic community it was meant to be.

One striking aspect of modern change which has contributed much to the weakening of interpersonal relationships is the fact that people move so often. There are few close-knit neighborhoods any more to help stabilize conduct standards through feeling themselves groups with a sense of group values. People tend to "follow the crowd" where they happen to be. Gabriel Marcel points out that the ease with which one today becomes anonymous constitutes a grave danger for those who lack strong personal convictions or do not have the support of a strong "base group." The sad effects are often seen among young people particularly, when they go into the armed forces or leave home for school or to seek work. A priest friend called on cousins who had moved to a large city from a small town and found they had stopped going to church. The same may happen even when people move from one part of the same city to another, if no one looks them up to welcome them into a living parish community. Our housing developments are full of Catholics who have "lost themselves" where they are not known.

From New York, Chicago, San Francisco to Tokyo, Manila, Bombay, in Africa and Latin America, priests told me that constant moving causes the traditional census to become obsolete even before it is completed. The parish priest of a new workers' suburb in Los Angeles described how he accidentally hit upon a census plan based on the fact that the people of a neighborhood can most easily know who move in or out. One Sunday at Mass he told the people he was sorry he could not call on the newcomers, but he was alone and tied down by building a church. Some weeks later a young mother brought in the names and addresses of thirty families in her neighborhood. She had taken her two children by the hand and walked from door to door. "It opened my eyes," he told me, "to what the laity can do and their willingness to help if they feel needed. In my seminary days I had looked forward to what I would do as a priest and given little thought to the part of the laity. The parish now has 1500 families and a force of 100 housewives visit every home twice a year to keep the census up to date. In their visits they have become aware of other parish needs such as religious instruction and many who began as census-takers are now engaged in other forms of lay action."

A missionary in Korea emphasized the place of Catholic men in developing organic parish community. "Our people," he said, "are extremely poor and move constantly in search of work, some stay only a short time in one place. We do not have enough priests to keep making the parish rounds and the relatively few Legion of Mary members have other essential work to do. Besides, keeping track of those who move in and out can often be done by those not in the Legion and so the parish workers are multiplied. The parish is divided into neighborhoods or blocks with men leaders who keep the census up to date and also integrate all the newcomers into the Catholic community life. They visit every family in their block once a month. In addition to the usual census information, they ask if any are sick, out of work or otherwise in need and make a list of those who require religious instruction. They ask if any new families have moved in and arrange with Catholic neighbors to make them welcome. The leaders find out if any plan to leave and their expected destination in order to secure an introduction for them to the priest of their new parish. If their future address is not certain, the leader gives them an addressed envelope so they can send it to him after they arrive.

"We not only have a perpetual, living census, but all newcomers become at once integrated into parish life without the danger of indifference creeping in. The neighborhood groups under their leaders become real centers of Catholic community. Before this we found that even devout Catholics did not realize how the people of a parish need to help one another lead a truly Christian life in this unstable world of change. It was not their fault; we had simply not provided them with a simple method that they could follow. Now each neighborhood is like one large family and even the newcomers fit in quickly. We found, moreover, that a few specialized apostolic groups could not of themselves develop a true parish spirit. People acquire it only by their own action of sharing at their own level in mutually cooperative action for the faith and for one another. Having men as the leaders gives them a role appropriate to their temperament as men and helps overcome their common tendency to look on religion as mainly for women and children. In reality much is done by their wives while the men are at work, particularly in the development of neighborliness. But that is based on the responsibility and action of their husbands as official leaders.

"From experience we have learned that this action with other parishioners must be primarily at the level of their local community, of daily life together as families, though special parish activities also have a part to play. But the parish is, in reality, the people in it and not the parish institution, as is very clearly evident when a parish decays. It must be so organized that they feel a part of it in their whole life of every day, not alone in the life of worship and the sacraments or of parish-centered work. Many of our people used to speak of the parish as 'they' and felt free to criticize. Now they tell proudly of 'what we do in our parish,' but it is chiefly in reference to their neighborhood action. Vocation candidates have also greatly increased as a result of this identification with the parish and hence the Church. Good vocations rarely develop in families which have such an impersonal attitude towards the parish that they feel free to criticize it before their children. We now have, furthermore, little of the leakage that was once so disturbing among the families who had lived in various parishes. The moment they arrive among us they are taken into the bosom of the 'clan Christian' by their Catholic neighbors."

One notable aspect of my trip to the different countries around the world was the way in which facts or ideas in one region would illuminate those from somewhere else. I recalled the remark of a lieutenant in the U.S. marines some years ago when a lay group was discussing the problem of integrating newcomers into the parish. "You know," he said, "that in the Services we are transferred frequently, sometimes after one year or even less in a place. Yet we are always integrated into a definite unit from the moment we arrive at a new station. Where the parish is concerned, however, we must each time find our own way as best we can. I have been transferred fifteen times, but only once did Catholics seek us out to make us welcome. Protestants, however, called on us each time." In far-off Korea I saw how this need was being met by the people themselves. It became clear that meeting newcomers in a neighborhood should not be the work of the priest or even of some special "welcome" group. The neighborhood community should be the "unit" which in the name of the parish both receives the new family and integrates it into parish life by incorporation into itself.

C. Social Change and Modern Youth

In Japan I visited Father Bosch, dean of students in Tokyo's Sophia Catholic University. "The young people of Japan," said Father Bosch, "are intoxicated with the new freedom they have acquired since the war. It has led many to do some foolish things, especially morally, because they have been freed from the former traditional restrictions. I tell them: 'Yes, freedom gives us the personal right to choose what we wish to do, but to fulfill ourselves as human beings we must choose what is right. In everything that a man does, there are a right and a wrong way of doing it. Only one who does things the right way will make a success in his studies, or in business, in farming or in any other occupation. It is also necessary in order to make a success of our personal life. God created man as His representative to develop the earth. He gave man powers over nature and over himself. God respects man so much that He leaves him free in his life. But to achieve our highest fulfillment in the humanity that God gave us we must try to choose what is right in every aspect of life. If, for example, someone suggests that we do wrong, we must exercise our freedom to say, 'No!' "

In a group discussion among missionaries in Japan, one of them observed: "For me, one of the most disquieting aspects of today's rapid social change is that it seems to produce a sort of dissolving process in values. The standards that should normally guide men's lives are neglected for what we may call 'possession' values. A man comes to value himself for his superiority over others, real or imagined, whether in work, or sports or even wrong activities. The successful gangster may become a hero to the young. The fixed social pattern of traditional Japanese culture at least insured the transmission of definite human values which had been the development of many generations. In the present situation there is a kind of fluidity in values which makes parents and others uncertain about how to give character training. There are fewer clear and agreed standards presented to the young by modern culture. A growing number of young people here are self-centered, sexually morbid, uncooperative, even truculent, almost completely lacking in self-discipline. The great challenge of today is to activate the essential good that is buried inside them.

"Many non-Christian parents are becoming deeply concerned, but past tradition does not give them an answer to the problems of today. Our explanation of the natural law is for most a completely new idea, and though implicit in their tradition it needs to be spelled out. I have been considering the organization of home discussions on family education for the 20th century. The discussion leaders would be Catholic laymen trained by the 'on-the-job' method. The priest would meet with the discussion leaders from a number of neighborhoods, explain one idea and discuss it with them. Each then gives a brief presentation of this idea in the home meeting where he presides and leads discussion there. This is followed by another meeting with the priest which includes reports on the home meeting held and development of a second idea, and so on. Perhaps a good opening for the first home meeting would be to ask those present to tell how they were trained as children in the matter of the topic to be presented. This would put them at their ease and give an opportunity to relate the traditional training to the natural law. The meetings would be announced in series of 3 or 4 sessions and progressively recruited by asking each couple to bring another couple."

"Since meeting these problems," he continued; "I have been doing some reading in cultural sociology, particularly of the family. Though self-discipline is individual to each one, it is always the product of a social formation in religious, moral and social values. It is primarily social approval of certain values that causes them to be accepted by an individual. This social formation takes place first in the family and it is the family's chief role as primary educator. Much has been written about the insecurity of youth today to explain why so many act contrary to good values. I have become convinced that it is first the parents who are not secure in their own sense of values. The chief source of a sense of security, whether in the family itself or in the community, is confidence in common relationships. But modern social change tends to isolate the family from other families. It presents parents with discipline situations where they may feel unable to make firm decisions from lack of a common pattern of values with other families to which they can appeal. Children play off one family against another, 'The kids down the street don't have to do that.' Parents may doubt it, but when the community no longer exists they do not feel backed up by clear community standards.

"Related to this, there is evident today a growing emotional gap between parents and children which is cause for deep concern. It exists in many Catholic families and on a world-wide scale. In the traditional society of former times, there was far greater sharing of life between parents and children. The latter had much more part in work at home and recreation took place either in the family or its extension, the neighborhood. The child was constantly learning from its parents through the common life they shared, not alone information about things but above all how a good man or woman acted. Unconsciously the child absorbed his parents' wisdom, gained from them a sense of responsibility and a taste for work. Most children would normally follow in their parents' footsteps, so that the present life of father and mother had an interest directly related to their own future. This interest they would show, for example, by making it the subject of their childish games.

"Today, however, the life led by one's parents seems to many youth impossibly old-fashioned. It is today's changes and contrasts that impinge most on their immature experience. Furthermore, modern children are much more away from the family for education and recreation, where they are involved in relationships of more formal and temporary character, shallow-rooted. These qualities may even be carried over into home relationships, showing themselves in early assertions of independence and a noticeable casualness towards the family. May not the depersonalizing influences of modern life on parents themselves also sometimes make it difficult for them to manifest the full warmth of love that children need from parents? If the child fails to find satisfying emotional relationships in the family, he seeks a substitute elsewhere. It may be in a gang, in early steady dating, in precipitate marriage, even in sexual promiscuity, in hero-worship of unheroic gangsters, popular entertainers or film stars.

"In this parish the 'welcome' idea is extended to all relationships. The neighborhood groups are constantly urged to do things together. They go on outings of two or three families, often with stronger families inviting weaker ones, and share expenses. They have backyard picnics for the children and Buddhist neighbors are invited to share the community spirit. Thus the transmission of good values takes place between families as well as within families. There is a continuing parish program of education through the leaders to help the families fulfill their responsibility as primary educators of their children by the quality of family life itself. The groups arrange that children where both parents must work are not left to their own devices when the mother is not at home. A group may hire a lady to 'baby-sit' with small children from several families and older children go after school to play with those of neighbors until their mother returns. The families have other mutual assistance services which help unite them; maternity funds, new baby help, burial societies, and whatever else they may find useful in their circumstances.

"We lay strong emphasis on the responsibility of adult Catholics to cultivate the friendship of all youth in their neighborhood and make them feel valued by the adult community. One duty of the neighborhood group leader is to see that this is done for the youth of his area, since he knows exactly who they are and their background. The young people are encouraged to cooperate with the adults in the group activities as well as in particular ones of their own. They help work with younger children as one of their special contributions. The number of adults naturally interested in individual young persons from the ties of family relationship, such as uncles and aunts, has been tragically reduced by today's predominance of the single household family over the joint family of former times. Many youths today do not have a single adult whom they consider a personal friend and often there are no uncles or aunts nearby with whom they have a natural bond. All need adults not their parents with whom they can feel free to discuss personal problems, but they will confide in an adult only if he has previously shown himself friendly and approachable. The adult must first welcome the young person."

D. Social Support in the Parish

In all the areas that I visited, the problems arising from social change tended to manifest a similar basic character. A missionary in Taiwan (Formosa) remarked that social change could be seen taking place there day by day, though the island entered into full contact with the outside world less than twenty years ago after the war. The first step of change was in modern communications, which tend to modify ideas and arouse expectations that outstrip the far slower growth of economic ability to satisfy them. "The latest world news," said the missionary, "is as eagerly discussed in Taiwan as anywhere else. The same moving pictures are molding the language, the fashions, the ideals. The mission peoples view everything, often with little discrimination between the good and the bad. Hong Kong was the only large city of the world that rated a notoriously immoral picture among the top ten in popularity. At the same time, the newspapers play up the same sensual titillations as in the West."

"Before the coming of the films," he went on, "the missionary could appeal to 'civilized' moral standards. Now the floodgates are open." Another recalled the statement of Pope Pius XII that the impact of modern change on less advanced peoples may well have a more seriously upsetting effect than on the more advanced who "grew up," so to speak, with social change. The developing peoples must leap from the sixteenth century, some from even further back, into the middle of the twentieth. They must change "over night" from a traditional society with its "built-in" rules of conduct to an open, dynamic society which keeps facing the individual with new and unfamiliar situations. He is forced into making a choice for which he is often not prepared. The importance of belonging to a group that will encourage the individual to follow certain agreed ideals is obvious.

In Canon Brien's talk at Eichstatt from which we quoted earlier, he went on to say that today we must develop Christian community to counteract the dehumanizing effects of depersonalization. Here is a new kind of mission method for the new age. We must demonstrate a life of interpersonal community among Catholics which others are invited to share. This invitation is necessary because it is only by entering into our community that they can discover it; like a cathedral window its beauty is seen from within. All the people of a parish must be such apostles "in the front lines" of the Church. They must not leave the reality of their oneness in the People of God as simply a fact of grace, but make it "experiential" in all aspects of life. It would be practiced by the family in charity and hospitality, by the neighborhood in mutual cooperation, with those one meets at work or in other outside contacts by manifesting the charity of Christ in one or another appropriate form. The clear teaching and example of Christ shows us a social ideal of charity, for our love of God can bear true witness to itself only as it enters into the life of our neighbor.

Man is a composite of soul and body in whom human action can result only from the interaction and reaction of both. We realize that being a Catholic does not insulate him from the influences of the social environment in which God has placed him. While giving him all the religious helps we can, we must face up to the problem of the many bad situations that the individual meets in the society within which he works out his life. Does the here and now local society of the parish community show him truly Christian concern as a person beloved of God conducive to the development of a fully Christian personality? Recent follow-up studies in various parts of the world indicate that mass conversions have tended to persevere better than individuals or small groups from having the support of living in a Christian community. It was my impression in the Philippines and Latin America, for example, that in spite of little instruction the faith was more deeply rooted in the personality than among some relatively well instructed converts in other mission areas who formed only a minority.

Once the close inter-relation between religious and social factors in the matter of fidelity to the Faith receives closer study, some old mistakes in missionary and apostolic endeavor will be corrected. The sciences of religious sociology, of missiology and of practical theology should devote much research to this question. It should form an essential part of the young priest's preparation. There is, for example, no stronger support than a good parish community spirit in the matter of desiring religious instruction and receiving the Sacraments. This is particularly true of youth. Conversely, if the Catholic community spirit is weak, youth tends to be little interested in learning about their Faith and careless about receiving the sacraments. Man is not a disembodied soul who lives only an interior religious life, he needs also to "experience" his faith socially as he does life in general. The young, above all, who begin life as a "blank" ready for imprinting, need to receive the good social impressions of a mutually loving parish community.

The life of man in community is the primary school of the Christian social virtues, justice and charity. If we merely preach about them without developing a parish atmosphere conducive to their practice, our people will get an intellectual idea of them without being moved to demonstrate them towards their fellow men. During this tour I was struck by the fact that often the rank and file of Catholics in the missions were little, if at all, more helpful to others than the non-Christians. And in our homeland Protestants seem generally more zealous in works of personal service than Catholics. Is it that we tend to transmit an idea of religion which is, in the words of Abbot Vonier, too mystical and too internal? In Japan, almost all the volunteers helping a priest who works in the great slums around the Kyoto railway station are Buddhist university students. A Catholic social worker in India set up a center in the slums of a large city which has many fervent Catholics, yet those who offered to help were mostly Hindus and Parsees. The chief influence that the parish community should exert around it, to show by charity the presence of Christ, is largely wanting as a habit of life.

Today's atomized, depersonalized world hopes for a new society, a new community of men, and we fail to bring out into the light the one we have from God. Many who have not experienced the Mystical Body in us turn therefore to the unity that they do see in the pseudo-mystical body of Communism. We may say that men should be able to detect the difference, but do we show them the Mystical Body in action as the Communists present their community so that men can make a comparison? We must manifest the Mystical Body socially and visibly in every aspect of family and neighborhood life, in all working and other areas of human relationships. Else the Faith will have little appeal to men who feel most insecure and unhappy precisely in their day to day existence. The honor and glory we give to God by prayer and worship, by our individual moral lives, do not move them from not penetrating into their lives and touching their felt problems. We are like the examining physician whose hands have not yet discovered the sore spot that would tell him what is needed to cure.

In every part of the world I found priests concerned about the same problem, the loss of interest in religion by youth, among Catholics as well as others. The outlook for the future in many places seemed truly dark and ominous. Have we perhaps failed to understand the religious implications of the fact that mankind today, and especially youth, see life as dynamic? Should we not present religion, our relationship to

God, also in the dynamic terms of cooperation with Him to build a new world? Our social structure today is a free and open one that invites everyone to strike out for himself. Those growing up in it are not ready to accept religion as consisting chiefly of formal "duties" as they would when the social climate was more authoritarian. Today we must present religion as a relationship to God that is in full accordance with modern man's new awareness of human powers. It would be fatal for it to seem a sort of "strait jacket" out of the past. Even God does not command free men to love Him, but invites them. Christ did not say, "If you keep my commandments, you will love me."

3. CHRISTIAN DYNAMISM IN TODAY'S WORLD

The dynamism inherent in the world from God's creative action has in our time become suddenly much more apparent. It has generated a great acceleration of human development which seems "self-propelled" towards an ever more rapid rate of change that makes us almost dizzy in the contemplation. The People of God have been given the role of penetrating and transforming this dynamism with their own superior dynamism, fired by a vision of man's attaining unheard of spiritual and social heights. How can they be content with any concept of Christianity as a system of routine "duties"?

To look upon Christian life simply as a kind of passive fidelity, avoiding sin and enduring the difficulties of the present existence in view of a better one hereafter, would be to miss the whole point of our being created in God's image. For God has shared with us His own dynamism and given us the world in which to exercise it. Pope Pius XII said in his famous 1955 Christmas radio broadcast to the world, "At present the social order is not the result of a varied labor directed by conviction of the members of the community towards the common good. This is the task that devolves on Catholics; this is their great responsibility. It is necessary that they work efficaciously so that the Christian and social sense may penetrate into the consciousness of men and bring about the return of modern society to the sources rendered sacred by the Word of God made flesh. If ever Christians neglect this duty . . . they will be committing treason against the

God-Man." These strong words from the vicar of Christ are a solemn declaration that the fruit of Redemption is social and not only individual, that the two are inseparable.

Again in 1957, the same Pontiff told the delegates of the Second World Congress for the Lay Apostolate gathered in Rome: "Aside from the shortage of priests, the relations between the Church and the world require the intervention of lay apostles. The "consecration" of the world is essentially the work of the laity, of men who are intimately a part of economic and social life, and those who participate in the government and in legislative assemblies. In the same way, only the workers themselves can form the Catholic cells which must be created in every factory and in all working environments to bring back to the Church those who have strayed away from her." The Holy Father here states clearly the dynamic role of the Catholic laity in modern society, all 500 million of them in every state of life where God has placed them. What a transforming social force they would be, if they made every one of the nearly 200,000 parishes in the world dynamic centers for the program the popes have outlined. What is stopping us?

A. The Church and Social Change

True to her calling as a loving mother, the Church ardently desires to see her children develop to the highest degree all the potentialities given them by God. She is concerned, of course, that the precious human material which comes from God be not spoiled by a lack of balance in its development. But she is in perfect accord with God's plan of creation. He did not make man to His own dynamic image for him to wrap up his talents in the napkin of timidity. Dynamic human society is the image of the dynamic divine society of the Holy Trinity, whose inner life is pure, ceaseless act. The divine dynamism, of course, expresses itself with infinite perfection in the divine community of the Holy Trinity. Man must pick his halting way along the road of human relations in his effort to express the divine dynamism ever more fully in human community. Now it is through Christ, also a man, that we participate directly in the dynamic life of the divine community. Hence the Christian vocation, as the Holy Father tells us, is to "bring about the return of modern society to the sources rendered sacred by the Word of God made flesh." It is to "consecrate" the world in and by the divine dynamism flowing from Christ through us into the community of men.

The Church rejoices that social change has caused her children to grow in spiritual as well as intellectual and technological awareness. The natural sciences have helped us acquire a more spiritual, less anthropomorphic, idea of God. They have helped us understand better the great human potential of the dynamism which we have from God and shown us God's dynamic action in the material world itself. Only two generations ago science thought of matter as composed of solid molecules but now our concept of it keeps getting less "material." Today, matter is seen as made up of countless minute systems of synchronized forces, so that if God withdrew His creative hand, all those forces would cease to act and the universe would instantly fall back into nothingness. All of nature is constituted in every part of such synchronized systems, from the tiny atom up to our sun and its planets and the galaxies of the stars. Scientific evidence contradicts the idea that such systems could come into being by chance.

As her divine founder promised she would, the Church has vastly grown in wisdom by the human dynamism within her infused with the Holy Spirit. "I have still much to say to you, but it is beyond your reach as yet" (John 18:12). The Holy Spirit will continue to the end of time to bring out of the Bible still unimagined treasures of wisdom about God's purpose for man. The Church learns from human experience, sometimes difficult like the storm over the ideas of Galileo. But the fact that many churchmen were wrong about his "innovations," as men are so often wrong and will be, in no way invalidates her dynamic mission under the Holy Spirit. She is deeply concerned about certain unbalanced trends in social change, but towards social change in general she has learned to maintain a serene attitude. She has full confidence in the divine wisdom that formed men in society and put a spark of the divine dynamism into their vitals. Indeed, it is her precise vocation to fan that spark into a flame that mounts up to heaven. Pope Pius XI openly rejoiced that he was given to live in a time of great social change.

One fact is clear: the Catholic can no more escape this changing world than he can escape being human. Social change involves the very matrix of our being, for we are this society that is changing. A Catholic of the city may flee to the suburbs where he can enjoy the fruits of industrialism without having to take part in the struggle to give it Christian guidance. He thereby abandons the toiling masses who make his suburban comforts possible, perhaps at the cost of their own spiritual and social insecurity, even degradation! How could one "square" his conscience with an attitude so unworthy of his Christian calling? During the solemn hour after the Last Supper while Judas went about his diabolical errand, our Lord was quietly giving His last message to the Apostles and thus to us. He prayed His Father to help them fulfill their mission to the world, not to take them out of the world, and that applies also to us today. In modern society, a "static" Catholic who did not try to bring the divine dynamism of Christ into the marketplaces where men are would be a contradiction. Pius XII said it would be treason to our Lord. "But I have children!" protests a father. Would they not become better men and women for being brought up where life is real, if hard, and in an apostolic atmosphere rather than among the false values and status symbols so prevalent today in suburban life?

The Catholic laity must live in society to leaven it from

within; leaven must be mixed with the mass. If they do not find in the life of their parish the means to fulfill that dynamic role from God, we must also not be surprised if they lack motivation to undertake the harder way of life for the sake of Christ and their brother. Religion tends to lose its central place in their lives as a dynamic force and to seem unrelated to the dynamic present of their weekdays among men. A Catholic of exemplary life high in the business world of a large American city told me, "Father, I know that my religion is the most important thing in my life, but it is the least interesting. Every day I have the satisfaction of applying my talents, of seeing my work develop and beholding its results. But the only activity offered me in the parish is to help move chairs at a bazaar." In the world of work, business and other areas of modern society, our laity find scope for every talent and at every moment meet dynamic challenges. But what happens to their dynamism religion-wise if in the parish the chief lay talent called upon may be the materialistic one of money-making to provide funds? Can the laity be blamed if they fail to understand their dynamic role in a dynamic Church?

It would be most unrealistic, of course, to expect the laity to fulfill their Christian role in this changing social context without guidance and training. First the bishop of the diocese and under him the parish priests must take steps to motivate and direct the dynamism of the laity. This raises the question of how well the priest himself has been alerted during his preparation to the realities of social change constantly taking place meanwhile in the world outside the seminary. One cannot ask of the young priest that he be an expert in economic and social questions, but he should at least have been taught to recognize the relation between his own special study as a priest and the key problems of today. The seminary must not overload its curriculum with special courses in social sciences, and even were there place for such courses the problem of their integration with the sacred sciences would still remain.

If, however, the teachers of the sacred sciences also did research and field work in the social sciences, they could give their students a properly correlated view of both. That would seem a natural and logical solution.

In the newly developing countries the burdens of the Church fall more and more every year on the national clergy. They need far different equipment to face the future than might have been thought necessary in the more traditional culture of the past. They will not be formed to guide the laity in apostolic action by seminary teaching methods which themselves belong to traditional times. They must be brought to take an active part in the learning process viewed as a development of the whole person and not merely as the passive absorption of certain information. The young priest should not get the idea that the high point of his seminary career is the ability to carry on a disputation in Latin against errors of the distant past. We must help him understand the impact of today's social change on the culture of his own people as well as in the world at large, also the appeal and methods of Communism and how to guide the Catholic laity in a dynamic facing up to these problems. He needs for this not only classroom instruction but also guided field study and action in order to acquire an integrated body of knowledge.

B. Social Changes Favoring Communism

For man to make proper use of the freedom that he demands in the modern world, he has need of dedication and self-discipline in a much wider area than of his own personal conduct and in relations with individuals. He needs also social and professional dedication, to perform the duties of his state in life with competence and integrity and concern for the common good. The socio-economic codes of the more developed societies that enable them to function successfully in the modern world of social complexity were developed at a gradual pace over a long period of time. In the simpler traditional social patterns of the emerging nations emphasis has been on loyalty to one's family, clan or tribe, and little attention given to the general community welfare. This private loyalty is one of the chief obstacles that gets in the way of proper regard for the public and national good. Now catapulted into the complex social structures of the 20th century, these peoples are faced with their greatest challenges precisely in the areas of public service, to set up representative government truly devoted to the common good, to develop industry and improve agriculture in order to feed an exploding population. Even when the beginnings of advance are slowly and painfully made, they are in many cases wiped out by old private loyalties or by new population pressures.

The confidence of the Communists that they will eventually win the newly developing nations as they won China is based on the postulate that these countries cannot solve such problems fast enough by themselves and that even we who are known as Christian peoples cannot discipline ourselves sufficiently to give them the necessary vast-scale assistance. A chief evidence of that lack of discipline, say the Communists, is our pre-occupation with the comforts and luxuries of life while so many in the world suffer want. Indeed, the pursuit of our vaunted "high standard of living"—in reality a high standard of consumption—precludes our really understanding the needs and insecurities that afflict the vast majority of mankind. It also sets up a barrier of the heart on the side of the struggling peoples that prevents their accepting our version of the "good life." The emerging peoples feel closer in some ways to the Communist nations because they have had the same problems. Communism has great fascination for the youth of the developing countries, because they see how Russia in one generation achieved the status of a great power. The ferment of expectation no longer stirs the American people as it once did, and the emerging nations feel that we put little heart into the new life dialogue which is for them the dominant consideration of international relations.

Communists who know something of the Gospels—more of them were once Christians than most of us realize—reproach us that we did not give mankind the social message of Christ. "And now," they say, "you are too late, for Communism offers a social doctrine more suited to the needs of the new world of technology." How can Catholics who know the Gospels present religion almost entirely in terms of the individual, of his own personal duties and conduct? Not only do the problems of mankind grow increasingly social, but in a world of social change the individual also finds it more and more difficult to integrate his life. Yet how seldom do we hear religious instruction which begins from God's plan that men should build together a new world fit for all to dwell in with dignity? A world that will be ready on the last day to be taken up by God to become part of the new heaven and new earth? In how many of our 200,000 parishes in the world are there Catholics leading discussions on social justice, decent livelihood, the equal rights of all to use the good things that God has made for mankind? The present great need is for action; the apostolate will not be judged by the programs it presents but by the action it carries out.

Douglas Hyde, former editor of the Communist *Daily Worker* in England, converted Louis Taruc, leader of the Communist *Huk* rebellion, now serving a life sentence in a Manila prison. Mr. Hyde tells us in *Christ to the World* (1960, No. 3), how he went to live with Taruc in the prison. When he outlined to him the Catholic social doctrine, Taruc's reaction was, "Why did no one tell me about this when I was a kid? I used to go to church through a porch on one side of which was St. Joseph and on the other St. Isidore. You are the first to tell me about the Church's social teaching and that they represented it. When I joined the Communists, I thought the Church had nothing at all to say on the social question." Mr. Hyde makes a further comment to explain why the Communists are able to attract so many. "I believe," he says, "that any people who are faced with a choice as between the Christian who is trying to apply his Christianity and a Communist, they will choose the Christian every time. Too often they choose the Communist, because they believe that no one else cares and no one does anything."

Mr. Hyde also gives some reflections on how people are attracted to Communism and then trapped by it. "Almost all the people who go to Communism are young, and youth is a period of idealism. The Communists take this idealism of youth, this vital force and use it for their own purposes. Too often we have neglected it, when we might have used it. To the overwhelming majority of Communists, Communism first and foremost is to them an ideal, a dream of a good society. I believe that Communism does not attract the worst of people and use the worst of qualities; it takes, instead, the best of people and the best of qualities and uses them for evil purposes. It takes loyalty and devotion to a cause, willingness to sacrifice and other such qualities, and uses them. This is part of the tragedy of Communism, that you have these sincere young people going into the Communist Party anxious to change the world and then accepting a totally evil philosophy, which leads inevitably to their lives becoming evil too." Elsewhere Mr. Hyde states that "joining the Communist Party was the most unselfish thing I ever did."

One reason why the Communists are able to have such vast influence is that they make clear to recruits from the very beginning that every activity of their life must be dedicated to the Party. They do not devote so many hours a week to their "apostolate," they are at it all the time in whatever they do. Says Mr. Hyde: "The Communists believe that if you make mean demands upon people, you will get a mean little response, which is all you deserve. If you make big demands upon them, you will get a heroic response." He remarks that so often our religious instruction seems to give the idea that a Catholic's positive obligations to the faith begin and end with attending Sunday Mass. By contrast, he declares, "When new members come into the Communist Party they come in expecting to have to sacrifice, sacrifice their time, their energy, themselves. They do not have any illusions." It is by such discipline that a small number often dominate a labor union or a school.

The Communist formation technique is nevertheless designed, observes Mr. Hyde, to give each member support and encouragement in the demands made on him. Situations are set up in which the recruit is almost certain to have some success to give him confidence. Communists are willing to take risks, but if defeated they restore morale by launching at once another effort where success is more sure. After each campaign there is a merciless inquest in which the members ruthlessly criticize their own mistakes and the mistakes of other members. They seldom make the same mistake twice and are in no danger of becoming complacent. The Communist is taught to think in terms of action about every situation. He never says, "Somebody ought to do something about this." He learns to say, "What can I do about it? We ought to do so and so." The Communists are taught to take action to help solve local problems and difficulties, to show the people that the Communists care about them. They are willing to take over any unwanted job, no matter how distasteful, in any organization from a labor union to a garden club. This makes them acceptable and helps open the way for spreading their ideas.

"You see the sheer tragedy of it," comments Mr. Hyde, "see the tragedy of those people giving all this dedication, giving all this zeal, giving all this energy, giving all this sacrifice to the worst thing that men ever had. The Communists have the worst creed on earth and they shout it from the housetops. Too often those of us who have the best creed speak with a muted voice if we speak at all. I do not see any reason why the devil should have all the best techniques."

C. Communist Leader Training Methods

This section is inserted, even at the risk of being found dry, because the practical technique it describes could well be adapted to the training of Catholic apostolic leaders. In *Christ to the World* (1961, No. 2), Douglas Hyde describes how he himself during his 20 years as a Communist conducted study circles in which leaders were trained to form the famous "action cells." Here we have exact details from one who had personally proved, he now wryly observes, that anyone willing to attend the study sessions could be made into a dedicated Communist leader. "Not more than 14 or 15 people," explains Mr. Hyde, "are assembled in a semi-circle around the 'tutor' in a relaxed, informal yet serious atmosphere. The number is important, and so is the seating arrangement. The idea is to create an intimate atmosphere in which everyone may be brought to participate in discussion." The key of the method, we learn, is "controlled discussion," which has been found most effective for the great majority of people at all levels.

"The aim of the tutor," Mr. Hyde continues, "will be to get just two or three major points accepted by his class and literally by every single one in the class at each session, and in such a way as to make them feel that the views they are brought to accept are ones which they themselves have arrived at. The class members will have been given in advance what is called 'necessary reading.' This is cut to the minimum: a few pages perhaps in one book, a chapter in another. But if they fail to do the required reading they quickly discover they will be exposed before their comrades in the course of the discussion." We know from other sources that this bit of reading is considered to have great value in developing the person's self-confidence, making him feel that he has ideas from authoritative sources to contribute. If any of the group cannot read, they are helped with this by fellow members of the class.

"The tutor leads off," states Mr. Hyde, "with what is called the 'opening statement.' In it he very briefly outlines the purpose of the session. This lasts only 4 to 5 minutes, but leads up to all the points for which he wishes to gain acceptance. Then he puts a question to the talkative member, one who will not be put off by the direct approach and so is useful at this stage even though later he will have to be controlled. The question takes the form of: 'What do you think of such and such a point which I have made?' When the person in question has expressed his point of view, the tutor switches to another member, asking for his opinion of what the first man has said. So the ball is passed from one to another, with the tutor skillfully steering the discussion so that all come in time to accept the point he wants them to accept." We note that by this method the members develop by the self-activity that is essential, yet always in the direction of a single goal.

"In each group there is always at least one 'silent' member —the type who is driven into himself if asked a direct question in front of a group of others. Or, it may be, there is one who is silent because he still has doubts. But the tutor aims to get such types into the discussion, too, and will not be satisfied, nor pass on to the next point, until they have actually expressed support for the right view. In such cases his line is to ask if the person concerned is in agreement or has some doubts. Or is it that he approves but finds it difficult to express his views in such circumstances? If there are doubts, then the tutor asks the others to 'help their comrade who is having some difficulty in getting the point.' Most of the group are now pleased at their own ability to grasp the point quickly and therefore eagerly cooperate in convincing the slow member, who in turn begins to feel that perhaps he is indeed being slow or is peculiarly 'dumb,' and so becomes receptive to their persuasion.

"When the first point is finally accepted by all, the tutor moves on to the next one. But each member feels that the point accepted is his, he helped to think it out, he contributed to the discussion and by his own efforts eventually got around to it. It is not something pumped into him by the tutor, but thought of, or argued out, by himself. It will henceforth be his and he will defend it as his own. This method is used in any well ordered Communist Party for every type of member, from the housewife to the university professor, and for every subject including dialectic materialism. By this means they succeed in turning the whole thought, outlook and moral code of those who come to the Party completely upside down by persuading them to accept dialectic materialism as their philosophy and Marxism as a way of life."

Some extracts are also given by Mr. Hyde from a pamphlet published recently by the British Communist Party, entitled *Hints for Party Tutors.* The pamphlet states: "There are a number of fundamental principles . . . which you will be endeavoring to teach . . . But these principles will come to life and be really understood to the extent that they are *applied to real, concrete problems* . . . Try and teach the principles in their relation to living reality . . . The more you get to *know your students,* talk their language, draw on their experience to help them understand new things, the more successful you will be . . . Some tutors *like to acquire prestige* by looking up rare questions from books out of print, or not yet translated. It may be good for the tutor's prestige, but it does not help the students. You will get deserved prestige if you help people to understand things, not through the display of your own erudition . . .

"The great test of your success as a tutor will be the degree to which you *draw the students into discussion.* The tutor's introductory remarks in branch classes should be as far as possible informal, almost conversational, encouraging interruptions, at least up to a point. But the important thing is to *create the atmosphere* in which everyone feels absolutely free to come in, to have his or her say, however short, and however much in disagreement with the tutor . . . There is something which is every tutor's reward—that is the look of understanding on the face of the young worker when he or she has come to understand, with the aid of the tutor, some fundamental point of socialism for the first time."

Douglas Hyde comments, "From my own experience since I left the Communist Party, I would say that the Christian tutor can get that same reward of 'seeing the look of understanding' which comes from suddenly seeing everything fall into place and become more meaningful. This comes when someone for whom the Christian teachings have been quite unrelated to ordinary everyday life suddenly realize that they contain the key of life instead."

D. Laymen in a Layman's World

The world of today which the Communists, themselves lay people, are trained to penetrate and conquer for atheism is the world of the layman and particularly the marketplace. How well is the Catholic layman prepared to bring Christ to this world? The Church cannot penetrate it through the priest directly because it is not his world. He does not have a family, he is not permitted to engage in business, industry or the other pursuits that laymen carry on in the marketplace. In a simpler society the priest was probably the best or even the only educated person in the community and had a corresponding influence, but today he is surpassed by many laymen in all kinds of new intellectual areas. As society grows more complex, its new fields of human endeavor are dominated by laymen. As a result, the priest has little or no part in the new social institutions or the transformed older ones of modern society—for example, general education—which increasingly form the framework of people's lives. The area of his human relations becomes more and more restricted to the field of religion, which is itself no longer regarded by a great part of mankind as central to all social institutions but simply as one institution among many.

The task facing the Church in her world mission is quite different from what it was in the time of St. Francis Xavier. Then it was chiefly to present Christ as the fulfillment of human aspirations which people viewed quite simply under a predominantly religious aspect. Now life has been divided by social change into a great diversity of areas that claim man's attention and tend to weaken religion's traditional role as the unifying center of life. The Church must today present a synthesis of religion and life in which the relation between God and all the diverse areas of human endeavor are clearly seen. Only the laity, each one in the particular social areas where he lives out his life, can demonstrate this synthesis just as the Communist demonstrates the synthesis of Marxism no matter what he is doing. The Christian synthesis would be worked out by experts, but it must be visibly demonstrated by ordinary laymen by their Christian participation throughout all the lay areas of society in a typical pattern belonging to the People of God.

It is clear, therefore, that the modern lay apostolate is not simply a matter of getting individuals to practice the Faith but also of applying it in social institutions as the leaven of a new society. While we tend to concentrate on individual conversions, the Communists never lose sight for a moment that theirs is a social mission, to change society. Michael de la Bedoyere, in *The Layman in the Church* (Burns & Oates, 1954), gives the Young Christian Workers (Jocists) as an example of lay Catholics who are devoted to a social mission. Catholic youth in the YCW carry Christian principles of life and work into one of the socially most important contemporary fields, the factory and the workshop. Youth is not there in a preaching or teaching capacity, or as an example of piety and devotion, but in its natural and normal worker capacity, by which in any case it must live its life, spiritual and temporal. Daily it becomes more evident that there can be no Christian penetration of modern society so engrossed in technology until the laity are taught this true relation between religion and their daily life where they encounter technology at every turn. But the average Catholic today, and even many an apostle, divides his life with so much time for religion and so much for work and other activities that even priests fall into calling "profane" or "secular."

Speaking of this question of Christian influence in the manifold social areas of our time, Mr. de la Bedoyere says: "What is needed is an apostolic laity gradually coming to influence and change the texture of values in the world and thus preparing it, however remotely, for that change of mind and heart which will dispose it, socially as well as individually, to grace. One may also note here the evident fact that if the materialist and totalitarian ideology of Communism is to be finally overcome, it can only be done by a Christian penetration of this kind . . . The 'free' world has, as a world, lost the sense of conviction of the spiritual order as that within which alone freedom can flourish sufficiently and be translated into firm institutions and relations powerful enough to challenge the attraction and logical development of Communism." We note here that this "logical development" of Communism is directed particularly towards certain key institutions such as labor, education and communications. Today's secularized "free world" is no longer able to convey to the emerging peoples a sense of the true basis on which our free institutions are built and only the Christian layman whose world it is can restore that sense.

In view, however, of the present very slow development of such an apostolate, Mr. de la Bedoyere raises the question if there is not still too great a dependence on "clerical" means in carrying out the Church's mission. There can be no doubt that the Church today is being brought to public attention in many new ways, such as by radio and television. Advertising and instruction by correspondence have been used with success. The laity are being called upon in constantly increasing numbers to make the faith known and to help instruct converts. As the yearly conversion statistics prove, many are thus brought to the truth. But there is strong evidence that the number of such conversions is probably no greater than that of those who drift away from the Church under the influence of secularized institutions. Even were the statistics much more favorable, it would still leave the great world of humanity in its many areas of daily life and occupations relatively untouched by the Church.

One example of our slowness to understand the social mission of the Church was seen when such pioneer Catholic Action movements as the YCW were launched, and some priests were critical that they spent so much time at meetings and were not active in the devotional life of the parish church. Canon Cardijn, the YCW founder, met many obstacles in keeping it to the special kind of training that he saw its members required in order to achieve their purpose. The purpose was by example, conversation and leadership to carry into their work and daily responsibilities the values and experience of Christianity fully lived in relation to the social environment. This difficulty was largely because Catholic education and training had generally conceived the Christian life almost exclusively in personal and sacramental terms rather than of the Mystical Body community in the world where God placed mankind. Mr. de la Bedoyere expresses the hope that, ". . . with the wider realization of all that is implied in the liturgical, intellectual and social movements within the Church, the present specialization of Catholic Action and the extra training which it needs, with perhaps even a form of community life at any rate for the leaders, will become less necessary. For at bottom Catholic life and Catholic Action are one and the same thing." If that day arrives, what a grand mobilization there would be of Christian apostolic forces.

"In order to work effectively towards such an end," Mr. de la Bedoyere continues, "the laity must come to feel that it possesses within itself a *certain autonomy and status* which is different from that of the clergy, while springing equally directly from the Church which is the Mystical Body of Christ . . . If there is an age of the Church which corresponds most nearly to our own it is that of the early Church in which the New Testament emphasizes so clearly both the ecclesiastically authoritative and God-founded function of the chosen Apostles, together with their successors, and the *living community of the faithful* which corresponds to and completes the Body of Christ . . . The importance attached to this sense of unity within differences of function, and of community or fellowship, is attested again and again in such Scriptural phrases as 'brotherhood,' 'same charity,' 'united in mind and judgment,' 'co-partners in Jesus,' and in the common life and sharing of those times."

It would appear that our present Catholic problem of separation between the Catholic's religious life and his participation in the marketplace has arisen primarily in the context of European history. After the fall of Rome it was the clergy and religious who played the main part in civilizing the barbarian tribes. They thus tended to become the chief authority on which people depended in the new society, even wielding temporal power over lands and fiefs. Then came the rise of the towns with new economic and political elements entering into the social structure and the long period of humanism that set men along new paths of discovery and culture. There arose also Protestantism and ideologies such as Nationalism, Liberalism, Socialism and Communism. The energies of the Church were directed to saving the faith of exposed Catholics, but chiefly in the form of a counter-reaction expressed in terms of obedience to Church authority in religious practice. Only in the later stages did it become clear to churchmen that the mass of the people were settling down to a society and life which no longer felt itself related to the religion which that authority represented. Now the same kind of society and life is becoming that of the whole world.

This is the specific challenge that the modern world presents to the Catholic laity. They are called upon to live their life, not merely in an environment of unprecedented religious indifference, but in daily relationship of work and partnership of activities with men and women who may be wholly alien to our spiritual and often to our moral values. At the same time, these people are by no means devoid of much genuine idealism and goodness. The Catholic laity are called upon to create in every working and other social environment a climate that encourages their fellows in acts of idealism and goodness from which they will derive an inner satisfaction perhaps new in their experience. Such acts and their interior effects tend to open hearts to the witness born by Catholics that it is because man is made in the image of God he is able to do such God-like things. Note carefully the sequence. The Catholic does not begin by speaking to his neighbors or fellow workers about religious ideas which would not be accepted, but bypasses their prejudice by getting them to do what they accept as good and then explaining how men are God's delegates to diffuse goodness upon the earth. Quite clearly, this is a job that only the layman can do in the multitude of human contacts that are part of his day by day living.

At a 1959 study day on the lay apostolate held in Toronto, Canada, the keynote speech was given by Lawrence Lynch, a professor at St. Michael's College. He told the 250 participants: "When the Marxist defines man in economic terms, he succeeds much better in saying what economic man is than we, in speaking of man as God's image. I say, we have not begun to challenge our contemporaries on the dignity of man! . . . We must prove to our fellows that the reason we want them to become Catholics is that only so will they be able to achieve the fullest realization of their best natural ambitions, no less; that actually the powers of man cannot reach their maximum except through God's love." These words of Professor Lynch indicate some positive values in our faith that we should emphasize, at the same time remembering that they are so unbelievable that to gain credence they must be visibly demonstrated in our own lives.

4. THE CHRISTIAN IN A WORLD OF ACTION

A Maryknoll seminarian told me recently of an incident in the "released time" religion class he taught to Catholic youth attending a government high school. A senior boy said, "Brother, when I went to the parish primary school the Sisters told us that if we made a good morning offering and did not revoke it by sin, our whole life during the day would be pleasing to God. My father and mother say, 'Keep the commandments and you'll be all right.' But I think God made me to accomplish something in the world."

That young man hit upon a fundamental question for the relation between religion and modern life. There seems in the minds of many a sense of separation between what are considered specifically spiritual acts and the work of daily life as if only the former had religious meaning. The worship of God on Sunday seems to such a person to have little connection with what he does during the week at work, business or recreation except in an indirect way. He recognizes that if he commits serious sin in the course of these activities it is a serious obstacle to his contact with God, but he does not see that these activities are involved in the sin as well because they also belong to God. The Christian who has such an outlook on life cannot possibly play his full part in bringing God into the marketplace. Yes he knows that the Church has a social teaching, but it seems to him somehow irreverent to think of God having any interest in the hurlyburly of the marketplace. When technological modern man encounters this outlook among Christians, is it any wonder that he becomes convinced the Church has little to offer towards the ordering of a dynamic new society?

The first essential, therefore, is for the Catholic layman to acquire a correct concept of man's role in the world. God was not playing jokes when He made man different from all other creation, uniting in his soul and body both spiritual and material worlds so closely that man can achieve his destiny only as a creature of both. God created man, moreover, in His own image and likeness and placed him over this combined world. This means that man's role in the world has a likeness to that of God Himself. Man is not merely a sort of care-taker in the world, but a co-creator. Today we see creation as a continuing process, not completed already from the beginning as was once thought. The Christian dialectic which we must present to mankind today is that God does not desire us to share the divine life in only an "interior and mystic" way, but in our whole being of body and soul as truly God's co-creators upon earth. This concept provides an approach to God for the modern mind that thinks of life in terms of man's vast potential for self-development. It also overcomes a very real danger for the Catholic of today, a tendency to separate his religious life on Sunday from his daily life as a man.

A. The Christian Mystique of Work

The Christian "mystique" of human work is the mystery of its place in God's plan for man's development and the glory he gives to God through use of the material world. The factory worker by his labor transforms and ennobles raw materials for our use, the farmer by his work feeds mankind, and in the working both fulfill a high destiny. God made the primary materials, the iron and metals in the ground, the land and all the plants. But man must use the creative power he has as God's image to make them serve human use and in so doing his own creation develops. Man is himself born "raw material," the helpless baby whose creation must be continued by parents, teachers, the community and his own action. It is a mystery of God's wisdom and goodness that He thus gives man a share in the divine creative work. He made us to His own likeness and to "stand tall" before Him by giving us completely free responsibility as His co-creators on earth. Our Lord Himself was a worker: growing up as a child and as a carpenter, then in His public life, finally when on the cross He performed the work of our redemption.

Both the Christian and the Communist, when they present their beliefs to others, usually begin from the meaning of life. For the Communist it is easy to arouse interest because his concern is directly with the visible life of man. The Christian, on the other hand, may tend to speak of life in its ultimate meaning, as salvation or sharing the supernatural life of God. Such an approach is likely to produce a "pie in the sky" reaction if he does not see man's role in the world as well. Though the Christian cannot imitate the Communist in promising the cure of all human frustrations, he should still deal with the daily life questions of his hearers. He would emphasize the worker's human dignity and his consequent rights in social justice, then show that these are inherent in his human nature from being made in God's image as His co-creator. Hence they are not given him by an entity called "society." Man's work is to be considered, as Pope John XXIII declared in *Mater et Magistra*, "not a commodity but an expression of the human person." If our time, our skill, our energy, are treated as commodities to be bargained for in a "labor market" or whose use can be dictated by others in the name of society or of the working class, then work loses its true character as the creative activity of free men and becomes the drudgery of slaves.

Today man by his work is bringing about the development of this planet at an astounding rate. From his beginning on earth until almost the present day, he had only the power of his own hands and of a few domesticated animals. Then came the harnessing of water power and in quick succession of steam, burning gases and finally atomic energy. It is said that within 80 years our present oil and gas supplies will be 80 per cent exhausted, but atomic energy can multiply itself and supply all of man's future needs. The discovery of electricity made it possible to transmit power everywhere to run factories, light our homes, create great irrigation schemes that transform vast desert regions into fields and pastures. With atomic energy it will be possible to multiply indefinitely the supply of electricity and of fresh water from sea-water in the same plant. These developments make possible great cities and their suburbs which are in the process of changing not only the face of the earth, but the face of life itself for a great part of humanity.

The diffusion of these transformations has, however, remained very unequal. They have created a great economic gulf among nations and between the classes of a population itself, or increased one already existing. A relative few enjoy their benefits. For instance, each inhabitant of the United States has at his disposal the energy of ten tons of coal a year, while the people of the underdeveloped lands still have by and large only their hands. This problem would not be solved by dividing the wealth of those who "have" among the great masses of those who "have not," for each would receive only a small amount and soon spent. It is a question of properly organizing the work of man, the creator. Karl Marx advocated forced organization, even to the point of making Communism's opponents slaves for the benefit of Communist society, and the Russians did just that by sending them to slave labor camps.

Such a concept simply degrades the dignity of all men and of their work, which should be organized by free cooperation. The conception of work required to solve the problem is that all, rich and poor, learned and illiterate, share together the creative power of each one's work as God has shared His creative power with mankind. But today each one thinks only of himself. Each acts as if he were himself the source of his own intelligence and strength, of the training given by family and teachers, of his social and national environment that makes possible the exercise of his powers and the enjoyment of their fruits. The problem is primarily of each man looking at his neighbor and saying, "Freely have I received, freely must I give. What does God wish me to do with the creative gifts He has shared with me?"

The problem of the world today lies in a paradox that threatens man's own existence. The greater our progress, the more do scientific, economic and cultural problems surpass the strength of present communities. Hence the great planning projects, which involve the investment of enormous capital, the employment of armies of men, the dealing out of contracts and materials, the direction and utilization of scientific research on a vast scale. The urgent and immediate need of measures to solve such problems favors the growth of bureaucracy, anonymity, totalitarianism and state control. The human person is lost, submerged, forgotten. Even those with some wealth may become virtual proletarians, for it is not lack of property in itself that makes the proletarian but lack of a place in the social pattern which seems meaningful to the individual. We must restore to man his sense of being treated as a person, as a "somebody" having value for himself. God considered him worth creating, one by one in the family where he is valued for himself. The single solution is to organize work according to the principle of subsidiarity, by which each man shares in responsibility at his own level. Otherwise technological progress will degrade him to the level of a faceless robot.

Thomas Merton writes, "The task of restoring work to its proper place in the Christian life is then more than a personal, interior project for the individual. It is a cooperative and objective obligation of the Church and of human society. The individual Christian will do more to 'sanctify' his work by becoming intelligently concerned with the social order and with effective political means to improve social conditions, than he will ever be able to do by merely interior and personal spiritual efforts to overcome the tedium and meaninglessness of a subhuman battle for money. It goes without saying that the task is enormous. It has almost endless ramifications. They lead in all directions, into politics, economics, business, and everything that seriously affects the life of the nation and the international community" (*Life and Holiness,* Herder and Herder, 1963).

B. Man Offers His Work at Mass

Here we meet a question that is fundamental to Christian life. What sense of real relationship do we have between the creative role that God has given us in daily life and the central act of Christian worship? Much stress is now being laid on the people's participation in worship by the dialogue Mass, use of the vernacular, Mass facing the people and "The Prayer of the Faithful" after the sermon. But this Sunday participation so often has little community counterpart in their lives during the week. When the priest says, "Go forth, the Mass is ended," the community action also ends in many cases, having no machinery for its continuance in daily life. Each one departs to his own individual world, where he finds neither the Mystical Body community that was expressed in the Mass participation nor the means to help build it. The few parish groups of the lay apostolate are far from embracing the congregation of those who come to Mass. Rarely do they rally the other Catholics around them to show forth the Mystical Body as a dynamic force in daily life, as the Gospels make clear they ought to do and the early Christians carried out in practice.

Participation in the Mass rite does not of itself integrate our life with the Mass, nor does "Mass preparation" of the Missal text. We ourselves must offer our lives to God in terms of the human realities that make up the life of each one as a co-creator. In the early Church, the congregation discussed before Mass the work each one did as a member of the community; that was the gift he brought to the Offertory. A letter attributed to St. Clement, disciple of Peter and third pope, has these instructions: "Let them (the deacons) find out who are sick in the flesh and bring them to the attention of the main body, who knew nothing of them, that they may visit them and supply their wants, as the one presiding may judge fit." The assemblage discussed how they would assist the widows and orphans of the martyrs, rejoiced over reports of new believers and were concerned for those who had grown careless. Each one undertook some task for what St. Paul calls "the upbuilding of the Church of God." Apostolic works were considered a normal and essential part of the liturgy (Greek: service to the community), the Christian's counterpart to the work that Christ was about to renew in the Mass. Indeed, He there renews the work of His whole life that we may unite all our work with it: as a growing child, a carpenter, as Apostle and Redeemer.

The key of integrating Christian life with the Mass lies really in what we bring to it, then the follow-up will take care of itself. It is not enough to make a vague, general offering of our life which has no reference to the creative purpose of life. Of course, if one is dying of a disease or is to be shot at sunrise, the offering of his life is itself a work. But the average Catholic should offer his week's work as God's co-creator and apostle that Christ may unite it with His infinitely productive work. The Mass is particularly the renewal of the sacrifice on the cross, but Christ did not simply die there. He performed the great work of our redemption. It was not a passive acceptance of death, but an active work of life. The bread and wine offered by the priest represent the life that we spend working for God, not just life in the abstract. They are the products of human work, used for the nurture of life. At the Offertory they are withdrawn from human use in preparation for being changed into the Body and Blood of Christ at the Consecration. We offer up to God the productive human work we have been doing during the week that it may be united with the eternally productive work of Christ.

A little story from Africa illustrates how natural and universal is the idea of sacrifice and its relation to human work. One morning a pagan neighbor of the mission found that a ewe of his little flock had given birth to a perfect white lamb. "Ah," said he, "I will raise this lamb until the autumn and have the priest sacrifice it in thanksgiving for the blessings my family has received." Every day he went out to look at the lamb, washed and fed it, offering up daily the best of his lambs instead of raising it for a profit. Peoples everywhere have the idea of offering the best they have in sacrifice. The Jews in the Bible offered countless animals on God's altar. The basic idea is always the same. Man recognizes that he is not the source of his own life, of his power to work and act as a man. To show his acknowledgment, he offered an animal to signify giving not only life but the powers of life. Food and drink, the nurture of life, might also be offered but always in a form that cost the offerer something. Life and work, or action, are synonymous, and a merely general offering of our lives at Mass is unrelated to their reality of productive action.

Modern man tends to abandon the idea of offering sacrifice, seeing in it what he considers a primitive way to express man's relationship to God. But our Lord gave the notion of sacrifice a new dimension, as man's offering of his work to God in union with that of Christ. "Greater love than this no man hath, that a man lay down his life for His friend." We can bring to the Mass not only the daily work which represents our lives as God's co-creators, but also works of self-sacrifice for love of God and fellow man. This idea of uniting our work to that of Christ appeals even to those who are not Catholics. How sad if we allow individualistic religious traditions to direct our attention towards multiplied prayers and devotions not related to the Mass, or personal acts of mortification rather than apostolic ones. All these are good in themselves, but the sacrifice of our Lord in which we participate at Mass was a social work for others. When we sacrifice our time, our personal inclinations, to help another it opens up great new horizons of love. The communication of love with our human brother is already a communication with our Elder Brother in preparation for our Mass.

With such as our Offertory, participation in the Mass is seen as much more than individuals coming from their separate lives to worship together only briefly at a certain hour in the church and symbolizing chiefly a spiritual community of the Mystical Body. It becomes rather the action of those who live the Mystical Body visibly and productively with their brother in daily life, coming to express their community and revitalize it in union with Christ at the Consecration. At the Offertory we offer our material of sacrifice, specific, concrete works that we have been preparing in daily life, and at the Consecration our Lord offers them to the Father as His own. All our daily occupations as God's co-creators, our mutual relationships with others, become countless occasions for sharing through the Mass in the work of the Son of God from all eternity. Even one tied to a bed of pain should be active, not passive, co-offerer with Christ. Not only sufferings, but also cheerful cooperation with doctors and nurses, a quiet joy in Christ towards visitors and fellow patients, all can be material of sacrifice united with the Mass.

At the Assisi International Congress of Pastoral Liturgy in 1956, Bishop Wilhelm van Bekkum, of Ruteng, Flores, Indonesia, advocated restoration of the Offertory procession as an invitation to the faithful to bring to the altar a concrete expression of their offering. Otherwise, he said, "At the Mass the convert will, above all, get the impression that a real sacrificial celebration is wanting. In his eyes, the actions of the Mass will have more of a symbolic than an actual sacrificial character. This is true of the actions of the priest as well as those, above all, of the community. For him it is puzzling and unsatisfactory that the community as a whole or at least its representatives (the heads of the villages or families, or other leading persons) cannot perform that part of the ritual which devolves upon them. To the new convert, who has experienced a genuine ritual in his pagan religion, a mere 'attendance' at a celebration is truly pitiful, not to say primitive."

In India I saw an Offertory procession where rice was brought up. It had been put aside pinch by pinch when the housewives prepared the family meal, with a beautiful little prayer recalling the Mass. The sale of the rice, incidentally, multiplied by three to six times the former money offerings. At the parish of St. Francis Cabrini which I visited in Rome, the collection includes a community fund to provide bread for the poor in secret through orders on bake-shops. Where envelopes are used, a place could be provided to note sacrifices made for others. The Procession may be led by two boys carrying the filled cruets and filled ciborium on trays to the altar and the priest would proceed with the Offertory. In large churches the procession would use several aisles so as to finish by the Preface.

Before the Offertory processional hymn a lay reader could read a brief invitation to offer our material of sacrifice. After the Consecration another invitation could be made to co-offer our lives and work with Christ to His Father. A third reading would be at the end of the Canon to beg God's blessing on the offering we have made Him in Christ and to ask admittance to the heavenly banquet of Holy Communion which He prepares for us. I have found that visitors at Mass are much impressed by these invitations. "Now we understand what the Mass is about." They are also interested when told that the Mass stipend is simply a special sacrifice-offering on our part.

C. Reflections on Lay Spirituality

In *Sanctity for the Married,* an Ave Maria pamphlet, Donald H. Thorman tells the story of a young couple who took their sanctity in marriage very seriously from the time they became engaged. During the first months after their wedding, they worked out a neat plan of the way in which their home would be built on religious practices. They had set aside time each day for at least a little spiritual reading; they went to Mass and received the sacraments together regularly; they made a married couples' retreat. Then came the first baby and difficulties for the well-planned program. As the family grew, the mother complained: "Now I even have a hard time getting to Sunday Mass. If I'm not washing diapers, I'm wiping noses or preparing meals. I barely get the children dressed and out for the morning when they're back for lunch. When the dishes are washed I try to straighten out the house a little. Then it's time to begin supper. There's no time to pray or read any more."

When they were single they could stop by the parish church for morning Mass or a visit on the way home from work. Even after marriage, before the children came, the wife could get to a later Mass after her husband left for work; she could find time for visits to the church, spiritual reading, acts of charity for the neighbors. But the arrival of children puts an end to some of these activities, it curtails others. On the surface, such problems seem to discourage a vital spiritual life for the mother or father. They may even say, "I miss the spiritual life I used to have. I haven't time any more to concentrate on spiritual values." This type of person is trying to borrow a spirituality proper to monks and nuns and fit it to the life of those engaged as God's co-creators in a quite different kind of life than that of the monastery or convent. Unless lay people find in everyday activity the source of their spiritual life, they are doomed to a continued state of spiritual frustration. What a sorry situation for mankind if the vast mass of the laity should seem to be condemned to a life which is an obstacle to their closer union with God.

It is very important in this connection that we have a proper understanding of values in human life as God created it and their relation to one another. The oft-told story of two men working on a great cathedral bears repeating here. One was a master workman engaged in carving beautiful statues, but he complained that his work was monotonous. The second was an ordinary laborer who was helper to the master. When asked what he did the reply came proudly, "I am helping to build a cathedral." The Catholic layman, whether working in a factory or office, in field or mine, a woman as housewife, nurse or teacher, is helping to build the wondrous cathedral of God's world. And they are not building it of granite or marble, but of "living stones." That is the fundamental value assigned by God to human work. The material development of the world should itself be directed to the total human fulfillment of those whom God has made responsible for creation in His place.

These considerations lead us to the fundamental question: "What is the spiritual life? What is the goal of Christian life?" Strange as it may seem at first thought, our goal on earth is not a life of prayer as such. The real goal of human striving is union with God by cooperating with His purpose for man as His co-creator, and prayer is one way to achieve that union. Prayer is itself a human work, but is only one kind of work by which man cooperates with God. In general, we may say that God's purpose in creation is man's perfection, hence whatever we do in our state of life should be done with the intention of cooperating in this purpose of God. Some are called to make their contribution to man's perfection by a life spent in the work of prayer and contemplation which sacrifices the attractions of the world. Others are called to work for man's perfection chiefly through the external activities of raising a family and contributing to the development of a society in which man can work out his true fulfillment as a human composite of body and soul. The highest spiritual wisdom for each one consists in reflecting before God on how he can best carry out in his state of life God's creative plan for the growth of all men in the perfection of His love.

It would be a fatal mistake to think that the exterior life of work is in some way incompatible with the interior life of union with God. And to equate the interior life of being united to God with prayer life alone would be what Pope Pius XII called "angelism." It would border on the heresy of believing that the body has no role to play in union with God. rather that it distracts and leads us away from Him. The soul and body are not created for separate purposes. The soul animates the body, but it needs the life of the body for its own awakening and unfolding. The soul and body must grow together in knowledge and wisdom in man's fullest union with God and to play his part for the upbuilding of Christ's Body. The old Greeks considered the human body a mere instrument of the soul that is discarded once its work is done. They believed only in the soul's immortality, while the Jewish-Christian concept is of a bodily resurrection when it will be reunited with the soul for eternal life together. Easter is the feastday which reminds us of this fact and every Sunday is a "little Easter" when we unite our human work with the divine and immortal work of Christ.

If now we return to the young married couple, the main lines of their spiritual life become evident. First of all, no daily duty proper to their lives should be looked on as an obstacle to grace, or union with God. Slaving at a desk or a machine, caring for children or preparing meals, must be viewed in their creative context for human fulfillment as planned by God's wisdom. The mother feeding her baby is not simply helping it to grow, which has its own merit, but the way she handles it will basically influence the child's personality for its whole life. Her creative work in child raising is infinitely more important from the point of view of cooperating with God than any other activity in which she could engage. The husband's work is similarly vital because of the part it plays in the social context of human development. Their life in the world is for both a vocation from God to be lay apostles bearing witness as God's co-creators in order to draw those with whom they are in daily relationship to a recognition that this is life's essential meaning.

Here it may be helpful for us to recall the relation of the Apostles and faithful with our Lord when He was on earth, how human it was. Now that our Lord is not visible we tend towards the internal as an expression of our relationship to Him, while at that time it was entirely through the senses. Today also we have a relationship with Him through the senses in the members of His Mystical Body. They are Christ present to our bodily senses and we are Christ to them. If, for example, a poor widow prays for help to God how will her prayer be answered? Clearly it must be by God's children as His representatives on earth. If they are not alert to this external, social role which they have from God because they attend too exclusively to the internal and mystical aspect of religion, then what happens? The poor widow will tend to lose confidence in the power of prayer and religion will be brought into disrepute among men as having no place in the realities of human life. Now, as Abbot Vonier points out, it was no part of God's plan that this should happen.

It is essential, of course, to recognize our human limitations and the danger of allowing material things to absorb our attention away from the real meaning of work. The result could be that our consciousness of union with God in work would become foggy and might even disappear. God has taken this into account by asking us to give back to Him one day in the seven that He gives us in order that then we may reflect more fully on our relationship to Him. And our loving mother the Church teaches us the necessity of regular prayer to elevate our minds and hearts to God. On the other hand we must not fall into the trap which snares some souls of allowing so much time for prayer and so much time for work as if they were not both part of one life lived for God. A very excellent practice is to give at least part of our prayer time to talking with God about our work, to ask His light and guidance. The important thing is our habitual attitude. When we try to know and do what God wants us to do in all aspects of our state in life with willingness to forget ourselves in His service and that of our neighbor, then we are leading the true life of a Christian.

D. The Christian Among Dynamic Men

The most striking thing that I noticed on my visit to mission lands after an absence of more than ten years, was a greatly increased awareness of human powers and human rights among people everywhere. They desire a world of justice and equity, though not always with clear understanding. I was told by missionaries who knew the races of primitive culture in Africa, even stone age tribes of New Guinea, that there are new stirrings among them all. A worldwide revolution of expectations is under way, the desire of sharing in the benefits promised by modern technology and of exercising the democratic right to manage their own national destiny. The world has become one and to use the term "foreign missions" now strikes a discordant note of separation. Henceforth there can be but one mission of the Church.

One notes among lay Catholics a growing maturity of thought and in most places gets a general impression of flourishing Catholicity—large churches, crowded schools and busy welfare activities. Often on Sundays, however, he wonders why there seem to be mostly women and children at Mass with a few older men, but a marked absence of younger men. In some dioceses of Africa, 80 to 90 per cent of the young men do not practice their religion and many have made polygamous marriages. I was told in Japan that the number who no longer practice about equals the conversions and is especially high among those who leave their native parish to find work. Among young workers of the United States, it appears that in many areas between the ages of 17 and 30 who do not make their Easter duty are as many as 40 to 60 per cent. The loss to the Church of so many young people and the new families they form has become a universal problem.

At a discussion with several missionaries in Africa a brief analysis was worked out that seemed to embody in a few words some essential elements of the question. "Modern man," they said, "has entered upon a dynamic era of rapid development. We see that, even considering as an individual, his growth always takes place through social cooperation. This means that he himself undertakes constantly increasing responsibilities in society. Now if his religious growth is to keep pace with his social development, he must equally undertake more responsibilities in his religion. Tradition can no longer be counted on to keep people faithful to the Church, as is so often seen when African Catholic youth go from the village to the city for work. The character of city life itself, its dangers and attractions, require that Catholics become more closely identified with the Church by active participation in the life of Catholic community."

With reference to these conclusions, it is to be noted that modern man's increased social consciousness and interest are developed much less by formal study than by personal participation in social processes. The Church must apply the same principle of participation to the religious development of the laity, else interest in religious values is crowded out by the new interest in social and economic ones. A missionary research center in the former Belgian Congo reached the conclusion that the high loss of faith there since independence was due largely to the Catholics not feeling they had a community function as Christians. Both in the villages and city neighborhoods many were found to be seeking in political movements the satisfaction of their innate need for community participation which had not been given an outlet in parish life. This throws some light also on the missionary purpose of the Church. It is not alone to establish the Church as an institution with a native hierarchy, but also to establish it as an organic community able to grow with its own life from deep roots in the Catholic laity.

Missionaries in Africa pointed out how much more closely the lives of the non-Christians were related to religion than among Christians in the West. Some felt that our presentation of the Faith was often weak for this reason. The African cannot understand, for example, why we regard as religious only certain activities, the Mass and sacraments, prayer, spiritual exercises, acts of mortification and almsgiving. Why not also, he asks, consider as religious going on a journey, building a house, getting a job, planting the fields and gathering their fruits? Is it not important to offer the first-fruits of one's work to God? Are not all of these part of the life that has been given us to fulfill? Westerners easily assume an air of superiority towards the religious rites by which the African seeks blessings on all his undertakings, but the orientation of his life towards man's relation to God is more all-embracing than our own.

One effect of our regarding religion as a private and interior activity for special times is evident in the progressive secularization of western society. In spite of the fact that the majority of us profess some form of Christianity, our social institutions are becoming more and more secularized, more and more withdrawn from a sense of relation to God. People become unable to think of religion as having a direct part to play in guiding those institutions. We shall discuss this further in the next chapter. Here we note how far we in the United States have departed from the Preamble to the Declaration of Independence in our public recognition of man's relation to God, and the same is true elsewhere in the West. We bewail the prevalence of expediency as a norm of action among us, but given our narrow concept of religion these become inevitable. We expect right action from the individual but deny him an adequate measure of social support.

Those who come as students to our shores from the emerging countries find religion treated among us as an institution with individual members, not as a force that directs our community, for example, in race-relations. For a large proportion of them this becomes a scandal in the true sense of a stumbling-block, that religion often seems for us to have only a personal and supplementary value, like some kind of spiritual vitamins for individual good health. The secularism that dominates Western education tends to make those students ashamed of their own religion as something for the backward or for children. Many go back home to become leaders carrying a spiritual emptiness which Communism will seek to fill. They will rarely think of religion as an important element in the development of their people, as is quite clear from the majority of leaders trained in the West who are now guiding the destinies of their countries.

Bishop Fulton Sheen, speaking at a White House conference on foreign aid, declared: "The foreign aid of the United States must introduce some factor besides the economic, political and military, one which is strongest in our national traditions and one which the Soviets not only lack but repudiate. They have one fear in our dealings with the rest of the world, that we will take cognizance of that defect which makes them suspect by all the peoples of Asia and Africa, and that is our belief in God, the dignity of the human person, the freedom of conscience, and the principle that the state exists for man, and not man for the state. When we go along with the Communist line that matter alone matters, we are weak and they are strong, when we give economic aid on the basis that matter alone does not matter, they are powerless and we are strong."

Pope Paul VI has told us that the essential task of the Second Vatican Council is to consider the mystery of the Church in the light of today's world, of man's vastly increased understanding of the relation between religious and social forces. Much has been written about a new social order in the world, a Christian order, but for it to become a reality we must offer mankind much more than a few remedies for certain social symptoms: We must offer the world a Christian mystique that is able to transform the whole outlook of human life in all its aspects, not merely in the aspects of religious and social practice but of the composite produced by their interaction. The mystery of the Church must be seen as involved in the mystery of mankind created by God to build a new world.

A medical student in South America said not long ago: "From the free world I get no mystique of life as an integrated whole. From the Communists I do." Now the "free world" to which he referred is basically a Christian world and that student had most probably been baptized a Catholic in a Catholic culture, but a culture unaware that it must take into account spiritual and social wholeness of human development. As we contemplate the flight of modern society from God, or perhaps more truly, its ignorance of God's place in human development, we become aware of the necessity for very deep reflection on how the Christian mystique is to penetrate and animate human society. The new world will not be built by piecemeal application of certain Christian ideas. The People of God must typify what human life really means in its entirety, not only in certain spiritual or social aspects here or there.

5. NEW CHALLENGES TO CATHOLIC EDUCATION

The role of Catholic education may be simply stated as to put truth at the service of mankind. Now all truth is from God and is given us for the purpose of carrying out His creative plan for man's development. In order, therefore, that truth may truly serve mankind it must be projected beyond the classroom into life and its function made clear as God's directive for all human life. The enemies of God seek to subvert not only the mind of man but his whole being, and their weapons are not simply ideas but ideas applied to life.

Father Jean Daniélou is quoted in *Christ to the World* (1957, No. 1): "The modern atheistic humanism invented by the West is in the process of conquering the world. India, for example, which has been lucky enough to witness a revolution carried out by religious men . . . is ideologically infested by many movements of thought which are gradually detaching the country from its religious foundations and causing the infiltration of atheistic humanism into student environments." We may point out here that much of that influence is by men who never set foot in India, by teachers in western classrooms, literary men, the press and all the ways that another culture exerts its influence. So also the impact of Christianity on the East comes only partly from the missionary. Christian writers, artists, intellectuals, also have a positive missionary function as well as the negative one of counteracting atheistic humanism.

"How many young Africans," says Father Daniélou in another article quoted by the same issue, "are abandoning their traditional religion and being won over by Marxism and the atheistic humanism which are being offered them . . . We are responsible for drawing them into the conflict between the materialist West and the Christian West. For it seems evident that the ancient Eastern and African civilizations cannot resist the pressure of the West, that they are crumbling away. Only the Christian West can save the East from the materialist West." The editor comments: "Who in the West has the intellectual prestige to reverse that flow? The only ones capable of creating a powerful enough current of ideas are our Catholic universities and intellectuals of the West . . . That is the role incumbent on them, a vital role that cannot be undertaken by anyone else." Here I would add that they must not allow themselves to think that the presentation of ideas alone will save the modern world. Marxism is intensely pragmatic and aggressively carries its ideas out into the key areas of human life. Communists are able to educate even the illiterate in the school of everyday life to be apostles of their doctrines. Catholic ideas must never be presented in isolation but always in relation to man as a creator, a maker.

A. The Question of Religion and Science

"The anti-religious campaign, so virulent in Russia and Communist countries, is everywhere waged in the name of science," states the editor of *Christ to the World* (1955, No. 5). "The famous resolution of the Central Committee of the Communist Party of the Soviet Union, signed by Khrushchev himself on November 10, 1954, states that to eradicate religious thought it is . . . indispensable to carry on, thoroughly and systematically, scientific atheist thought." Here are some passages of that resolution, as translated in *Christ to the World* from the French version:

–The Communist Party struggles against religious ideology as being unscientific ideology. The essential opposition of religion and science is obvious.

—The struggle against religious prejudice must be considered as the ideological struggle of scientific and materialist conscience against the religious and anti-scientific conception.

—The results at which science has at present arrived, in the field of natural sciences and in that of social sciences, refutes religious dogmas beyond all doubt.

—Science and religion are incompatible.

The editor of *Christ to the World* continues: "This propaganda goes on continually, everywhere—in schools, study circles, by means of newspapers, books, radio and all the powerful means at the disposal of the Soviets. It exercises a deep influence, especially on younger people. The modern world is scientifically minded and full of admiration for scientific progress, and in regions affected by Communist propaganda, there are few prejudices more widely spread than that religion is opposed to science." The editor states further that persons who work among refugees from Russia and Communist-held countries are much concerned to find that even those who have religious aspirations are affected. Irene Prosnoff, a convert from Orthodoxy, asks, "How can those influenced by this propaganda be dis-intoxicated?" She observes that abstract reasoning and the classical arguments of apologists have very little effect on such refugees.

"The Christian West must save the East from the materialist West." Discussing these words of Father Daniélou and the problem they imply with Catholic leaders from Japan to India, in Africa and even Catholic Latin America, I found this materialist influence of the West even where little Communist propaganda existed. It is summed up and epitomized in one short phrase that the West has given the East: "Religion is opposed to science." This phrase was not invented by the Communists, yet it provides a perfect preparation for atheistic Communism almost as if it had been copied from the Soviet resolution instead of the other way around. This idea is found in most textbooks of history as well as science based on western authors in practically all educational institutions outside of Catholic ones. In a questionnaire distributed among Japanese students some years ago one question was on the relation between religion and science. A typical reply read: "My history book states that religion has been consistently opposed to science and I have no reason to believe otherwise."

Such claims made in the name of truth by teachers and intellectual leaders of Asia, Africa and Latin America can be refuted only by the prestige of intellectuals from the West. For example, Catholic universities of the West could set up university extension institutes in key educational areas of various countries, which are usually centered around the national and state capitals. There has been for many years a Yale-in-China, and several U.S. universities sponsor counterparts in various Latin American countries. Our program would be much more modest, yet not the less effective. A team of perhaps 3 or 4 Catholic specialists would go out to set up an "extension (or, associate) institute" of their home university. The team might comprise a topflight physicist or other natural science expert, a social scientist, an expert in the philosophy of education and perhaps one in history. Others would be added according to further indications. Each year the institute would sponsor "visiting experts" of high enough standing in their respective fields to be accorded a hearing by the intellectual circles of the country. For example, Father D'Arcy, the English Jesuit, and Gabriel Marcel, the French Catholic philosopher, made a real impression a few years ago by their lectures before the intellectuals of Japan.

It appears that the team would do well to avoid getting involved in a demanding schedule of classwork at local schools. Classroom teaching is determined by the school's program and one's opportunities for direct influence on the class are usually very limited. Correcting test papers for the large classes of these schools would consume a vast amount of time. The key of influence is rather through personal contacts with teachers and students outside the classroom and through special lectures. One might act as "guest lecturer" in various schools in order to become better known. It is essential, however, to leave oneself free for "parlor work" and personal visits, to conduct discussion groups at the institute and to brief student leaders. One should also be free for field trips to other cities for personal contact with intellectuals there. Such a program would give the necessary freedom of action and permit multiplication of contacts, the more valuable because more personal. The personal cultivation of teachers, for example, would be an excellent means to counteract the "religion is opposed to science" idea.

At the level of secondary education, which is rapidly becoming widespread, the missionaries themselves can do much. In the town of Miaoli, Taiwan, with 40,000 people, there are four large government middle schools. The Maryknoll Fathers set up a reading room and students' reference library in a location within easy access to the schools. The shelves with their more than 3,000 volumes are open and there is someone taking advantage of this service practically all day long and late into the night. Books may be taken to a quiet study room for undisturbed work. Around the public reading room are placed large panels which form a permanent Catholic exhibit, with particular themes changed every two months. From the theme, "Catholics in Science," students were surprised to find that many names with which they were familiar in their textbooks belong to Catholics. Other subjects are: Catholics in Art, in Music, in Education; Rome and the Holy Father. Another subject, "Christ the Ideal of Youth," is presented by a large painting done locally of Christ with young people and photographs of Catholic youth activities in many parts of the world.

B. A University More Fully Catholic

The Catholic university which organizes extension work in the newly developing countries thereby adds a very important dimension to its own universality of outlook. For there it can actually take part in the fascinating jump from 13-16th century culture to the 20th. Catholic specialists from the West would enjoy more than ordinary prestige and could help guide the emerging society along the right lines. Some education areas in those countries often suffer from a considerable time-lag, especially in the secondary schools, for many now teaching there studied under men who went abroad a generation ago. That was the time when anti-religion was probably at its height among western intellectuals and the notions then brought back have tended to crystallize into academic traditions. In Taiwan, for example, education is dominated by the ideas of John Dewey, officially adopted on the Chinese mainland in the 1920's. The result is relativism in moral science, with conscience considered simply a social product.

Though some mission areas have Catholic universities, only in rare instances do they equal in prestige the highly subsidized government universities, often for lack of sufficient help from Catholics in other parts of the world. An extension institute of a western university established near a government one would be far easier to finance and would not be looked on as in competition. At the same time, if it had several topflight specialists, even if for only a certain period a year, it would attract the interest of both teachers and students. The institute would also be a residence for selected homeside students taking courses at the government school. Both faculty and students consider it a compliment that foreign students follow their courses. As many as 20 extension institutes could be staffed with the foreign personnel required for one small Catholic university. Several such institutes in a country could give precious assistance to the idealism of those who desire to aid their people but need help to evaluate social change in the light of unchanging values. In Japan, for instance, the need of moral education is recognized, but what principles are to be stressed in place of tradition? Because of the lack of a natural law concept, which they do not discover in their traditions, those responsible tend to propose directives based on a secular concept of morality.

Work in the newly developing countries would help the homeside Catholic University to become more directly aware of its role and responsibility in the Church's Mission at home as well as abroad. For example, it is my impression that Catholic students in the United States tend to enter the "bread and butter" professions. One would expect rather, in view of the Catholic layman's social responsibility, to find Catholic Universities leading in research on special problems and human welfare. Monsignor Ligutti, who represents the Vatican at the Food and Agricultural Organization of the United Nations, has stated that, in spite of our strong stand against contraception, Catholic schools "are not doing much, if anything" in food production and distribution research. Catholic Universities should prepare many more technicians to work in areas where population pressures are great and food production low. By far the major part of serious study along those lines is at present being done by persons who do not accept the Church's position on birth control.

There seems to be relatively little dialogue between the Catholic university and the modern world on the mystique of truth and the meaning of life. Indeed, recently the spirit of exchange seems stronger between Catholic seminaries and Protestant divinity schools—at least, it comes more to public attention. Is it that our statement of life's meaning is still so much in terms borrowed from the more static past that we are unable to communicate with modern man who sees life as a dynamic and continuing human ascent? Yet what could be more dynamic than the Christian view of life as not simply the ascent towards God of the individual but of the community, in which he also is born upward? Sin did not deprive man of this original heritage but only weakened his ability to use it to the full except by long and arduous self-discipline. Does not such a dynamic concept of life open the way to dialogue with those who also view it dynamically, even if primarily from the material point of view? If we are really committed to the spirit of ecumenism, we must try to understand the reality represented by other approaches to truth than our own and give credit to the good will of man always in search of his heritage. Perhaps we do not give enough consideration to the material part of man in the whole. To paraphrase a witty Japanese philosopher: The westerner believes that he thinks with his mind alone, and won't acknowledge that he thinks also with his guts.

It has been said that the Catholic school tends to build a fence around its students as a protection to faith and morals. May not that fence also tend to so cut them off from the world that they do not see the relation between Christian education and the world of today and be therefore unable to enter into the apostolic dialogue by word and action which the popes have said is the layman's vocation? What proportion of Catholic college graduates in the average parish are active in the lay apostolate? The modern trends of social evolution make it more than ever imperative that the Catholic student grow in socio-religious awareness of the world into which he will go and his relation to it as a Catholic. That is not something to be acquired "sometime" in the vague future, but needs to be made an integral part of his preparation for life as an educated Catholic. The question has been raised as to whether Catholic education is producing a sufficient number of top lay leaders in todays marketplaces. Would this perhaps be due in some measure to the fact that so many Catholic educators are priests, who by their vocation cannot be fully involved in the marketplace? Do not many Catholic students acquire a sort of "clerical" outlook that makes them feel uncomfortable in the public forum of ideas?

Almost every valedictorian at a commencement speaks about the life of action into which the graduates are entering. In modern education there is provision for vocational guidance to help students orient themselves for their careers. But the Catholic school by its very nature ought to give all students an orientation towards Catholic Action in the sense that the whole of every Catholic's life is involved in God's creative purpose for mankind, not for himself alone. To have some students engaged in the lay apostolate as an extra-curricular activity is not enough; every course should be set in a human context from the Christian point of view. It is now general practice in the study of cultures, social conditions, human attitudes, to have field work, contact with people. But in such professions as law or medicine, the student also needs to have personal experience of the human context, of the social and apostolic as well as professional responsibilities inherent for the Catholic in his state of life. If the student has not learned to see his own life's work in relation to the Christian's mission in the world, how can he fulfill the role chosen for him by the design of God in that state of life?

It is very important that Catholic universities of the West not only welcome foreign students but form them in this social awareness. It is critical for our Church-related institutions everywhere in the world. Several years ago I met a young priest from Latin America studying in the United States. He told me that his city had a Catholic university of perhaps 10,000 students, mostly baptized but few practicing. They were in general little concerned about the urgent problems among the poor in that city and would later go out to work in their chosen field of life with little likelihood of making much contribution towards social improvement. I suggested that the medical students spend perhaps two hours a week helping in free clinics for the poor, law students in legal clinics, liberal arts and students of other faculties conducting various types of evening classes. He found the idea "impractical," yet almost in the same breath deplored the growing influence of Communism among the poor. When I visited West Pakistan in 1961, the Moslem Minister of Education had just decreed that all students, even in secondary schools, must spend a certain number of hours weekly in some form of social action in order to graduate. One wonders if our own conviction of possessing religious truth does not sometimes tend to make us socially smug and ingrown.

C. The Christian Mystique of Education

The great harm done by secular education to the sense of God in man's life does not result so much from teaching positive religious error in certain aspects as from the negative effect of leaving out God altogether. To the student in such a school, God seems less needful in life than the least important subject of the curriculum, for that does receive some positive attention. Religion thus becomes a "no-value" in the very environment that prepares the vast majority of citizens to take their part in society. The fruits are evident in the galloping secularism and lack of value standards that envelopes the whole life of our culture in spite of there being so many individual church-goers. And among the underdeveloped peoples no missionary effort can stem the steady religious breakdown that occurs when their political and educational leaders become convinced from the example of western countries that secularist culture is the mark of modern progress. In the first chapter we mentioned that this is a time of great missionary opportunity, because those peoples are seeking a new religious identity as well as political and social identity. Yet in widely separated mission areas I heard expressed the belief that 5 to 10 years would see a great decline in religious conversions because of progressive secularization.

In Catholic schools the students are not ignorant of God since they have a class in religion. But the essential quality of Catholic education, that it should relate all knowledge to God's creative purpose for man, is often under-stressed. What happens if God is absent also in the Catholic school from the body of general knowledge on which the students' future participation in social institutions is built? When they come in later life to use this knowledge, the thought of its place in God's plan will not be automatically associated with it. In view particularly of the large place held by the school today in forming our life-pattern and social outlook, this question assumes critical importance for the Church's mission and for Catholics themselves in our so strongly secularist society. Even the Catholic school is often trapped into over-emphasis on the economic aspect of the student's future career.

The student takes his cue from his teachers. His lifetime view of the relation of temporal things to God's purpose, of the meaning of work, of man's part in perfecting God's creation—all will depend on the attitude he acquired at school. If he enters upon his state in life without a proper correlation between them, he will never have a clear view of his state of life as the appointed field of his lay vocation to render the social institutions in which he there participates conformable to the spirit of Christ. How can the parish priest, how can Catholic Action, give the faithful a real sense of their vocation to Christianize the institutions of society unless Catholic education has made it a part of their basic formation?

Some years ago Pope Pius XII told a group of educators, "Catholic education must become more Catholic . . . It must aim at confronting its pupils with all their responsibilities." The popes do not look on the Catholic responsibility to bring Christ into the marketplace and into all social institutions as an "extra-curricular" activity of the Catholic, but as an essential part of Christian life. Now if the lay apostolate is to hold this place in the Catholic's life, it cannot be properly prepared for simply by having some extra-curricular apostolic activities in the Catholic school, excellent as they may be. It must be seen and emphasized as an essential part of the official course of studies by which the student is prepared for life. The trend in our changing society is for life to lose its unity and religion to be separated from the other elements. Shall the Catholic school itself be guilty of this—so much time for religion, so much time for general knowledge? Should not the healing of this dichotomy which already works such great harm in Catholic life and the restoration of that unity be considered the highest function of Catholic education? If not, on what other institution shall it fall?

The "mystique," or mystery, of Catholic education lies in its function as itself a co-creator with God to restore the unity of God's plan for man by giving its students the proper formation in their role as His co-creators. As we saw in discussing the mystique of work, God made men His co-creators for the perfecting of men and things, chiefly through their cooperation in society. Obviously, man cannot fulfill this role if he is neither aware of it nor trained for it. Catholic education has the irreplaceable function in God's plan of not only giving man the tools to fulfill his role but also of teaching him their use. The commonly accepted definition of the lay vocation from the fact itself of being that of the layman is to bring Christ into the marketplace and into the institutions of society as himself a participant there. It would seem a truism that the chief influence of the Catholic school against secularism in our society must be through its students, but we do not appear to do very well. May this be related to the goals our students have in mind during their long years of training? Is it "success," or is it to act as God's co-creator in the world for the perfecting of man both directly and through the perfecting of things?

No other organ of the Church can fulfill the function proper to Catholic education of formally relating all knowledge to God's creative purpose. Cardinal Newman wrote, "God has relations of His own towards the subject-matter of each particular science . . . Religious truth is not only a portion, but the condition of general knowledge" (*On the Scope and Nature of University Education).* Edward B. Pusey, Anglican friend of Newman, stated, "All sciences . . . will tend to exclude the thought of God if they are not cultivated with reference to Him" *(Collegiate and Professional Teaching and Discipline).* Yet people outside the Church today look on the Catholic school as simply teaching general knowledge in a certain Catholic atmosphere, not as offering a radically different outlook on knowledge. More and more social institutions are growing up divorced from religion and the newly independent countries are almost all organized under secular constitutions. I have even heard Catholic educators speak of the "secular" subjects in their curriculum!

Sometimes Catholic teachers say that the object or matter of "profane" knowledge is the same whether taught by an agnostic or a Catholic. But we must make two distinctions here. One is that, though the object of knowledge is the same, the baptized Catholic "subject" acquiring the knowledge is of quite a different order from an unbaptized subject. He has a very specific and positive supernatural responsibility for using his knowledge in a certain way. The second distinction is even more fundamental. Despite ignorance on the part of the agnostic teacher or the unbaptized student, both must refer their knowledge to God and use it in accordance with His plan as they have light to do so. But the Catholic educator or student does not have the excuse of ignorance if he fails to make clear the divine source and purpose of all knowledge.

Let us take the example of a Catholic professor who teaches atomic energy. The facts and laws that he explains are identical with those presented by his agnostic colleague in a secular school, following the strictly scientific method. But is that all for the Catholic teacher? Perhaps he may warn his class not to commit sin by using atomic energy to do harm, but that is a further example of the merely negative approach which renders sterile so much of Catholic teaching. Why can he not say, does he not say, to his students that God bestows on them a high honor to live in this great dynamic age and to act as His co-creators in providing the fuel needed for the further progress of the world? When I expressed this idea to a chemist in Caracas, his reaction was, "Why, that gives me an entirely new outlook on the relation between my religion and my work in the 'miracle' science of organic chemistry?"

"But how," some will say, "can you do that with a course in arithmetic, or in typing and shorthand, or calculus or heating systems?" The answer lies in a twofold emphasis. One is that all knowledge comes from God, but this relation will not be sensed as a living reality unless each form of knowledge is cultivated with reference to His plan for mankind. The other is that all studies should be so projected into the future that the student understands how the state of life where he will use them is precisely the field of his particular vocation to cooperate in God's plan. Without this projection, the student is likely to go out into the world unaware of his role to promote the kingdom of God precisely in the field where he uses arithmetic, typing, shorthand, calculus or knowledge of heating systems. Is not that unawareness a chief reason why the lay apostolate so often seems something super-added or "extra-curricular" to life and fails to have a truly dynamic influence in the parish and the world? The young Communist is urged to become expert in, for example, the field of mathematics or typing and shorthand precisely because it will help him to promote Communism.

The modern world stands in dire need of an up to date correlation of all truth with life as related to God's plan for human development, and the pursuit of this correlation is the primary justification for Catholic education. The entire education program should be set in that context. This suggests the need in each school of an organization to promote such integration. There should be periodic meetings to discuss the ways to achieve a real integration, not only of the various branches of knowledge with one another, but of all together for serving the fullest good of man under God's plan. Catholic education needs not only to provide its students with the tools for life but also to show them how God meant these tools to be used. The great strength of Communism lies precisely in the fact that it integrates all knowledge, all formation, all action, with the Communist view of life's meaning. What a dynamic new force Catholic education would introduce into the world if it infused students with a concept of the Christian life that would lead them to look for ways and means to apply it of themselves? Is not such self-activation in the line of cooperation with God the essential purpose of true education as well as of the lay apostolate?

D. Sharing the Gifts of God

At a gathering of intellectuals in Bombay several years ago, a Mr. Masani asked, "Why do so many of our educated young men turn towards Communism?" His answer: "Because they have given up their ancestral beliefs and have replaced them with nothing else." A non-Christian professor put this challenge to the missionaries of India. "What frightens me about this youth is their lack of prayer. . . . Why don't you teach our young men to pray before it is too late? You do all kinds of things less important, for which you are less qualified, but the spiritual is your realm and your responsibility." In a college of South India, a Brahmin asked a young priest in his class: "What is it you do before lectures? You pray to God, don't you? Teach me how to pray." Years later he was baptized.

In *Christ to the World* (1959, No. 3), Father G. E. Watrin wrote from India: "Young people are always led by ideals. Do they get these in the colleges and universities of India? Not if you exclude the enticing ideal of Communism. . . . In government schools religious education is excluded and in the other schools it is held to a bare minimum, and often neglected altogether. The Hindus and Mohammedans who come to our (Catholic) schools are not trained in their own religion and religious practices, and hence quickly discard and forget them. Nor are they taught any other religion. 'Oh, but we teach them Moral Science' some will object. True, but we all know, only too well, that a knowledge of right and wrong does not give the strength to do the right and avoid the wrong. . . . Except for a few students who come under the influence of their 'religious' teachers, our students receive nothing but a vague feeling of religiosity from our schools. Since this is not backed up by external practices, many of them lose all religion in a short time after leaving our schools. We educate them to atheism."

The problem raised by Father Watrin troubles the missionaries in many countries to varying degrees. In India, not only is religious propaganda forbidden in the schools, but any Hindu who became a Catholic would be accused of betraying his own culture and might well be assassinated by religious fanatics as Gandhi was. Missionaries are now beginning to consider the idea that it may often be necessary to bring people to the fullness of the Faith by slow stages according as they are able to correspond with grace. The great English convert, Gilbert K. Chesterton, is said to have been defending the Church for twenty years before he actually became a Catholic. This does not mean that we should fail to bear witness to the Faith, quite the contrary. But in each situation the various modifying elements must be taken into account. There might be people of good will who, like Chesterton, would remain for a certain period at one or another stage. Our aim would be to get them to perform religious acts at each stage which would open to them further channels of grace.

During my visit to India in 1961 I found an example of a movement towards the Faith by stages organized by Father E. J. Briffa, S.J., in a Catholic high school for boys where almost all are Hindus. Faced with the problem described by Father Watrin, he proposed to the boys an organization under the title, "God's Leaders' Group," with emphasis on preparing to be worthy leaders in the new India. The boys themselves recruited fourteen outstanding students from the three upper classes, about one in ten of the student body. The priest, as "spiritual guide," began by telling them that they should never be ashamed as many boys are nowadays of their mothers' religious teaching, which was in reality a gift from God. Their mothers had taught them to pray, but then they were small and did not have a clear idea of the full meaning of prayer. Now they were becoming adults and should understand how to pray as adults. He proposed to explain to them four kinds of prayer: adoration, praise, thanksgiving, petition, and suggested that they pray in their own words according to these ideas. Some wrote out prayers for themselves. He thus weaned them from the old prayer formulas without imposing formal Catholic ones. Each morning they have a ten-minute meditation and every two months make a day of recollection.

A second channel of grace was opened to them of charity towards the needy and social justice towards the worker because all are made in God's image. Concern for the hardships of the masses was developed through conferences by the spiritual guide and field trips, while practice in leadership was chiefly in the area of school responsibilities. The school principal expressed amazement at the changed spirit brought about within two years among the predominantly non-Christian students. The boys in the group developed greatly in a personal love of God and neighbor, but they were not yet ready to accept Christ because of community prejudices. The spiritual guide showed me an example of the "progress notes" which each boy makes during the recollection day on three points: the group's progress, the spiritual guidance, each member's contribution. This boy commented that he liked the talks by the spiritual guide and that one on the condition of the poor made an impression he would never forget, but he criticized bringing in Christ so exclusively as an example of love towards others.

Though these boys will not perhaps become Catholics in the near future, they will always feel a real bond with the Church because they now share with her prayer and charity as channels of grace.

Also in India, the priest director of a labor school praised the workers for their spirit of mutual aid and told them that by it they were manifesting God's goodness which man shares from being God's image. The workers do not for the most part practice any religion, but are not anti-religious at heart. They simply have not seen any value in its formal expression. The praise for sharing God's goodness with fellow workers and their families gives them a sense of themselves having value at a higher level than the merely economic one and tends to lift their hearts a little towards God. All men have within them an innate sense of religion that only needs to be touched at the proper point. The director tells them also that what their mother taught them was a gift of God's goodness and now that they have children of their own they realize the importance of family training. He points out that, as adults with responsibility to train their own children, they need to appeal to an authority higher than themselves for standards of conduct. Now to teach their children man's relationship to God, they themselves need a better understanding of prayer and religion than they themselves had only from their childhood training.

It would seem that our college graduates and others with leadership ability could use a similar method to share Catholic values with those not yet drawn to the Church. They would present to some others outside the Church the idea of cooperating in works of charity in a simple, positive way as God's deputies to manifest His goodness on earth. Most will accept this idea which is essential to constitute an apostolate and not simple philanthropy. The Catholic originators of the group would keep relating its activities to the concept that we are God's deputies, co-creators, everywhere—in the family, the neighborhood and all the relationships of life. This supernatural orientation opens up a common channel of grace for both the Catholic members and those who are not. As they experience an inner satisfaction from doing good, they will come to understand that our relationship to God includes all our social responsibilities. It is easy then to suggest that the members offer to God by prayer the work they are doing, thank Him for the light He gives them, ask His help to do it well. Thus the second channel of grace, prayer.

Would not such initiative on the part of Catholics be an excellent form of practical "ecumenism"? It would create bonds of charity and prayer between Catholics and those outside the Church, open up many lines of communication that would work a change in relations between the Church and the general community. For our cooperators in good works would be our apostles there, they would receive a hearing that we could not hope to get. The awareness of common spiritual values with us that they acquire in the groups, and the lack of which is one of the great obstacles to Christian influence, will make them real witnesses to the Church in the general community. Their apostolate will have all the greater impact because they will declare among their own how the Catholic spiritual values of prayer and charity correspond to the inner religious sense common to all men. Perhaps such groups organized among students would like a study-action program based on the Gospels. In India, if a priest led it he would be regarded as a proselytizer, but Catholic students briefed by him would be less likely to face that handicap. The Gospel study, moreover, would be undertaken by the students as a guide of life rather than from a theological point of view.

6. WE AND GOD'S PEOPLE OF TOMORROW

The story is told of a business tycoon who went to a famous psychologist. "Look," he said, "I have four children, from five to eleven. Your specialty is human nature, mine is business. I'd like you to see those children about once a week. Money is no object if you will undertake to make them good men and women." The psychologist replied, "No fee could be large enough to insure that. It is something only you can do."

Each human soul is created by God to fit its genetic inheritance of intelligence and constitution from parents, but the child comes helpless into the world. God has made man to pass a long tutelage under parents and teachers in order that his natural gifts may be developed in the accrued wisdom of the past, each generation rising to a higher level of progress. From the first moment of its existence, the child depends on human contact and communication in order to acquire this wisdom of the race and it is parents who provide the basic formation on which all other growth must be built. Today this is sometimes forgotten owing to emphasis on education in schools as a preparation to take one's place in modern life. The child's first educators are its parents, who mold the basic quality of its life by the home atmosphere they create rather than by formal teaching. No school can later make up for failure on their part. It is a fact of everyday life for example, that the child learns to speak from hearing conversation. If the speech of parents shows mutual respect and affection, that is what he learns; if angry and rough, he will speak the same way. If a young father and mother pray devoutly beside the infant's crib, the special cadence of their voices prepares him to take part in prayer later.

The child's nervous system is, in reality, like a living tape recorder which registers everything he hears, sees or feels. Nothing is ever erased, though the output may be modified by later recordings as well as by our free choices. Thus habits are acquired and thus may be changed. All impressions combine with our genetic heritage to form each one's basic personality pattern. Specialists tell us that when a child is wet or hungry he suffers a "specific" anxiety which disappears when the cause is removed. But if a mother picks up her infant when she is under tension from a quarrel or other reason, her tension is transmitted to the child's nervous system as a "general" anxiety that remains and is aggravated by each repeated experience. Crying for no apparent reason, bed-wetting by older children, are often results of tension in the home. A child's behavior is always "a mirror that reflects what is going on round about him."

A. The Process of Growing Up

The child begins at about the age of four to leave its mother's arms and explore the world around it. From then up to twelve is the first stage of growing up, the time of the child's basic formation through taking part in the life of the family where he is loved. Medical psychology tells us that without love a child's personality does not unfold, for example, an infant left for even six months in an institution without constant "mothering" can be stunted for life. Social workers nowadays much prefer to deal with a problem child within its own family environment by helping the parents, 'unfit' as they may often be, than to put it in an institution. The function of parenthood is not only physical but psychological as well. Modern thought tends sometimes to emphasize the mutual fulfillment of husband and wife more than the needs of children. In reality, this fulfillment is meant to provide children with a proper atmosphere of mutual love rather than be a separate end in itself.

When our society was one of family farms and family businesses, a boy was much with his father, imitated his actions and unconsciously absorbed his father's wisdom. He gained a sense of responsibility and a taste for work. Girls learned from their mothers in a similar way. Today children go off to school at an early age, into relationships that are impermanent and unrelated to the family bond. One often sees school children who tend to show a casual and self-centered attitude at home. To counteract such tendencies, parents need to talk over with children the daily experiences of school and play in order to relate them to family values, such as an out-going sense of responsibility towards others. One family where the father returned rather late from work solved this problem by a rule that if the children took an afternoon rest they could stay up in the evening to "be with daddy." The father would gather the children around him while the mother brought on the supper and during the meal they were encouraged to talk about their day. This kept the father close to them and also gave him the opportunity to bring a father's influence into their attitudes and conduct. For the father to play his proper role as family educator is essential in family life, not the least to avoid husband and wife growing apart.

In modern society where the father works away from home there is grave danger that the child's formation will be left too much to the mother alone. The result is that it may lack the masculine element needed for completeness. A French writer holds that modern fathers are unconsciously abdicating their role with their sons, partly from leaving formation to the mother and partly because fathers of this generation have often themselves been a product of the system. As a result, the young male in our culture tends to be lacking in the proper sense of what a man ought to be. Instead of having a clear idea from his father of masculine responsibility in the family and in society, he is afflicted with a basic insecurity. A growing number of young men today allow their wives to work for support of the family. The modern decline in filial respect, states the same writer, results largely from the father's failure to share a man's life with his son. A boy needs identification with his father to know how a man should act. Many years later, both as husband and citizen, he will almost surely be a copy of his father. A daughter learns from her father what to expect in a husband. Similarly, both boys and girls acquire from a good mother the right ideal of womanhood.

In the matter of religion, only from their fathers can boys and girls learn that to praise and honor God is a manly ideal. If a father rarely kneels down, his children will grow up like that no matter how much catechism they memorize. If they are sent to Holy Communion but parents do not go, it seems something that only children do, like going to school. One objection to a separate children's Mass on Sunday is that they do not see with their own eyes how grown-ups value Holy Communion. Children take their standards from what parents do, not from what they say. Boys copy their fathers, girls their mothers. It is a law of life. Now that there is a growing trend to drop the lower grades of Catholic schools for lack of personnel and financial resources, this question of family training in religion becomes all the more pressing. Some parents, unfortunately, have tended to abdicate their role as religious educators to the Catholic school from a mistaken notion that school education in religious knowledge could supply for lack of home education in the religious spirit. If a good program for restoring religious formation in family life is not set up, it seems inevitable that the next generation will see increased religious laxity.

One reads much today about the need of education for the "under-privileged" in order that they may take their proper place in modern life. It is now being discovered that many of them lack the basic human experiences from their home life on which the school can build. Among the human experiences essential for the child are: The opportunity to express and receive affection and to learn about his life environment in a context of family security. Other basic experiences are praise and rewards for success, as well as just punishments for doing things expressly forbidden or that are not to be repeated because of their danger, such as playing with matches. Just as a flower cannot unfold in all its beauty in an unfavorable environment, so the child's personality cannot unfold as it should in a parent-child relationship which either does not promote his development or gives indulgence to his impulses. In the one case he will lack the basic human experiences, in the other he will be unable to manage normal human freedom of action. In either case he will be ill-fitted to handle adult life effectively in this rapidly changing and uncertain world.

The age from twelve to sixteen is one of profound physical, mental and personality transformations leading to maturity. In school it is the age for the adolescent to learn how to study "on his own," and the high school that fails in this ill-prepares him for continued progress in life. The adolescent is puzzled and perplexed by the unfamiliarity of his new inward experiences, may be ashamed to discuss them for fear of being considered odd or bad. He does not know what to confide, and often lacks the words to express his still vaguely apprehended emotions. Today he may be friendly and accessible, tomorrow hostile and withdrawn. At this stage he is being pulled two ways by the old habit of compliance and a new need of personal autonomy. It would be a serious error to expect from him the same unquestioned obedience he gave perhaps only last year. One who would help the adolescent must be wise enough to see that the external inconsistencies arise from a turmoil within and to view apparent rebelliousness as a tentative trying out the new sense of independence. The adolescent needs to experience from adults a tranquil acceptance that tells him plainly, "I believe in you."

This transition period will obviously be much easier for young people who already have a sense of security grounded in mutually confident relationships with parents and other adults from their early years. Unless the foundations of emotional security have been laid during the period of formation up to the age of twelve, the 12-16 period of learning to use the new powers will be a most difficult one. The young person who was neglected by parents for other interests during his childhood or manipulated like a puppet to satisfy certain parental drives, has not acquired the sense of having value in himself which is the basic human need. He feels rejected and unwanted by those who represent to him the adult world, very often guilty as well that he has not pleased them. Such frustration almost always generates anger towards the adult world, developing quickly into habitual hostility of attitude. This is the story of the delinquent and of most maladjusted adolescents. The world is not to them a friendly place where they are at ease.

There is quite wide agreement among those who work with youth that the 12-16 year period marks the definitive emergence of the kind of person one will eventually be, though the foundation was already laid in childhood. Some have considered sexual development as the central fact of adolescence, but it is really a question of the total personality with sex forming part of the pattern. For example, the young person who has experienced "wholeness" in his home life, real mutual affection between parents and with children, tends naturally to see relations between the sexes as based on mutual respect and not selfish desires. On the other hand, for those emotionally insecure as a result of home tensions, seeking sex pleasure for itself tends to be a substitute for normal emotional relationships that are lacking. Over-eating or heavy drinking usually have a similar cause. Here we may add that today's focusing of adolescent interest on a boy-girl social life with resulting precocious sexuality is a regression to the mores of primitive culture. Such a youth cannot develop the emotional maturity, the responsibility and self-discipline which are required for the progress and maintenance of our technically advanced society.

B. Formation of Youth by Action

Canon Cardijn has constantly said that youth are not formed for emotional, religious and apostolic maturity by picnics, outings, or amusements. They are formed only by responsible action, by winning victories over problems and over themselves. They are not formed by the talks of a youth director who does not at the same time guide them in related action. St. Thomas says that we grow and develop only by our own self-activity. Canon Cardijn worked with many Catholic young men who did not make their Easter duty or attend Mass. In *Christ to the World* (1958, No. 4), he states that our purpose should not be simply to bring such youth into a good environment for an hour or two a week, for when they go back to their own environment the effort is wasted. We must help them undertake responsible action within their environment to change it and in doing so they themselves are changed. It is the only successful formula for social and moral improvement. A youth center which did not have a really effective program in that kind of action would be, in the Canon's eyes, a waste of time. "What do youths need?" he asks. "They need a philosophy of life, a purpose of life, independence of life. If we try to give them this in lectures or in classes, few will come. Youths must have action; it belongs to their age."

Youths are best formed, says the Canon, by what he calls "the pedagogy of action." He began by asking them to do little things: "Would you mail this letter for me? Thank you." He gets them started making contacts: "Do you know so-and-so? Would you say hello to him for me when you see him, then engage him in conversation to show him you are his friend? Would you invite him to come with you next time? Would you give me the name of the fellows you work with? How many of them do you talk with as friends? Could you cultivate friendship with more of them?" Such acts may seem rather trivial, but most of these youths had not the habit of thinking about anyone but themselves, or of doing things for others. Then they went on to more difficult actions. "I have been to visit the attic apartment of an aged couple, it hasn't been cleaned for months. Can you get some boys to help clean it?" He tells us. "The key is to act yourself for them to see, then get them to act, first individually and later as a team. . . . Always show appreciation for what they do; begin every talk with words of praise." The Canon's secret was to make them feel valued and needed, perhaps for the first time in their lives.

The formation of youths to be apostles takes place, the Canon states, in four specific areas: 1) in the apostolate of action; 2) in the apostolic concept of life and the Church; 3) in the supernatural, sacramental life; 4) in the sense of sharing the apostolate of the hierarchy. Progress is by stages in accordance with human psychology—go from passing and occasional acts to more regular ones that entail a more permanent responsibility. No matter how distasteful the job he asked, they would not "let him down." They knew that he praised them to everyone, to their parents, their teachers. He showed that he believed in them and they felt challenged to respond. "We must have faith," he tells us, "in the worth of action to form and transform. I have seen young fellows steeped in vice, the poor fellows pretty morbidly sensual. I have saved them all, everyone without exception, by action. After a time they would come alone and tell me, 'I don't seem to have time for that sort of thing now.' "

Catechists and lay apostles can learn vital lessons from the Canon's approach. They will often work in areas of bad environments, where even the children are in daily contact with all sorts of evil. It is useless to take the negative approach of warning them against what is wrong; often it is the parents they love who do evil and such warning might cause an inner conflict. The great need is to develop the good potentialities that are in them all, through positive action which enlarges the pattern of their lives with good elements. Bad habits and attitudes can be driven out only by good ones that "take over." The qualities of goodness inherent in every human being as God's image must be nourished and encouraged by self-activity in acts of goodness, above all of goodness towards others and with others to overcome the self-centeredness that characterises all evil. Even prayer should be encouraged by "teams" and for others. The leaven of generosity thus gradually penetrates the environment and purifies it, beginning at the human level and mounting towards God.

When Canon Cardijn saw that the youths were beginning to "taste" the goodness of action for others, he would talk to them about life, about relations with their families, relations with girls. "What time do you get up? How often does your mother have to call you? Do you say good morning? Do you spend your wages on yourself, even beg carfare from your mother? When did you last go out with your father? Do you feel separated from him? Why not invite him to go with you to the cinema?" They may laugh a little, joke about it, but deep inside they realize that something is wanting. "All right, then, will you do that?" Slowly the boys begin to realize that there are other values to life besides "having a good time." "You are not a brute beast, you are a human being. You know what is right. You know that every girl should be respected because God made her to be a mother." Finally they get down on their knees and pray with a true desire for God's help.

Summarizing, the Canon tells us, "First get them to act, to help others, to perform acts of religion and to act in their family, where perhaps relations had been bad or at least they were growing apart. Gradually the whole family is transformed. They greet their father and mother with affection, they lend a hand in the home. Even parents who had been anti-Catholic were won over. Boys who were once careless about their faith, themselves find the secret of true joy and desire to share it with all around them. I am not saying that such a tremendous effort is to be asked of a great number, but the stronger will help the weaker. And you must not leave them without further assistance. They must never be allowed to feel forgotten; someone must keep in contact with them, tell them he prays for them. I asked the cloistered Sisters to pray for them and told them I did, for their happy marriage, for a good family life. It helped keep up their ideals in the face of the world.

"But let us beware of separating acts from doctrine, because acts will have transforming value only in the measure that the young folks understand why they must do this and not that, how to act and how not to act. 'Are you an animal? Are you a dog? Is that girl one? Why not?' They must discover the worth of their human personality, the image of God. 'You are not a machine. Well, why behave like one? Have you freedom to choose? You must use it then.' They must always be seeking and discovering the purpose of their lives . . . 'Why work?' They must understand the importance of work, the greatness of work that is always done with God, for God and in God. 'Young workers, it is you who give the Church the wherewithal for sacrifice, the host, the chalice, the altar. You offer your week's work on the altar that it may be united with the work of Christ. In the Mass your work is transformed to become the work of God, of Christ who by your work continues to spread the fruits of your part in His redemptive sacrifice among young people, in the working class, in the whole human race. By your work you are helping to build a truly new world, not merely by transforming matter, but by transforming men."

C. Young Christian Workers in Japan

At the Young Christian Workers' National Center in Tokyo I met Father Murgue, the director. He told me that one of the chief problems of the Church in Japan was to reach the working classes. "Marxism," he said, "is favored by many intellectuals as the 'social wave of the future' and penetrates down among the workers. The leaders of Japan's largest labor union are extreme leftists. I had made many attempts to set up the YCW here but the first successful Japanese section dates back just ten years. Now it is a national movement, comprising 1200 members of 16-20 years old in nearly 200 section groups. As Japan has few Catholics among the workers, it is out of the question to try to create a strong movement of Catholics alone. The 200 sections are really that many catechumenate centers in the heart of the working class areas of the principal cities. Only the leaders must be Catholics. All non-Christians who accept the Church's social doctrines may belong to the YCW, and most eventually become Catholics." Father Murgue was an "ecumenist" before the term become common!

"The YCW has thus taken on a new character in Japan. It reveals itself as an invaluable means of the apostolate among the masses of the young workers. Indeed, it is the only movement so far that can reach them. In one year I have baptized almost 100 young workers, all of whom came to the Church because they were attracted by her social doctrines where a direct presentation of religion would not appeal. Most of them express surprise that a religion would be interested in social problems; they had been led to believe that was a monopoly of the Marxists. [The present writer had the impression in Japan that converts in the parishes were almost all from the middle class, many of them office workers.] The social revolution creates new problems that do not seem to be covered by the neighborhood associations which the Japanese have everywhere. The Marxists receive special training to take over leadership in meeting modern problems, but the relatively few Catholic workers do not have such preparation and keep much to themselves. One non-Christian worker told a YCW leader, 'You are not like the other Catholics; I can talk to you.'

"The hard experience of many failures taught us to give a great amount of personal attention to all newly founded YCW units. It appears that Japanese youth do not take up a new plan of action and persevere in it without a great deal of encouragement. The National Chaplain always goes to a new unit's first meeting, the National President to others, and during the first year someone representing the National Center is present at every meeting. Thereafter someone goes frequently from older units nearby, and a representative of the National Center now and then. In larger countries it could be representatives from a Regional Center. The Gospel discussion with which the weekly meeting always opens makes a strong impression on young workers. They are called materialists, but deep down they have an innate religious thirst and sense of what is right. They also have a good deal of hero-worship in their make-up. The young workers are impressed to learn that Jesus taught human rights and social principles, while the common Japanese conception of religion is as mere sentiment.

"The YCW publishes a magazine, *New World,* which sells 50,000 copies on the street and door to door by the members—an average of 40 copies are sold by each member. This shows that it has many sympathizers. Recently the YCW approached the police about the pornographic magazines being sold openly to young workers, minors, but were told, 'We can act only if it is a public issue.' When this was made known in *New World,* 40,000 letters of protest against the flood of filth were written to the newspapers. The police then declared that the magazines had failed in the public responsibility and raided both publishers and distributors. One publication of a million circulation was suppressed. On the local level the objective is concrete and visible solutions for everyday problems of the worker's life, both at work and in the neighborhood. At Tobata, for instance, the YCW collected materials from merchants to build a home for a poor family and got enough to provide houses for three families. In addition to the direct good done, there was much comment favorable to the YCW and the Church, especially valuable because the ones responsible were Japanese. The ordinary worker here tends to accept bad conditions, 'It has always been like that,' but the YCW members are taught to seek improvements. As a result, the others look up to them. If we only had 12,000 members instead of 1200!

"The Japanese like lectures and cultural meetings and a short series of two or three lectures will attract good crowds. One YCW section organized monthly record concerts for young people and in four months has a regular attendance of over 100. Six months later one of them suggested a 'friendship circle.' Here about 30 young workers meet to discuss work, Communism, marriage, the Church's social doctrine, the YCW. About one-third of this group will eventually become Catholics. In another area, a boys' and a girls' section started a choir. After five months they had fifty voices, mostly non-Christians, singing Masses at the request of other non-Christians. A number of sections organize lecture-study courses on the Church's social doctrines with invited speakers. Some girls' sections form discussion groups among the many thousand non-Christian girls from the country who work in factories for some years to get money for their trousseau and live in dormitories provided by the management. They discuss preparation for marriage, child training, working life and similar questions, always based on the Christian viewpoint."

Father Murgue's experience that the YCW groups needed a great deal of personal attention at the beginning corresponds with what Canon Cardijn said about his method of transforming the lives of youth. It is the application of our Lord's method of training disciples by sharing life which He commanded the Church to carry out everywhere: "Go, make disciples of all peoples" (Matthew 28:20). Encouragement is particularly necessary at the age before they have come to full adult independence of thought and action. At the same time, if young people are to develop their own powers towards adult autonomy, it is necessary to give them all the responsibility of which they are capable. It is true of people at any age, that their interest in carrying through an action is in direct proportion to their feeling that they have had a part in planning it. If they are not accorded this as a right, the leader or director will quickly find himself at the head of only the compliant ones, and more girls than boys. Reality teaches the unchanging lesson that all, especially men, are best formed in responsible action by offering them gradually more difficult challenges.

D. Adults Help Youth to Grow

Since the time of youth is one of reaching towards the self-decision and responsibility of adulthood, it is normal for young people to feel more secure during this period of transition if they have confident relationships with adults. Modern society, however, tends to deprive them in three ways of the close contacts they had in a simpler society with adults not their parents. One is that many young people today have no uncles and aunts living nearby who have a natural interest in them. Another is that they are far less associated with adults in work and recreation than in former days. Finally, a far greater part of young people's lives is spent in school with those of their own age, thus tending to lengthen the period of juvenile outlook. It is not surprising, then, to find many at 18-20 whose emotional and psychological maturity do not match their physical and intellectual development. Another serious result of this separation is a breakdown in the emotional bond between the generations which is essential as a communications channel for the transmission of human values.

A teacher in a typical small American city states that so many modern children do not have a true sense of "self-value" because they do not feel close to adults whose interest in them should embody such value. They tend to make their own scale of values at an immature level, engaging in dangerous and even unlawful actions to demonstrate, in the face of adult indifference, that they do have value. By their actions they repudiate many of the values that society accepts. An example of this is the wanton destruction of property or even of human life in which they may engage, seemingly without any real motive except frustration and hostility towards the world. Recent studies indicate that these young people feel hopelessly detached from their parents and society. Their emotional communications which would make them accept values have been cut. The professors call this condition *anomie,* rootlessness.

One of today's most pressing needs is to open new lines of communication between youth and adults as well as to restore old ones. We are only beginning to become aware of the great danger to society arising from the gap of emotional separation that rapid social change tends to open between the generations from even the earliest days of childhood. There is much bemoaning the dangers to youth assailed on every side by paganizing attitudes towards the basic values that are essential for maintaining decent human standards. Yet few seem aware that the growing emotional separation between adults and youth is responsible more than any other factor for leaving youth open and defenseless against these dangers. Nothing is more likely to make young people accept and imitate our values than giving them personal friendship. Some time ago I asked a member of the Christian Family Movement, "Have you any neighbors whose family life is weak with whom you could share the graces of the insights you receive in the movement?" Discussion revealed that in a large family nearby several adolescents were on the verge of delinquency. "Say," he exclaimed on a note of discovery, "when I take my boy fishing I could invite them to go along."

Organizing youth groups in the traditional sense will not solve the problem because the need of young people is for personal acceptance. This would be done by adult lay people becoming friends with the children and young people of their neighborhood. In place of trying to set up formal groups, the adults would act on the basis of personal friendship towards individuals or informal groups. This should also be considered an important work of the organized lay apostolate. For example, when lay apostles visit families they should not speak only with the parents, but also talk to the children. The latter will look forward to their further visits as of friends instead of feeling left out as they do now, and the apostolic influence will be much the stronger from embracing all the family. As the children grow older, they should be invited to visit the homes of their new friends. How sad if even lay apostles fall in with the modern trend towards separation of adults and youth, in face of the principle that the strongest factor in Christian formation of young people is a sense of being loved for themselves as God's children.

All Catholic adults, even those who for some reason cannot engage in the formal apostolate, should cultivate the friendship of children in their neighborhoods. There is no better way of reaching parents. And as the children grow older they will discuss with their adult friends things about which they would be embarrassed to speak with their parents. Moreover, they will be unwilling to "let them down" by bad conduct. I met a mother of several children who told me that one of her best friends was a girl of eighteen who would come to her with the personal problems typical of that age. How had they become friends? The girl's family had moved into the neighborhood four years previously and the lady went to welcome them. She met the girl, then fourteen, and invited her for a friendly visit, since she did not yet have young friends there. Many young people today have no adult friends to whom they can go. The police commissioner of Detroit declared recently that if every young person had an adult he could trust, there would be no delinquency. Today, in place of the uncles and aunts of the Kelly or the Smith clan, Catholics must assume the responsibility as members of the "clan Christian" to help the young become God's co-creators in their turn.

In many mission lands, it is almost impossible to secure the conversion of unmarried young men because the gratification of sex as part of their social life is taken for granted. The missionary tries to form active groups of young men with Catholic ideals to welcome other young men and enable them to share a social life that is chaste, perhaps with emphasis on sports activities. They need, however, the friendship and interest of good adult men to encourage them and give them moral support to follow Christian ideals. In some areas, young girls are exposed to grave dangers, either from pagan customs or from intoxication with woman's new freedom. To form apostolic groups of young girls is not enough, they need also the friendship of apostolic Catholic women to provide a personal ideal. To really be able to help them supposes, in the words of Cardinal Suenens, ". . . a close intimacy, a psychological sense, a penetration of the feminine soul, and inside knowledge of the concrete circumstances of their life." It is clear that the priest working with youth needs adults who belong to the same lay environment to lend the help of their personal acceptance in counteracting unfavorable conditions which have so serious an effect on those who have not yet reached emotional maturity.

Father John P. Reid, O.P., discussing the lay apostolate in the *American Ecclesiastical Review* (Catholic University, September, 1960), takes up the problem of why so many young workers give up practicing their religion while still more are so ineffectual in witnessing to it. He offers as one reason that the faith as they possess it is inadequate for them to interpret their contemporary experience. The young worker faced with a trade union problem, for example, is not mature enough to himself apply Catholic social principles. So he turns to the fellow worker who seems to have ideas on the subject, very likely a Communist. Or when the young worker discovers the existence of "factory marriages" he does not know whom to consult, and from being at first troubled in conscience he may come to accept them. Father Reid concludes that the development of the young workers' faith was usually arrested at about the 13-15 age level, when to be a good Catholic meant mainly Sunday Mass and the sacraments.

Every reader will recognize the sad situation presented by Father Reid. It is the reason why a more or less minimum of 50 per cent of young Catholics give up the practice of their faith within a short time after going to work, in some places as many as 80 per cent. At the same time, it is admitted that relatively few of them can be induced to attend religious instruction appropriate to their situation. Indeed, it is very difficult to even get those at school to come to religion class after the age of fourteen unless they are in a Catholic school. The solution lies in the fulfillment by Catholic adults of their responsibility as Christian teachers and leaders in society to which we have already referred. It is really they that should help the young people who are their neighbors or workers with them to meet the problems of life in today's world in a Christian way. Who else can help modern youth adjust to life as wage-earners except adults whom they feel understand their situation from being also in the same environment?

In a survey by the YCW in England, one of the questions asked young workers was, "Where do you get your ideas of love and marriage?" The almost 100 per cent answer was, including the Catholics, "From the 'flicks.'" Many young people tend to "shy away" from formal marriage preparation courses organized by the parish. The conferences for young people called "Pre-Cana" in which factual presentations are given by happily married couples to those contemplating marriage have a strong appeal. The proportion that come, however, is still relatively small. Moreover, youth should have learned about ideals of love and marriage long before to guide their social relationships. There is no better way of achieving this than for good Catholic couples of each neighborhood to show personal friendship towards the young people growing up around them, welcome them into their homes that they may see for themselves what a happy married life means. Young married couples nearer the age of youth find this a most rewarding apostolate. Some hold "open house" perhaps twice a month for young neighbors and their friends from sixteen years old and up. After introductions and small talk, someone brings up a topic: dating, love, marriage, children, budgeting, and the discussion is on. The particular value of such sessions is that the young people are educating themselves, which is by far the most effective way, and painlessly.

What a change could be wrought in a parish if one couple in each 25-30 undertook this form of the apostolate. Where it has been tried the results have been most gratifying, not only in transmitting good values but in converting non-Catholics before marriage. Parents tied down by young children can do it and there is no problem of baby-sitters. Indeed, the presence of the children at the beginning of the meeting can be an aid in the apostolate. Today's young people are subject to many tensions that can easily make family relationships difficult. It is the best lesson possible for young people to see how the child blossoms out in a tranquil home where parents give it praise and encouragement. If, on the other hand, they are demanding and critical, how withdrawn and confused it becomes.

The following is a little gem by an unknown author which I found in a daily newspaper.

If a child lives with criticism he learns to condemn—with hostility he learns to fight—with fear he learns to be apprehensive—with complaining he learns self-pity—with jealousy he learns to hate—with encouragement he learns confidence—with praise he learns to be appreciative—with acceptance he learns to love—with approval he learns to respect himself—with recognition he learns to have a goal—with fairness he learns justice—with honesty he learns to value truth—with friendliness he learns that the world is a friendly place in which to live.

All parents in the People of God have a responsibility to seek the proper development of all children and not their own only, to help them learn that the adult world is really a friendly place in which to live. If that were carried out we should no longer have to deplore the emotional gap now so often evident between adults and youth.

7. THE TRUE IMAGE OF THE CHURCH

There is one question basic to the entire apostolate: how far do Catholics here and now present a true image of Christ in His Church, comprehensible to the people around us? We follow our religious ideals, but they also follow theirs. Our faithfulness to certain religious practices as such does not move them. The image of the Church which best reveals her inner being is that of Christ made visible in the lives of Catholics today.

Often the Catholic parish forms a sort of separate enclave in the midst of the larger community. Though we are associated with the people around us in business, in work, in politics, have we really entered into a dialogue with them about the meaning of life? Sometimes, perhaps, we try to speak of our faith, but we use so many terms known only to Catholics that people do not really understand us. They often feel, therefore, that they do not know us as we are. We are their neighbors, yet in the fundamental sector of religion we are strangers. It is a chief reason why churches in the missions are so often called "foreign" even after many years. There is, however, one universal language in which even the least learned can communicate, if he wishes, with any person he meets. It is the language without words, when heart speaks to heart in love. If a man shows love and kindness towards another, or seeks them from him, the other automatically tends to respond in kind. All human hearts are attuned to this universal mode of expression.

That love, however, is still only as between creatures and no more than an image of the divine love. Many a missionary has been surprised and disappointed that his works of charity did not seem to bring the recipients to God but only to himself in human gratitude. Even an action that has clearly involved great self-sacrifice they attribute to some human motive. They may be moved by the missionary's kindness, but knowing nothing of the Gospel cannot conceive of an act being done for love of God. No matter how good a non-Christian may be in his life, he does not possess this supreme richness of Christian life. God he knows, but being a child of God he cannot know unless he is told. We must build a bridge in his heart from the human to the divine by teaching him to say, "Our Father." Then he sees a great light: the goodness of Catholics towards others is because they love God. To achieve this is the great reason for missionary sacrifice.

A. The Laity as Christ Today

During the Second International Congress of the Lay Apostolate, held at Rome in 1957, Pope Pius XII told the assembled delegates that the parish must be a "community of all the baptized, mobilized in apostolic charity for the service of the Church." The Holy Father's address initiated a new concept of the part to be played by the Catholic laity, not just a few but all of them. He said that if the lay apostle is to "change the face of the world—particularly in towns, which have a dominant influence in modern life" it is not enough for the parish to have a few dozen lay apostles. Every Catholic must visibly incarnate divine charity in all his social relationships, so that the Christ of the Gospels will be recognized again today in him. Prayer and liturgy alone are not enough to show forth Christ before today's men and women who are not interested in them or even reject them. Christ must be seen among them, speaking with them, eating with them, be united with them first under His human form of today, the members of His Mystical Body.

"The Catholic laity," says Frank Sheed, the famous speaker of the London Catholic Evidence Guild, "are in touch with everybody; there is scarcely a person in the country who does not know at least one Catholic. Unless the laity are equipped to give the kind of preliminary explanation of the Faith that will get the non-Catholic really interested and willing to consult a priest, then the vast masses will never be touched at all. I simply do not see how we can reach these throngs in any other way." A layman in Tokyo told me that Japanese workers are accustomed to gather in little groups of neighbors after the evening meal, hundreds of thousands of groups in that one city alone. He suggested to a group of his own neighbors that on one night a week he discuss with them a book which explained the Catholic Faith in a simple way and they said it gave them answers about life they never got from Buddhism. But not one of them would have been willing to go with him to an inquiry forum at the parish church. We are reminded of Father Murgue's statement quoted earlier that the young workers in Japan are surprised to learn that the Church has a social doctrine.

In fact, I was told in Japan that for every man who would be willing to go for information at the parish church, there are as many as ten who would like to learn more about the Faith from laymen. Social change has greatly weakened the traditional securities and there is searching for new spiritual values in life. We must penetrate below today's more visible socio-economic expectations and see that the whole man is involved, with expectations in the spiritual order as well. In Africa, but also elsewhere, the seeking assumes or could easily assume the proportions of a mass movement if it received the proper admixture of leaven from the laity. In India, despite strong Hindu prejudices against the Church as "foreign," many thoughtful people have a great desire to know what we think and believe, but would not go in search of this knowledge lest they seem to show that they have leanings towards the Church. Priests doing convert work in the United States estimate that there are 8-10 million persons, one in ten of the adults, who would willingly listen to lay friends tell them about our view of man's place in God's plan. If Catholic laity everywhere in the world would speak every day to one or more about this, what an ecumenical effect and what Christian penetration of social institutions could result.

Father Charles, S.J., a missiologist at Louvain, wrote after a visit to India that most of the 400 million non-Christians in 800,000 villages also gather in small groups after the evening meal. They discuss the news, politics, religion, there public opinion is formed. He observes further that for a missionary to approach such a group would cut off the natural flow of conversation. Nor can the missionary, continues Father Charles, "mix with the laborers on a construction job or squat in the shade with the rickshaw men. From all the evidence, the means of penetration among the masses, the true carrier of the Christian message, is the native layman. The clergy exercise their own function, which is to control, stimulate, encourage, absolve, bless the faithful, keep the Eucharistic Christ in their midst, guard the purity of doctrine, recall the duty of good conduct, and this manifold burden already fills their time . . . Native Catholic Action, the intensive action of the laity, is the *sine qua non* of all missionary progress. To believe that the christianization of a country can be produced only by the heroism of the missionary is a disastrous illusion (*Missiologie I*).

How would one go about making the Faith known by a large-scale plan in, for example, Japan or India in view of what has just been said? Since the Japanese are highly literate, leaflets might be used, but of a certain kind and distributed in a special way. The first leaflet could be entitled: *What is the Catholic Church?* since most have heard of it.

In very simple language it would say that the Catholic Church teaches what Jesus Christ, known everywhere as a great teacher of love and justice, taught in Palestine. The specific subject of the first leaflet would be how He taught and exemplified love of fellow man. A Bible story would be retold, for example, Christ's eating with those whom their self-righteous neighbors despised. The Church's teaching today would be related to this and an example or two given of how men ought to show love now. A second leaflet might deal with social justice, or several with various aspects of it. But in all the starting point must be our Lord's teaching and example in terms of today's life and needs. Spiritual lessons would be drawn from these rather than vice versa. For example, our Lord's teaching that God is our Father would be mentioned as an explanation or motive for love of others, but would never be used as the starting point.

The distribution of the leaflets would be as follows. Catholics, especially young people, would ask friends, perhaps not Catholics, to go with them on a religious survey. Each team of two persons would have an assigned area and call on a family in the area whose home seemed to indicate responsible standing. "We are making a religious survey and are asking the help of the leading families in each area." Would they be willing to distribute the leaflets to ten neighbors and get their reactions, whether the leaflets helped them understand the Catholic religion better? The team would return in a week or so for the results, of course, bringing other leaflets. If the family contacted did not wish to help, they might suggest another nearby. Each team would be responsible for a number of areas. The personal contacts with the families who undertake the distribution would, of course, serve as an opening into the area. In largely illiterate India the lay apostles would need rather to present the message orally at places where the people gather. But leaflets would still be given out, preferably having a drawing to illustrate the Bible story.

In both countries the aim would be to get the people talking about the Church, and the missionaries assured me that anything based on the life of Christ would be well received.

It would be interesting to make samplings in parishes of various areas throughout the world to find out what ideas people of the general community have about this Church that is in their midst. Many of the answers would astonish us. In one of the chief cities of India, the cathedral has stood for nearly 100 years on a main thoroughfare where tens of thousands pass every day. One evening at a social gathering the Archbishop met a professor of philosophy from a Hindu university. The conversation turned to religion and the professor explained that Hinduism was transmitted mainly by *guru,* or masters, who gather disciples around them. The Archbishop said that Jesus had followed the method of choosing and training disciples. Then He sent them to make disciples among all the peoples of the world. That is the work of the Catholic Church today. The professor answered in surprise, "I had never heard that. I thought the missionaries were here to conduct schools and hospitals and to give their followers political protection."

When I asked a thoughtful young man in Japan why the Church seemed to make slow progress in his country, he replied, "I think it may be that the Japanese people look on the Church as an educator of youth and preacher of a special way to worship God. But we have excellent schools and our own religion has become a part of ourselves that is not easily given up. I think that the Japanese people will be attracted to the Catholic Church only if she offers them a value which they recognize as unique in human life and is not found anywhere else. This unique value, it seems to me, is Christian charity, but it must be seen as the essential value of all Catholics, not of some groups alone. Then people will be attracted to the Church as the community of mutual love."
A letter from a missiologist in Europe was quoted in the

Japan *Missionary Bulletin* (December, 1959). "The success with your schools, hospitals and new churches exposes you to the risk of giving in to the desire for prestige as well as to the envy and scorn of those who want to see in you the bearers of moral and spiritual greatness."

B. The Apostolate of Personal Service

A missionary in Japan who is also a trained sociologist told me, "Apart from the results of relatively few activities among the masses, the Church in Japan is predominantly middle class, probably from conversions through our schools. And now these Catholics bring mostly their own class as converts. I believe there is a serious lack of work in the great community of the masses. A group of nuns in Wakayama have begun a new approach, service of the sick in their homes, and I suggest you visit them. They found situations that we could not imagine existed. They discovered a whole class of people not eligible for social insurance living in destitution, and even in comfortable pagan families chronic invalids receiving little care. One salaried man had built a hut behind the house for his mother who had tuberculosis and arthritis. There is great fear of tuberculosis. He collected her social insurance but the only care she received was that his wife brought her food. One university student who broke his back mountain climbing had lain paralyzed for seven years. The Sisters thought his legs were gangrenous but it turned out they were unwashed. Now he makes rosaries to support himself."

On visiting the Sisters I found that they had made a greater public impression on that industrial city in five years than two parishes had in fifty. Pagans stop them on the street to tell them of some neighbor in need of care. No one is afraid of them. It is above all among the masses that the word has spread. "The Communists never did anything like that—they only preached hate." The Sisters' novitiate is bulging with Japanese vocations. During the home visits they do not speak about religion, for a Japanese feels bound to give a benefactor whatever he desires. There are cases where recipients of help have studied with apparent sincerity and been baptized because they felt that this was what the benefactor desired. But having discharged their obligation, they never came again to the church. The Sisters send Catholic lay people to visit the patients and explain the supernatural motives that animate their service. A missionary who went with me on the visit has since organized a group among Catholic nurses in government hospitals to do similar work for his parish in another part of Japan.

Calcutta, India, has the distinction of possessing some of the worst slums in the world. There I met the Sister Missionaries of Charity, who take a fourth vow to "give whole-hearted service to the poor for life." They are regarded by every Indian, high or low, who knows them as veritable heroines of goodness. The congregation was started by Mother Theresa, from Albania, who came to India in 1929 as member of a teaching congregation whose school was near a slum area. Appalled by the terrible conditions, she received permission in 1948 to found a group of Sisters who would devote themselves to the needy. Her name is already a legend among all classes, an 'Open Sesame' for the pocketbooks of Hindu and Moslem businessmen and with the Calcutta government for anything that concerns helping the poor and abandoned. Some of the slum areas where the Sisters are now welcomed were formerly unsafe for a priest to enter because of Communist influence. The congregation is now rapidly opening new houses in all the large cities of India, and receives everywhere welcome and assistance.

The nuns direct 20 primary schools for the poor in Calcutta alone, under a simple shelter of matting or in the open air. Six general clinics provide free treatment for all who come and give milk to expectant mothers. In one year over 60,000 patients were treated. A mobile leprosy clinic treats about

1700 cases a week and Mother Theresa plans a project for rehabilitating 1000 leper families. "Of course," she says, "we cannot do all this ourselves. Doctors and many others give very generously of their time and energy. The Indian people, like people everywhere, possess a great amount of goodness. It is only a matter of organizing and channeling it. The question came naturally to my lips, "But how do you, a Catholic, approach the Hindus and Moslems for their cooperation?" Her answer revealed the magic key to hearts everywhere, "I say to them very simply, 'Come, let us do something good for God.' "

There were 127 nuns when I visited them in 1961, almost all from India. Their habit is in simple native style, a white cotton *sari* with lady-blue border, and their food is that of the poor. Sometimes when discontented women complain, "I have nothing to wear," a Sister will reply, "I have two *saris*, but can wear only one at a time." The convent is an old building in a side lane of the slums, with nuns crowded into every corner. Chairs are only for visitors with stiff knees. "Sitting and sleeping on the floor we need much less room." They bubble over with joy, so much more attractive than the very serious air which in some convents seemed to be considered proper for a nun. The Sisters told me that more than 300 educated women help them, forming committees to prepare bandages for the clinics, gather clothing and secondhand books for the children in their under-the-sky schools, and raise funds. These ladies say to the nuns, "You have given us a chance to do good."

Later I visited their newly opened house in New Delhi, capital of India. It was a small private residence, but already they had brought in several crippled and abandoned children who would be sent to their children's home in Calcutta until one could be established in New Delhi. The first thing they set up in every city to which they go is a hostel for sick and dying destitutes picked up in the streets each morning by a city ambulance. The one in Calcutta may receive as many as fifty in a single day. Young Hindu ladies who are abandoning the restrictions of caste come to help care for them. Protestants shave the men and cut fingernails. On Sundays the nuns help in outlying parishes, where they round up the people for Mass and teach catechism to old and young. They walk, even for several hours, in preference to riding. Previously the Communists had the slums to themselves and their voting strength there threatened to elect a Communist city government in Calcutta. Now the Sisters, without saying one word against them, have become the strongest anti-communist influence in the city.

The story is told that a Hindu doctor, superintendent of a large government hospital in Calcutta, once asked Mother Theresa, "Will you tell me, Mother, how it is that young Indian girls of good family can sacrifice their lives in this way for others and still be so happy?" She replied, "No, I cannot explain it. But please come with me, and perhaps we can find out." The doctor expected that she was going to ask the Sisters themselves, but she led him to the chapel where one of them was making a visit. The chapel has rugs on the floor with no pews and over the simple altar-table is an almost life-size crucifix. The doctor stood for a long moment silently taking in the scene, then as they left he whispered, "Mother, now I understand."

C. The Primacy of Christian Charity

In that great missionary encyclical, *Rerum Ecclesiae* (June 15, 1926), Pope Pius XI wrote, "Let Us remind you of what We said on another occasion, namely, that all who are interested in the health of the inhabitants, and minister to the sick, and all who are kind to infants and little children, win the good will and affection of all, so readily does the human heart respond to charity and kindness." From the very beginning in China I used medical dispensary work to win good will, but quickly learned that to bring to God people who had no concept of the supernatural, a further step was necessary. Our Catholic people were asked to explain to their neighbors that the Christian practice of charity was from love of God. Later we printed a small leaflet with a Chinese saying as the title: When you drink water, think of the source. The leaflet stated that the funds to buy medicines were given by ordinary people in America, often at the cost of personal sacrifice such as walking to work or school and giving the fare to help others. They did this to carry out the command of Christ: "Love your neighbor as yourself." This leaflet seemed to have a greater religious impact than any other approach.

Missionaries met during my recent tour were not always of one mind about the value of distributing relief goods. All agreed they were a godsend for hospitals, orphanages and for meals for school children, but some said that general distribution should be restricted to true emergencies and for a short time to avoid creating "relief mendicants." Others noted an increased sensitivenesss which caused teachers and professional people to hesitate in inquiring about the Faith at a parish where relief supplies were given out because of their fear of ridicule as "flour and milk" Christians. In Japan I was told of a town that had been badly damaged by a flood and a nearby missionary came to offer relief supplies. The mayor refused, saying, "You give them to win converts." When the missionary protested that he only desired to help, the mayor finally said, "We won't accept your food, but you can bring a team to work with us cleaning up the mud and debris." One of the best ways to use relief goods is in work projects by which the people earn them. One missionary became the "toast of the town" because he arranged with the authorities to have the streets paved and gave food to the workers in payment. The Catholics reported that the residents praised the community spirit of the Church.

Looking again at the encyclical, we note the Holy Father's

emphasis on the good will those gain who "minister to the sick, and all who are kind to infants and little children." In most missionary towns one can find local doctors who will give some time to a medical clinic and there it is easy to limit the relief supplies to those obviously in need of them. But there is no parish having poor within its boundaries that could not at least open a simple "Children's Nutrition Center" on certain days a week, even without a doctor, where relief food would go only to the under-nourished. The diet customary in many areas is so poor in proteins as to produce much 'kwashiorkor' in children of 3-7, with enlarged liver, dull hair and persistent diarrhea. In one slum I saw twenty cases within an hour's walk. To prevent it, vegetable proteins can usually be found in the area itself, or powdered milk may be available. The U.S. makers of baby foods are often willing to donate high protein ones from stocks being replaced.

Almost every child in warm climates has round worms, which often cause rickets and even vitamin A deficiency blindness by absorbing the few vitamins in the child's diet. The cure is to expel the worms, not to feed them with good food! In China we used one-fourth grain each of santonin and calomel, one tablet for each three years of age up to twelve and given two successive mornings on an empty stomach. I have cured children unable to walk, or with the cornea of the eyes already showing a ground-glass appearance. The infants of working mothers are commonly weak and a few drops of liquid vitamins daily for a short time work wonders. One missionary told me that the receptionist in a U.S. doctor's office collects and sends him from a number of doctors' offices liquid vitamin samples with which he has been able to put many such infants on the road to health.

But the priest and a few others must not be the only ones in a parish engaged in the works of mercy. As Jesus showed so graphically in His discourse on the Last Judgment, every Catholic must show His love for Christ in the least of His brothers. To reach the masses who are outside the Church or Catholics not practicing, goodness as a reflection of God's own goodness must be seen as part of the Catholic's whole everyday life. The neighborhood is the natural place to begin. When one Catholic says to another, or to one not a Catholic, "Come, let us do something good for God," he is showing love for that person as well as towards the recipient of their good deed. In fact, that is more often than not the more effective aspect. The most powerful missionary words on the lips of men are not those we utter but were said by the pagans of Rome, "See how these Christians love one another." If the Catholic parish is to be true to its inner nature as the Body of Christ, it must be constantly going out to others, giving itself in the person of its members. This is equally true of the long established parish and of the one just beginning. Neither can neglect its vocation of projecting upon the consciousness of the general community with all its strength the true image of the Church, which is the image of Christ.

Even where Catholics are few, they are the Church in that place. They must be conscious of acting in the name of the Church and under the inspiration of the Holy Spirit like the early Christians. Let us not think that they spent their time chiefly speaking in strange tongues. Each home had a room of hospitality near the entrance for travelers and the homeless. Every household was involved, not just the parish center. Tertullian warned his wife that if he died before her she should not marry a pagan, for then she could not continue the practice of hospitality. There should not be one Catholic in a parish who is not known as a kindly person who "makes you feel welcome," else in that much would the true image of the Body of Christ be falsified before the men of our time. In a predominantly middle class American parish that I studied briefly, most of the leakage was among the poor of one section who did not feel welcome in parish life. On Sundays after Mass, at socials and parish gatherings, the middle class tended to go with their own and the 'little ones of Christ' felt out of place. The lay apostles of the parish were concerned about the leakage, but did not seem to recognize its basic cause.

Catholics often find the practice of such charity difficult to carry out. Is it that as children, when the habits and attitudes of life are being formed, we have not been adequately trained in thoughtfulness towards those different from us or less fortunate? In Rome I visited St. Francis Cabrini parish where a well organized program of charity emphasizes the role of the family rather than of the individual. Children as well as adults have their part and one sees them happy to help their "friends," especially the aged and crippled that need the service of young hands and feet. That is the only way to insure that the future generation will not only be trained in charity but will rise even higher than the present one. If the whole family were concerned with spiritual and corporal works of mercy, would it not be an excellent means of closing the gap that tends to open today between parents and children? The family does not transmit good values to its children primarily by words or formal teaching, but by "acting them out" in life together.

Every Catholic needs to understand that men today have the same need of being shown the divine compassion that they had in the time of our Lord. There are so many modern equivalents of Zacchaeus whom men despised as a grasping tax-farmer, of the publicans and sinners with whom Christ ate, of all the masses who are treated as anonymous beings rather than human persons. Do we know our community, the needs of our fellow men? A parish priest in Madras, India, asked an exemplary Catholic to go with him for an evening walk and took him through a large slum area not far from the church. At the end his companion said, "Father, I have attended this church for twenty-two years and never suspected this." How many students in our Catholic high schools and colleges, our seminaries, have much personal knowledge about the conditions under which people live in the slums from apostolic work or social studies field work done there? Yet it is they who are destined to set the tone of Catholic life by which mankind will judge if the Christian image of man it offers corresponds to his true self.

D. A Wider View of Charity

There is no doubt that our hospitals, orphanages, social welfare and similar institutions are outstanding examples of Christian charity. Their influence is evident from the fact that they have so many imitators, but those institutions cannot be taken as fulfilling our whole Catholic responsibility. Charity, kindness, love, cannot be shown by proxy. The priests, nuns and lay workers in these institutions, though themselves examples of Christian goodness, cannot substitute for the Catholic families and individuals of the parish. The contributor to an institution of charity, like the officer of Catholic Action, is not thereby released from the need to practice goodness personally among the people of the community. Centralized institutions are often necessary for reasons of technical efficiency, but charity by its very nature involves a personal interchange from which both profit. The purpose of Frederick Ozanam in founding the St. Vincent de Paul Society was not merely material help of the poor. He prescribed that all members must visit the poor families regularly in order that they might feel one with them in Christ.

Every parish has various parochial societies and organizations. Their members must not consider only themselves for they are first members of Christ and His co-workers. Each group without exception should regard their being together as a call from God to employ their united strength in some way that manifests God's goodness through them to men. If they see that some kind of help is required which they cannot give, they should take united action to secure it elsewhere. In general, the primary work of the priest is to announce and explain the kingdom of God. That of lay Catholics is to make the kingdom of God a visible reality among men by animating all human affairs that they touch with God's truth and love. When ordinary Catholic laymen bear witness to Christ's truth by imitating Christ's love, they present a true image of Christ that is comprehensible to other laymen. They need not be learned in theology, since the others would not understand them. It is from seeing and experiencing the lives of laymen informed by charity that others begin to understand how the Catholic religion is not for religious devotees only, but is meant for ordinary people like themselves.

It is clear that guiding and encouraging his people in the way of charity is one of the priest's chief duties to help them more fully "put on Christ." He is not to manage everything, decide everything, yet he must be in the midst of things as the chief catalyst who brings about action for Christ. An essential part of preaching Christ is to make Christ known in the works of His members. The priest must keep in touch with the apostolic activities of the parish groups particularly, praise and encourage their zeal and self-sacrifice. He will praise his people from the pulpit. Appreciation shown for a job well done inspires to greater effort. This applies to all the priest's co-workers, his teachers, catechists, servants. He should show kindliness, respect and justice towards them, encourage them in the practice of charity towards others. Then they will use him as the strongest visible argument for the Faith. There is no greater help to the missionary than to have his co-workers and people say of him, "Do you see how good he is to all? It is because he wishes to show us the goodness of God towards men."

The priest's apostolic and ecumenical sense will lead him to promote cooperation in various works of charity between Catholics and those not of the Faith. He may invite doctors and nurses to serve in a clinic, teachers to help in schools for the poor and underprivileged, artisans to build homes for those without decent shelter and dealers to contribute materials. Here again it is essential to manifest appropriate recognition and praise, but adding to the "human" side of motivation some thought that lifts the heart towards God. One might say, for example, "You have acted as God's representative to help others," or, "You have shown yourself a true elder brother towards weaker members of God's family." The priest should keep telling his people that enlisting the cooperation of neighbors who are not Catholics to help others puts the parish on its way to becoming a true leaven in the general community. It is an authentic and necessary expression of the mission God gave His Church, of her proper place in the world.

It is evident, therefore, that the formation of the Catholic in today's world of rapid change requires careful attention, lest some key factor relevant to the change be overlooked. One such factor, for example, is that modern man's outlook on life is concentrated on its dynamic aspects in the marketplace rather than on philosophic or religious reflection. Catholics today must learn to relate to God and His plan for the world all the activities of the modern marketplace and of modern social institutions. Our failure to be aware of this and to take appropriate action causes Christ to be ignored in the marketplaces of the world and crowded more and more out of its social institutions. If Catholics are to be imbued with the insights and qualities needed to reverse that process, these must be made an integral part of their intellectual and dynamic formation. In the education of Catholics by family, school and pulpit, in the instruction of converts, care must be taken to use methods which correspond to these needs of today and to our present better understanding of man living in society.

If we offer modern man a Catholic culture that seems truncated, partial, failing to demonstrate in the lives of Catholics that its heart is the goodness of God, we only invite his scorn and indifference. Culture is not an abstract idea but the life lived by a people and ours must demonstrate in daily life how the divine goodness embraces and animates all human activity proper to man, social as well as individual, of body and soul together as one. Only a culture of such Christian wholeness can at once create and identify a People of God who will be everywhere and in all of life His visible, active representatives as a people. And it is only as a visibly united People dwelling together in a great City of God which permeates and illuminates the city of man that they can offer haven to all the men of good will who have become lost in the darkness of God's absence and stumble from one to the other dark turning of life.

Today, above all, we are pressed by a great urgency. For over against us the insistent and persuasive voice of Communism beams to all nations without ceasing its false messianic promise of redemption. Is our voice loud enough to be heard? Is our beacon clear enough to reach and light up the life of every human being? Do we kindle in every parish, every neighborhood, bright fires of love around which men lost and isolated in this cold world may gather to be warmed again into the life of God? Do we carry this warmth and light of love into our daily work? Canon Cardijn observes that over the doors of offices and factories there is often found the sign: "Employees Only." Yet Karl Marx enters there every day, brought by workers, but Christ does not enter because Catholics leave it to the priests. Even the small child in his neighborhood or at school, among Catholics or not, must have learned from the attitudes of his elders how to bear witness in love. If he has a positive outlook on life as a Catholic, he will be a good influence on the other children instead of being in danger of learning bad habits from them. Spreading and preserving the Faith are part of the same pattern. If we do not share our spiritual treasures it will be lost, if not in ourselves then in our children!

This practice of charity is truly life-giving because it helps develop the human personality as God meant it to be. In *Christ to the World* (1960, No. 4), Mother Marie Kostka describes how during the 1940's it changed the outlook of the several hundred students at the Helpers of the Holy Souls Morning Star School in Shanghai, China. The girls belonged for the most part to wealthy families and were spoiled, self-centered. Few were interested in the Faith. The school had little space for recreation, so the pupils were taken on outdoor walks for exercise. The teachers called to their attention the beggars that lined the roads. Then they began to give the unfortunates a coin, which at first they threw from a distance. Next they learned how to give graciously, kindly, respectfully, and later even asked naive questions: "Why are you poor?" "Why are your clothes so ragged?" They also learned to deprive themselves of cakes and sweets for a neighboring orphanage, but would go only to the door while the Sister went in to make the distribution. The next step was that the girls themselves took an interest in the children directly. Finally, they organized "Feasts of Friendship" to which they invited their "orphan sisters." Between 1942 and 1948 there were 68 baptisms of students at Morning Star. Many converted their families.

The highest perfection of the human person is found, of course, in union with God, but that can be achieved only in accordance with man's own psychological being and not as if he were an angel. Who can measure or delimit the transforming and fulfilling result of a Catholic saying to another person, "Let us do something good for God."? A divine-human dynamism is thereby activated that changes them both. Their environment is also influenced and through all these ways the direction of man's future itself is altered. It overcomes obstacles of communication that separate man from man, adults from youth, Catholics from their brethren of other beliefs. The need of communion in charity is particularly urgent today in view of the depersonalizing tendencies that arise from modern technology and produce such strong feelings of personal isolation and emotional insecurity. May we not say that such charity alone offers the key for man to control technology for his greater humanization rather than become dehumanized by it?

8. EVERY CHRISTIAN A BEARER OF LIFE

The Son of God become Man thus defined His mission, "I have come that they may have life and have it more abundantly" (John 10:10). Now if you ask the average Catholic where is Jesus in his parish today, he will most likely reply that Jesus is in the tabernacle on the altar of the parish church. His religious formation has not imbued him with the idea that he himself is Christ at work bringing life to men everywhere through a multiplicity of "little incarnations."

We need to reflect very carefully on the full meaning for us of our Lord's words, "I am the Vine, you are the branches." What is the nature of the life we thus have from Christ? The fruit of life is always other life. Out of each branch new ones grow and receive nourishment through it. Our Lord could have brought divine life directly to all men, but here also He gave us the honor and dignity of being His co-creators as well as in the human order itself. The sap of the vine produces new growth, but it must go through the branches. Any branch that does not produce buds and new shoots by means of the sap makes the vine barren of fruit at that point, for it is new growth that produces fruit. If the gardener sees that certain branches seem dormant, not sharing life, he cuts them off in the hope that others will come out in their place and make the sap fruitful in new growth that can produce more fruit.

The primary vocation of every Christian is to share life as the fruit of love rather than to give learned explanations.

Only certain ones have the responsibility to teach others in a formal way. No Catholic therefore should ever be under the impression that he cannot act in the apostolate because he is not learned. In reality, when he has God in his heart by grace, he possesses the very source of infinite life that was given him to be shared. It does not take learning to share God's life with others any more than it does for parents to give life to their children. Would not one who made sharing God's life with others secondary to his own convenience or to a certain way of living to which he has become accustomed, actually be practicing a form of spiritual birth control? We say of God that He created us to share His life because "Goodness tends to diffuse itself." How can we feel that we share God's life worthily unless we share goodness in our turn by transmitting that life to others?

A. Bishop, Priest, Layman

The bishop, as a successor of the Apostles themselves, is responsible for the over-all pattern of sharing divine life throughout his diocese. His first duty is to be a shepherd, as his bishop's staff shows, to feed the lambs and sheep of Christ. His qualities of learning, of eloquence, of management, are secondary to his role of developing his people to the full stature of Christ as life-bearers. The bishop ordains priests as his co-workers in this. If he did not make it his chief concern that the priests help those to whom they minister fulfill their responsibility of sharing God's life of love in their turn, he would fail his vocation in two ways. Countless souls that should have received the gift of life would remain without it and the faithful themselves would fail to develop in practicing the spiritual adulthood they received at confirmation. How often today the priest and lay apostles spend much time and effort trying to bolster up Catholics who never matured spiritually. In Africa, for example, a missionary told me he had spent four months regularizing one marriage and his parish had many such. But a spirit of sharing God's gifts infuses into parish life a vitality that means far fewer problem cases, and many that do occur will be taken care of by the mature Catholics on their own initiative.

The great pope of the lay apostolate, Pius XI, said in an address: "Where would the Twelve have been, lost in the world's immensity, if they had not called to others—men, women, the aged and children—'Help us distribute this treasure of heaven'?" So today our bishops who are the successors of the Apostles and our priests who are their co-workers must make the same appeal to their people: "Help us distribute this treasure of heaven." If, however, sermons and instructions deal chiefly with their individual religious duties, then the laity will never imagine that they have been chosen to help their bishop and priest in the exalted role of distributing this treasure of life. When parents are told that they are God's co-creators they acquire a far greater reverence for their role. Why should we not proceed from this physical transmission of life to give Catholics a vision of spiritual parenthood that involves sharing with spiritual children the life of God Himself? Once they have this vision and achieve this parenthood, their appreciation of the mystery of divine life within themselves will be immeasurably enhanced.

Sometimes in discussions on cooperation of the laity with the work of the priest, some may seem to think that it almost means being always at the side of the priest. But the primary lay vocation is not to act as parish secretary or to help manage parish funds, though such assistance from those competent in these things can be very valuable. The real lay vocation is not a "splinter" as it were off that of the priest, and the layman who assists the priest in his work still has his own personal vocation to share divine life with others. The lay vocation is to carry Christ into lay life where the layman belongs by the fact of his daily life as a layman. He may be working for the priest or he may be an officer in Catholic Action, but he still goes home to his family and his neighborhood as a layman. The priest's vocation is to go out daily into his parish to share divine life with his people by the special means that God has given into his hands. The layman's vocation is to go out daily into the layman's world and bring the divine life into every part of lay life by the special means that God has given him as a layman.

It is part of the priest's vocation to train his people as life-bearers. Pope Pius XII told the Women's Union of Catholic Action (July 2, 1958), that it was the priest's task "to communicate the sanctifying fire of the Holy Spirit." He should not give them a monastery type of spirituality or one drawn from his own seminary days. The average layman spends his life in a realm of the concrete and his action proceeds from concrete ideas. An abstract spiritual formation that is not related to the circumstances of lay life cannot elicit in him a strong enough impulse to make him act. That is why some who prepare to be lay apostles may fail to undertake action, their formation has not been geared to it. When the priest meets with a group, or with officers to prepare a group meeting, considerable time should be given to share with them his own apostolic ideals and motivation. The officers form an inner group who will inspire the others as Peter, James and John among the Twelve Apostles trained by Christ Himself.

The priest must often be on his guard lest the lay apostles he seems to have are only weak life-bearers in the parish. In South America, as elsewhere, I saw parishes where the members of the lay apostolate were chiefly women and girls, while few men practiced the faith. Those women would rarely, if ever, be able to bring men back to the Church, even their own husbands. They only reinforce the idea that the value of religion in society is a feminine contribution. The men must be made apostles of the idea that God created the masculine qualities of leadership and that to honor Him is therefore manly, masculine. The priest must show them a vision of God as making them His co-creators to build a new world and religion as a dynamic force in accomplishing this. They cannot expect that religion can remain indefinitely as something useful for their families and children if they do not restore giving honor to God as a manly ideal, for without their leadership it must eventually decay.

The primary motive of accepting the faith is not being convinced that the Church has the truth but that she puts us in contact with a lovable God. The transmission of life always flows from love. Now the Catholic community as members of Christ should be able to far outdo all others in their visible demonstration that God is lovable. Yet surveys made among new Catholics in many parts of the world reveal a surprisingly large proportion who say that few parishioners ever manifested a real interest in them. A well-known lady convert in Japan, foundress of a religious congregation, has said that Catholics in general did not show the warm spirit of Christ in their relations with those outside the Church. She laid it to the character of their religious formation, too intellectual and cold, centered on abstract truth rather than on Christ as a person. In Africa, the Moslems show a warm welcome to non-Moslems in order to win them. One of the chief techniques used by Communists to win over young people is to make them feel welcome and appreciated.

Our Lord told us how to distribute the "treasure of heaven" when He said, "Go, make disciples of all peoples." He Himself showed us how to do it by sharing His life for three years with disciples. Faith is transmitted personally as life is because it is life. That is why our Lord needs every Christian to go and make disciples if all men are to have that life. It is something everyone can do. It is necessary only to receive as many as possible as friends, sharing with them our own love in order to lead them to the Source of love. The Master trains his disciples in the apprenticeship of love as Christ did: "Come, let us do something good for God." From sharing this love of ours they come to experience such love as life's real meaning, as children learn it from sharing the love of parents. Beyond that there is need of relatively little formal instruction, for Faith comes from realizing that God is lovable.

To complete the picture, we say a word here about married deacons in the Church. They would provide the organic link between priest and laity. There would be no danger of priestly vocations growing less, because the deacons would be men of perhaps thirty-five or over, known as good husbands and fathers, self-supporting and already proven apostles. Living in various parts of the parish, they would gather the Catholics of their area around them and be considered their representatives with the parish priest. In districts far from the church they would preside at Sunday worship in the absence of the priest. If there were a safe chapel, the Blessed Sacrament could be reserved and the deacons distribute Holy Communion. In our present situation, the people of such areas tend to become careless from lack of attention. The deacons would also be able to promote the lay apostolate there as official representatives of the hierarchy.

B. Brothers and Nuns as Life-Bearers

The deeply dedicated lives of Catholic brothers and nuns have won the admiration of the world. They are apostles "sent" to teach in our schools, to care for the sick, to engage in social work and many other ways of serving Christ in our brother. But they too are under the necessity of being part of the life-bearing chain from Christ. To share the divine life with others and get them to transmit it in their turn is an integral part of the vocation received by every Catholic in baptism and confirmation. It is part of the cooperation that each one must give the Holy Spirit dwelling within him. The Catholic vocation is to become not only spiritual parents, but grandparents, to not only transmit spiritual life to others but to form them for passing it on in their turn. Otherwise those to whom we transmit spiritual life do not themselves achieve true Christian fulfillment! This requires a clear understanding by all "religious" congregations of their special vocation as related to the basic Christian vocation. Our responsibility does not end with the particular service for others to which we devote ourselves, but includes a true master-disciple relationship by which we make them sharers of our lives.

Cardinal Suenens, in *The Nun in the World* (Newman, 1963), quotes an account by Bishop Huyghe of France that he had from a nun whose community had spent thirty years nursing the sick poor of a certain town in their homes. "We are now in touch with the third generation," she said. "When we came we knew only the old and the sick; we nursed the next generation; today it is the grandchildren of our first contacts that come to us for help. We have been completely naturalized in this working-class quarter and are welcome in every home. We have, of course, been able to bring the priest to the bedside of the dying in many cases, but we have never succeeded in converting one single adult in good health. To anyone with eyes to see, it is clear that our quarter continues to become more and more de-christianized." The Sister says nothing about asking the people to do something for one another. By doing all themselves, the nuns also kept all the graces of working for God to themselves and life was not multiplied. When we get people to "do something good for God" and they experience the joy of acting as the agents of God's goodness, they have already begun to live His life actively.

Many Sisters are engaged in conducting retreat houses or play host to various Catholic Action gatherings, but often they meet the guests and the public chiefly in relation to the domestic arrangements. For them to engage actively in forming lay apostles appears the exception. The nuns who have residences for working girls and college students almost invariably restrict themselves to the material work of being "house-keepers." That they try to provide a "Catholic atmosphere" is undeniable, but they rarely influence any of these girls to be true apostles sharing with others the divine life within them. In most cases the girls have come to expect from them no more than board and lodging. From not having their generosity appealed to, these girls tend to be mostly concerned about their "freedom" to come and go at will rather than using their freedom to share God's life with others. All these works of convent hospitality are really precious occasions for the Sisters to share the dynamism of the divine life within them. They should be apostolic "activators," drawing from their own spirit of generosity not only to receive apostles but to "send" them.

The missionaries, as we have already mentioned, constantly encounter the problem that their works of charity win gratitude and admiration without bringing people to understand their supernatural motivation. In Latin America I met a number of nuns and lay papal volunteers engaged in social service who felt frustrated from failure of the people to show a religious response. Some thought that they lacked the personnel and equipment to do the thorough job that would make an impression. In a Lima, Peru, slum parish I suggested that instead of trying to carry out "Social Service" with their limited resources, they change the title to 'Family Service' and organize Mothers' Clubs to discuss family life and undertake some mutual assistance. One of the Sisters told me this story. A poor woman whom she had sent to the hospital with cancer was discharged after a month, but it would be some time before she could do her own housework. The Sister asked several poor neighbors, all lax Catholics, "Will you do something good for God?" They took care of her and her family for several weeks and have continued to give her assistance. The result? In the Sister's own words, "They have not yet come back to church, but now it is apparent that they feel they have something in common with us which they did not before."

The devoted service to the sick of countless nuns in our

hospitals has become proverbial, yet many are asking themselves what of the future. The modern hospital tends to be an institution where the nuns have perforce exchanged the angel of mercy role for that of supervisor, technician or surgery nurse. They are engaged in routine tasks rather than in personal service of the sick. Many young girls become nurses but relatively few enter the nursing sisterhoods. The hospitals grow at an ever-increasing rate, still more lay people must be engaged and the contacts of Sisters with the patients decreases further to a simple "How are you today?" The nun still wears her religious habit but her work becomes progressively laicized. What to do? Let us reflect: If more and more of the material responsibility can be given to lay people, why not also more and more of the spiritual? Why should those in religious garb be the only Catholics who can explain that divine goodness animates their service of others? It is the nurses who are now in closest contact with the patients and the Sisters should share with them their own apostolic spirit. The Legion of Mary is particularly suited as an apostolic organization for nurses and hospital workers.

A magnificent work is being done by the brothers and nuns in Catholic schools. Yet here, too, because of a growing institutionalism the religious tends to be absorbed in the teacher of algebra or history who has a schedule to complete and papers to correct. Have we not sometimes accepted in too absolute a sense the notion that to form the young is to assure the future? What can the teacher accomplish if he does not also influence home and community? Father Daniel A. Lord, S.J., devoted all his life to youth, but two years before he died of cancer he said publicly, "If I had my life to live over again I would work with the adults. It is grown-ups who run the world, create the community climate of self-discipline or laxity which is the predominant influence in young lives." A Communist boasts: "We leave you the children; we look after the young adults, whom your children will also be." How can the Catholic school influence the adult world on which their students unconsciously pattern their lives? Clearly, the teaching brothers and nuns must have closer contact with that world in order to help make the dynamism of divine life far more operative there than is now the case.

This need for brothers and nuns to be life-bearers in the world outside the school assumes special urgency today in view of the population explosion. More than half our Catholic children are not in Catholic schools and the proportion is on the increase. There is even serious question of giving up certain lower grades in the Catholic schools from lack of adequate resources in funds and personnel. The presence of a Catholic school has, however, lulled many parents into a false sense of security and they have tended to abdicate their own responsibility of religious instruction. Other influences that have helped bring this about are the progressive secularization of our culture and regarding religion as simply a system of duties rather than a life. In view of this situation we face the danger of a galloping tragedy of religious illiteracy unless all the trained Catholic forces become engaged in forming the Catholic laity to be also spiritual life-bearers for the young.

In spite of the obvious need for brothers and nuns to have closer contacts with families, many communities are prevented by their rule of enclosure. This seems to stem from the original concept of the religious life as one of being "enclosed" in a monastery, even for men. The first to abandon the traditional cloistered life to make the apostolate their aim were congregations of priests, such as the Barnabites and the Jesuits founded in the sixteenth century. St. Angela Merici founded the Ursulines without enclosure and received approval in 1544. The first twelve Sisters lived in their own parishes and devoted themselves especially to educating the girls of the poor who could not attend the schools of the enclosed nuns. But before long Canon Law was invoked and they had to accept enclosure. St. Francis de Sales and St. Joan Frances de Chantal had a similar experience with the Visitation Sisters. When St. Vincent de Paul founded the Daughters of Charity he called them, with holy shrewdness, a "company" and their residence just a "house" instead of a convent. "The Daughters of Charity," he said, "must be able to go everywhere."

Cardinal Suenens suggests study of whether such traditions from another day embodied in the rules of religious congregations may not be an obstacle to their role of transmitting divine life to others. Pope Pius XII, addressing the Second World Congress of the Lay Apostolate in 1957, explained why every Catholic must be an apostle. He said that it is by transmitting his own life of faith to others that the Christian becomes an adult and discovers the real value of his faith, as parenthood in the physical order reveals new human values. Brothers and nuns need to go beyond their professional duties in order to themselves experience these values of maturity by helping lay people to discover them. For "religious" to teach children their catechism is a very good thing, but it is still better if they get lay people involved in this work of sharing God that they also may become mature in their turn. In how many ways the brothers and nuns in an area could multiply the work of the priest by helping build up the laity in the true likeness of the self-giving Christ!

You are now disturbed about a scarcity of vocations? Look for the cause in the diminution of generosity in this self-centered age. You can fill your novitiates only if you yourselves act to renew the founts of generosity among the people from whom vocations come by getting them involved in sharing life with their neighbor.

C. The Legion of Mary Vocation

The lay vocation does not make sense unless we consider it a true call from God of spiritual life-bearing which requires appropriate formation to fulfill its responsibility. In one mission I visited, several priests felt that some Legion of

Mary groups had seemed to lose their first zeal. I asked why they had established the Legion and was told, "To help us with parish work." They had not thought of it as a call from God to share His life with others and one of the more difficult lay vocations. Lacking such a conception, the priests did not provide the appropriate formation in spiritual outlook and attitudes. For lay apostolic groups this formation is largely given both in the group meeting itself and individually in confession. Those priests had too often failed to provide group guidance by giving the 'allocution' called for by the Legion Handbook or to set a special time for the Legionaries' confessions.

One great value of the Legion of Mary in the lay apostolate is its definite program: the order of the weekly meeting, the reports on work done and specific assignment of work. The Legion is able to inspire zeal and self-sacrifice among Catholics at all levels, even illiterates who must learn the prayers by heart. The Legion's chief training method is that of master and apprentice, new members working with those more experienced. The discipline and definiteness of the Legion are very important for the apostolate, particularly in underdeveloped areas where the people may lack formation in those qualities. Yet even where the Church is more developed, many lay apostolate programs fail to bear full fruit from being indefinite as to the work each member should carry out. Great apostolic potential may be wasted if meetings are given mostly to theoretical discussion and work assignments are vague or routine, demanding little sacrifice. Generosity grows on sacrifice. The members of the Legion are ordinary people, the salt of the earth, yet its formation is such that almost any member can take on any task in it, even going to the ends of the earth. Edel Quinn went from Ireland to organize the Legion in Africa when already in an advanced stage of tuberculosis, yet before her death within three years it had spread across the continent.

It is best to start the Legion with one group or *Praesidium,* as many men as possible, and at the parish center where it can receive close attention as a model for other groups. At the same time, others not in the Legion should also be encouraged in apostolic works, perhaps as members of various parish societies. The Legion members should take an interest in them and cooperate with them, for we do not wish any organization to become self-centered. The Legion Handbook, moreover, states that the Legion should cooperate with them and encourage them. There are many different lay vocations just as there are in "religion," but all should be part of the same mutually helpful parish community. I visited one missionary parish where an attempt had been made to have the Legion as the only form of the lay apostolate, but it was quite obvious that not all the members had that vocation. Some failed to carry out their Legion assignments, which made meetings uninspiring for all. It is easy to say that they should be dropped, but that would probably lose them for apostolic work. In another parish all lay apostolate was centered in neighborhood groups, with the result that other forms of the lay vocation were neglected.

The question is often asked, "Since the priest should form the Legion groups, can we have it in outlying districts?" When preparing this book I wrote to Frank Duff, founder of the Legion, and he gave me examples of mission parishes that have dozens of village groups. One Filipino parish of 20,000 Catholics has 40 *Praesidia* in the villages. The priest arranges their care as follows. Each time he visits a village for Mass or other reason, a regular meeting of the Legion there is held. Furthermore, since a number of *Praesidia* form a *Curia,* the monthly *Curia* meetings attended by the officers of the various *Praesidia* brings them all under the eye and the guidance of the priest. Finally, this priest has a special *Praesidium* at the parish center composed of experienced members who are trained to go as "Spiritual Guides" for the village meetings held in the absence of the priest. The Spiritual Guides can give special help to new or weak *Praesidia*, but they have been found to increase the sense of united strength among all the groups from their contact with all.

One of the chief problems met by the missionary who has Catholics scattered in many villages is the tendency to laxity because of infrequent contact with the priest and isolation from the Catholic community. The experience of a missionary in the Congo is related in *Christ to the World* (1961, No. 1). His parish had 1000 Catholics at the center and 4000 scattered in 14 villages. Each visit several times a year to all the villages took two weeks and he felt that he could not spend more than a day in each lest work at the center suffered. Communions for the two weeks would be only about 25 altogether. He had established the Legion among the men at the center and, seeing the good results, asked the members' advice about the careless Catholics in the villages. The answer was, "We must give them the Legion." It was difficult to find candidates among careless Catholics, but the Legion-naires were finally able to set up a *Praesidium* in each of four larger villages. The Communions soon rose to 200 per trip, 150 irregular marriages were blessed, 25 polygamists put away their concubines and several became Legion members. The smaller villages? They were visited from the other villages until able to form their own groups, or several neighboring villages formed a group together.

In the Dahomey area of Africa, the position and mentality of women in the villages made it difficult to find suitable work for them in the Legion. Then they were assigned to the service of the sick and the aged, where it was discovered that they fulfilled a really important need and got entry everywhere. They were able to baptize many in danger of death and became angels of Christian charity to the sick and afflicted, who among pagans commonly receive indifferent care in even comfortable families. Pagan polygamists, who would have forbidden them entrance to the compounds containing the huts of their wives, now send for them if a wife or child is sick. To increase their acceptance, some lay apostles might be given short courses in practical nursing. In India and Pakistan I was told that there is an even more vast field for women apostles of charity to the afflicted of the villages, where *purdah* (enclosure!) of women is still widely observed.

The emphasis of the Legion program on home visiting makes it very easy for the members to be apostles also to the young, who in today's world have such need of adult friends. In every home visit, the Legionnaires should spend some time speaking with the children. It makes them feel that the visitors are their friends also and moreover wins the hearts of parents. We must not wait until the young people arrive at the age when it is difficult to reach them, or perhaps until they become part of our assignment as "problems." Legion members would also contact in the same friendly way all the children of their own neighborhood. They would invite their young friends from perhaps twelve years on to visit them in small groups. Some could be formed into the Junior Legion, but that should not mean neglect of the others. In certain areas of Africa, up to 80 per cent of graduates from Catholic schools give up the practice of their Faith when they go to the city for work. To provide an effective safeguard by previous friendship and putting apostolic groups of the city in contact with them is a challenge to the Legion's close-knit organization.

One of the most important tasks undertaken by Legionnaires is to act as voluntary catechists. The first envoys of the Legion sent from Dublin to Latin America established a general formula of half their time to home visiting and half to religious instruction. The two go together very obviously, for so often weakness in the faith is due mainly to ignorance of it. I do not know of any part of the world where this is not true. In the archdiocese of Chungju, Korea, which has a marvelous record of conversions even for Korea, there are nearly 1000 Legion-naires giving religious instruction. The less experienced teach children of Catholics, but a large proportion are engaged in convert instruction. Moreover, the classes are recruited by the Legion itself through home visits. The missionaries say that the Legion is the secret of their success, not only in winning so many converts but also in making them good Catholics.

D. Ecumenism as Sharing Life in God

When Pope John XXIII announced that he was calling an Ecumenical (universal) Council, he stated its purpose as to seek fulfillment of our Lord's words, ". . . there shall be one fold and one shepherd." Immediately an amazing current ran through the world and overnight a visible change of atmosphere took place both inside and outside the Church, even among non-Christians. Other popes had just as sincerely declared the same goal, yet with relatively little apparent impact. Pope John's words, on the other hand, not only became front-page news but stirred men everywhere to enter into "ecumenical dialogue" with one another. The Holy Father made clear that to achieve the purpose he set for it the Council must bring about a renewal within the Church and a spirit of *aggiornamento,* or "updating," among Christians. Only then can she fully make the words of Christ her own and say to all men: "Come to us." But the one thing that gave this call of the Holy Father real and personal meaning to mankind was his demonstration of complete openness in his own life.

What is the aim of Catholic ecumenism? Is it simply to assure the growth of the Church, of its ecumenical or universal visible extension over new territory where Christ's gifts have not yet been received or to bring back those who have become separated? Or is it not rather the very delicate task of discovering and respecting the gifts of God in others so that they may better understand the value of those gifts and desire even greater ones? Every page of the Gospel reveals the deep sympathy and openness that Christ showed for every human being made in God's image. They were first of all His brothers and clear recognition of that was always the first step in His apostolate. Ecumenical dialogue may, therefore, be held on many levels, even with non-Christians. With other Christians it is based, of course, on a common faith in Christ, while with Jews it is on the Old Testament alone. Ecumenical dialogue with non-Christians would not begin from revelation but from the innate "religious sense" in every man which causes him to seek God in some way or other. Theologians say that this religious sense is from our being made in God's image and that it enables the non-Christian to have a real supernatural relationship to God, though not as perfect as that from revelation. Two Congolese priests whom I met in Africa told me that some missionaries ignored this and spoke of religion as if the people had no sense of God in their lives.

An excellent illustration of what the Catholic ecumenical spirit means is found in an incident that occurred during a "Religious Emphasis Week" at West Texas State University. William Jacobs, who spent two years in the Amarillo diocese as a lay missionary, tells the story in "REW/Adventure in Understanding," published in *Ave Maria* (October 19, 1963). As introduction the writer explains that the students are chiefly from Baptist or Church of Christ backgrounds, with Catholics numbering scarcely more than 5 per cent. At a panel discussion on the campus, the Catholic bishop had stated that Protestants were clearly "moving closer to us" liturgically. A Methodist minister was prompted by this remark to say that anxiety was being felt over Catholic intimations that it all had to be their way, asking, "Must we always move towards you? Isn't the movement ever in the other direction?" The bishop's reply was that, in practice, "You must come our way; the movement is in one direction."

The next evening there was an invitation session at the Catholic rectory with twelve participants: four lay professors of different faiths, two Episcopalian priests, a Methodist and a Baptist minister, the bishop, two Catholic priests and Mr. Jacobs. The panel exchange of the evening before had been recorded and one of the priests turned on the tape to check its clarity. As Providence would have it, the first sound that filled the room was the Methodist minister's question of the night before. But the bishop's answer was not replayed, for he asked that it be shut off and said plainly that he had answered the question badly. "In regards to interfaith dialogue, I just don't know the language yet and you'll have to help me learn it . . . The Council was an overwhelming experience for us bishops; now we know how neglectful we have been in this area . . . Help me find the words to express our Catholic desire to see everyone grow in oneness with our Lord Jesus . . . to move all of us *toward Him.*"

Those words of the bishop express exactly what is the spirit of ecumenism, to move all of us together towards Christ. The most immediate and direct idea of ecumenism would probably be as a movement aiming towards religious unity of Christians, but not in a narrowly theological sense alone. It is being more and more seen also as a movement under God which embraces the entire visible world and all the human family that lives and labors within it, an ecumenism of love, social justice and intergroup harmony. Are we not justified in considering ecumenism in that sense not only from the words of Pope John when he discussed the Council but above all from the example of his loving openness to all men? What but an immense openness of charity led both John XXIII and Paul VI publicly to pray God's forgiveness for anything they might have done which would impede the movement of all men together toward Christ? The interfaith dialogue is therefore not to be carried out only at the level of discussion between theologians but at every human level in a humble and prayerful manner in the presence of Christ.

The pope is constantly asking us to pray for the Ecumenical

Council, but he means for the purposes of the Council and not only for the deliberations going on in Rome. In this sense even the ordinary Catholic who thinks he has no part in such a matter has the opportunity to help in the renewal of the Church. We should pray to be delivered from evil, from the evil of our smugness in our faith. We should ask our separated brethren to pray with us, that we all may be delivered from the evil of separation: that all prejudice and ignorance on both sides be removed, that suspicion and estrangement be overcome. We should pray for each other, not just in general, but in particular: Catholics for their Protestant neighbors, Protestants for their Catholic neighbors, that God may bless and guide them. The leaders of the Churches need our prayers, Catholics for Protestant leaders, Protestants for the pope and the Catholic bishops. This prayer is to be an expression of all-embracing love like the prayer of Christ for mankind, not a disagreeable duty imposed on us by unfortunate circumstances which we may be inclined to blame on the mistakes of others in the past. Each man here and now must be seen as beloved of God.

Father John L. Thomas, S.J., undertook a broad national sampling of the attitudes by members of the major American religious groups towards those of other groups. One of the questions asked was: "Do you think there is much ill-feeling towards Protestants, Catholics, or Jews among most people of your religious preference?" In the Protestant group, 24 per cent felt there was ill-feeling towards Catholics and 25 per cent towards Jews. Of the Catholics, 11 per cent felt there was ill-feeling towards Protestants and 21 per cent towards Jews. In the Jewish group, 5 per cent felt that there was ill-feeling towards Protestants and 15 per cent towards Catholics. Another question was about having people of other faiths as neighbors. Of the Protestants questioned, 13 per cent would prefer not to have Catholics and 27 per cent not to have Jews as neighbors. Among the Catholics, 4 per cent would prefer not to have Protestant neighbors, but 15 per cent would not wish Jews. In the Jewish group, 7 per cent said they would not want Protestants and 13 per cent would not want Catholics as neighbors.

Here, then, at the neighborhood level is where the ecumenical struggle against prejudice must begin. Nor is a negative absence of prejudice enough. There must be a positive love of neighbor, a positive seeking his good as an individual person whom God has placed beside us. The first step is to become aware of him as a person, as a human being with a name, worthy of respect in God's sight as we are. The basic obstacle to our drawing nearer to one another in Christ is often a human gulf among people which is often overlooked. It is the same human gulf that creates in the Negro, as James Baldwin writes, ". . . the doubt that he is worthy of life, since everyone around him denied it." All discrimination of whatever form is at bottom religious discrimination, because it restricts or denies the dignity among their fellows to which men have a right as made in the image of God. It is not enough for us only to tell men about the Christ of the Gospels. Men must be able to recognize Him and experience His love in the Catholic of today. That is the true spirit of ecumenism.

9. GOD'S WORD GIVES LIFE ITS MEANING

The heart of modern man cries out for certainty about the meaning of life, yet so often he has little confidence of finding it. He has innate within him a sense of God from being made to God's image, but sin has blurred and confused that image. Vainly he seeks to discover life's meaning in learned discussions, in technological progress, in devotion to pleasure. Only the word of God can give man the true answer to the essential question of life.

God alone can tell us why we came to be and reveal our relationship to Him. He does this by the concrete dramatic form of "salvation history" in the Bible. The best living pagan lacks this definitive revelation of life's meaning. In Hebrew, God's word is *dabar,* which includes the idea of action as well as speech. The Bible does not simply tell us what God said; it also relates how God acts and reacts with man in a personal relationship. The divine interchange culminates in God's becoming man. We could never have understood our relationship to God from explanation alone. As the child learns from seeing the conduct of his parents how he should act, so the ideals of the race as God's image have developed through concrete example. How do we know, for instance, that God is merciful as an example to us? It is from man's experience of God's mercy in salvation history, as when Peter denied Christ or the case of the woman taken in adultery. Where do we get a "real" idea of faith or hope as supernatural virtues, except from such Bible accounts as those of Abraham and Job? Missionaries say that it is impossible to give their converts a real conception of the Christian virtues in any other way than from Bible stories. A mere explanation of the catechism is not enough.

We are beginning to discover that this concrete character of man's relationship to God as expressed in the Bible is also essential that our own religious concepts may be seen in their proper life perspective. How often we meet "born Catholics" in whom religion seems almost completely divorced from life, who have little idea of a relation between what they do on Sunday and during the week. They need to learn from the Bible how all of human life is related to God. In an age when all their values are constantly under fire, it is our Catholic youth especially who need the Bible. Bishop Elchinger said at the Eichstatt Mission Study Week in 1960: "We must plunge our young people continually into a Bible atmosphere to make them feel more familiar with an order of values that is becoming more and more depreciated. If not, they will very soon discover that they are no longer in accord with the message of God; they will not know how to understand it, nor how to apply it" (*Teaching all Nations,* Herder and Herder, 1961).

A. The Bible Our Guide of Life

The Bible is, therefore, in a special way a direct line of communication between God and the heart of man. God's call to man is felt far more clearly and urgently when given in His own word than if presented in human speech, which is able to express the divine reality so faintly. If God Himself has spoken, it seems somewhat presumptuous not to make use of this majestic word of God which is able to pierce the curtain of human existence and speak directly to the heart of man. In *Christ to the World* (1960, No. 1), Father Albert Muthumalai of India writes, "There is a difference between a Hindu who has read the Life of Christ and one who hasn't.

When a Hindu has read or heard of the life of Christ, his very being is impressed by the dominant personality of our Lord. The Protestants in India have realized this fact and are making capital out of it by distributing Bibles and New Testaments among the educated Hindus . . . Most of the educated Catholic converts in India say they came to Christ and then to the Church through Protestant sources."

How well the Bible takes into account that man is not spirit alone, but body-spirit, a human person whose spiritual existence is conditioned by his bodily and emotional being. In a paper, "Psychology and Spiritual Guidance" *(The Furrow*, August, 1962), Sean O'Riordan shows how God in the Bible has always in view the actual life of man in his time, the bodily conditions of his existence, his temporal work and occupations. When the multitudes asked John the Baptist: "What is it, then, that we are to do?" He answered them, "The man who has two coats must share with the man who has none; and the man who has food to eat, must do the like." To the tax-gatherers he said, "Do not go beyond the scale appointed to you." And to the soldiers, "Do not use men roughly, do not lay false information against them; be content with your pay" (Luke 3:10-14). These men asked in simple faith guidance for their lives and John gave it to them in a practical way that would make faith a real motivating force in the concrete details of everyday living.

Or consider how our Lord made an apostle of the woman at the well who had had five husbands and converted Zacchaeus the wealthy tax-gatherer by showing the respect for him as a man that self-righteous neighbors had refused him. Sean O'Riordan describes a beautiful example of this type narrated in John 8. " 'The Scribes and Pharisees brought him a woman who had been found committing adultery, and made her stand there in full view.' It was her moment of shame, guilt and fear." The Gospel writer tells us that Jesus bent down and wrote on the ground with His finger, whereupon all the woman's accusers slunk away. "'Then Jesus looked up, and asked her, Woman, where are thy accusers? Has no one condemned thee?' It was an invitation not to deny or repress the shame, guilt and fear but to transcend them in hope and love. The response is implied, not stated. 'No one, Lord, she said. And Jesus said to her, I will not condemn thee either. Go, and do not sin again henceforward.' The woman caught in adultery is such no longer. She has been caught up into her true womanhood, created anew in true life, through an emotional-spiritual experience wrought round her and within her by the Master."

When our Lord speaks in Matthew 25 of the last judgment, how comprehensible He makes it to even the most dull of wit and how reasonable to all by relating it directly to simple facts of everyday experience. "When the Son of Man comes in his glory . . . all nations will be gathered in his presence, where he will divide men one from the other, as the shepherd divides the sheep from the goats; he will set the sheep on his right, and the goats on his left. Then the King will say to those who are on his right hand, Come, you that have received a blessing from my Father, take possession of the kingdom which has been prepared for you since the foundation of the world. For I was hungry, and you gave me food, thirsty, and you gave me drink; I was a stranger, and you brought me home, naked, and you clothed me, sick, and you cared for me, a prisoner, and you came to me. Whereupon the just will answer, Lord, when was it that we saw thee hungry . . . ? And the King will answer them, believe me, when you did it to one of the least of my brethren here, you did it to me."

What shall we say, however, of certain statements by our Lord that seem to express an extreme idealism? How can we practice such as the following in everyday life? "If a man strike thee on thy right cheek, turn the other cheek also towards him; if he is ready to go to law with thee over thy coat, let him have it and thy cloak with it" (Matthew 5:39-40).

Is there not danger that we would be constantly imposed upon by those without conscience? Dr. C. H. Dodd, the well-known Anglican commentator, states in his *Gospel and Law* that our Lord was concerned to help us understand the *quality* and *direction* that Christian life should have for man's highest development. He desired to arouse in each one of us a sense of personal responsibility to demonstrate the perfection of God in a greater or less degree according to our own life situation. "That you may be the children of your Father, who makes his sun to rise on the evil and equally on the good, his rain to fall on the just and equally on the unjust . . . But you are to be perfect, as your heavenly Father is perfect" (Matthew 5:45-48). How completely our Lord carried this out in His own life.

The one who seeks in the Bible divine guidance should not try to analyze it intellectually but be attentive to "listen" in his heart for God's response to his own deepest aspirations, which are in the heart and not in the mind. Today many "Bible Study Groups" are being formed, not to study the Bible as simply a document like others but to hear God's word together. "Speak, Lord, for thy servant heareth." What does God wish us to do? In the sense of God's own presence speaking to us, the idealism expressed by our Lord does not seem so impractical. It rather inspires to the love which sweeps away apparent difficulties. Within the heart that is attentive to God's word there is always a constant inspiration at work. Bible discussions provide the best possible incentives to the apostolate and lay apostles should learn to conduct Bible discussions themselves as a basic method of action. In the home, reverent reading and discussion of the Bible is the best guide to Christian living and source of family unity. Small children have an intense curiosity about themselves and the origin of things. Moreover, their open and uncluttered minds are particularly attuned to "hear" the Word of God.

B. Gospel Weeks for Italian Workers

An article by Sister San Martino of the Daughters of St. Paul in *Christ to the World* (1958, No. 4), tells of the Sisters' remarkable success with Gospel Weeks and Gospel Triduums among anti-clerical and pro-communist workers in Italy. This community is well prepared for such an apostolate, as a fair number of the Sisters take a full course in philosophy and theology, as well as special studies in Scripture, apologetics and social sciences. The usual form of the Gospel Week was daily conferences and discussions for three or six days in some part of the factory or other place of work. Typical subjects were: "Jesus, a Real Man"; "Jesus, the First Worker"; "The Kindness of Jesus"; "The Gospel, Fiction or Fact"; "The Gospel and Human Dignity"; "The Gospel and Man Today." It often required much patience and tact to secure permission from the managers or the workers' internal commission, but on promise to avoid politics or social questions and speak only of Christ it was usually forthcoming. Once this was arranged, a poster would be put up in the canteen or on the notice-board announcing the program and the subject of each day's conference.

In 1953 the first campaigns were held in about 30 factories of Naples, large and small: cigarette factory, cotton mill, brewery, glass works, canned food, naval mechanics. It took the Sisters assigned to the work six months to cover all the factories. The best results were among the naval mechanics, in spite of the fact that most of the 900 were Communists. In the 60 years of the factory's existence, no priest had ever entered it even as workers' chaplain. When the Sisters arrived in the dining room on the appointed day to speak during the lunch hour, they found it decorated with red flags and at the speaker's place photographs of Nenni, Togliatti and Stalin. As the Sister prepared to speak, the men began to hiss and to throw paper pellets. She waited quietly until things grew calmer, then gently invited the men to reflect. "You fathers," she said, "what would you say if one of your daughters were in my place? And you young men, if one of your sisters were here? I came here gladly among you, not to bring you just an idea, but to bring you the idea: the idea of God, the thought of God. It is not the word or the idea of a man, but the idea of the Creator, who is our most loving Father." She spoke of God in this simple way for a few minutes until the factory whistle blew for the return to work.

As she went out, however, the Sister approached individuals very cordially, asking each about his family and children. One poor man had a mentally sick wife, and needed to have her put in a hospital; another's children roamed the streets because his wife was sick. The Sister listened to them kindly, then went on to ask others about their work, their difficulties, and had words of consolation and encouragement for each one. At succeeding conferences there were larger and larger audiences. The one on "The Kindness of Jesus" made an especially deep impression and it was possible to pass from the kindness of Jesus to the duty of every Christian to be kind. The private conversations continued daily, speaking about God, why He created us, how much He loves us, even to sending His Son to be one of us. Today we take the place of Jesus as God's delegates to show love on the earth in our families, among fellow workers and towards all men.

The factory was transformed. The head of the workers' internal commission, a Communist, said publicly at the concluding "Gospel Celebration" when copies of the Gospels were distributed: "Sister, we feel it our duty to beg your pardon for our more than impolite manner in receiving you; we are on Christ's side and we want to be Christians; do not abandon us. Tell the pope, the bishops, that we workers want to belong to Christ. Never in all our lives have we heard kind words such as those you addressed to us these days. You have brought us calm, kind words, not those of men who promise much and then leave us in the deepest disillusionment, in the blackest bitterness. During these days we have felt the presence of God with us and our very life of toil and fatigue has been more bearable because we have felt the joy of being children of God." From that time many of the workers laid aside their anti-clerical and anti-Catholic prejudices. The Sisters go every week to distribute Catholic literature and to give a short catechism lesson.

At three days of conferences among railway workers in Sardinia, their Communist leader had warned: the Sister has been sent to interfere in politics; when she begins on politics we will all go out of the room. The first talk lasted 12 minutes and when the free discussion began the Communist leader tried to slip in a political question. The Sister addressed him, very politely but firmly: "Brother, I came here to talk about God and not about parties, much less about what Christian Democracy should do. I came to give you the joy, if only for a few moments, of tasting how wonderful it is to feel we are all children of a common Father, God, who loves us as any true father loves his own children. I would be false to my vocation and unjust to you if I failed to speak of this and began to deal with an entirely different subject." The Communist leader was most attentive to the two following talks. At the end of the Gospel Celebration he assisted at Mass and received Holy Communion. Two years later his wife said, "Sisters, since my husband received the Holy Gospel book from you he reads it to the children every evening and I must thank the Lord that he has left the Communist Party."

In the salt marshes of Sardinia, the Sisters had to begin by going out among the men engaged in tending the salt evaporation beds. They gather in groups of seven or eight at certain times to load the salt onto trucks. The first day the Sister walked almost continually from seven in the morning until seven at night under the hot sun in order to contact them all. She took advantage of their waiting for a truck to greet them, ask how their families were, always adding a spiritual thought: your toil is blessed by Christ who worked with His hands; offer it to the Lord and it will be meritorious in His sight. They were amazed when she said that she would come out there every day for a week to tell them about the Gospel. Talks lasting 7-15 minutes were held in little groups beside a truck or a heap of salt. At first they were frankly curious why a woman would come thus to speak to them, but daily the interest grew. Three years afterwards the reports of the Sisters' weekly visits to the families noted that 921 out of 1500 workers read a page of the Gospel regularly every day. One woman said, "Since my husband has been reading that book, he no longer swears or gets drunk, no longer goes to the Communist Party Center; every Sunday he attends Mass and receives Holy Communion."

In Rome a Sister arranged to conduct a Gospel Triduum to 1100 gardeners in preparation for Easter. Their leader had given the watchword: no one was to attend the conferences. In the morning punctually at 6:15 the Sister was at the San Sixto nursery garden, one of the largest. The workers came in but none would return her greeting, the same on the next day. The third day she came a little later after the men had gone to work and went around to the different hothouses, approaching them one by one. She spoke about their work, their worries, and other things that concerned them. Then she concluded: "Now that we know each other you can see that I have come to bring you a message and a book very different from those you have heard and read up till now. I expect you all at the talk by the gate, where I shall speak to you only of God and the nobility of our family, we are all God's family." The next day 650 workers came and on the last day over 1000. All came to the final Mass held in the garden and 43 per cent received Holy Communion.

During a campaign among the nearly 2000 street cleaners of Rome, 95 per cent Communists, the Sister walked through the streets for about a week to meet as many as possible where they worked. She invited all to be present on a certain day at the meeting to be held in the *camerette* (little room) where they kept their working equipment. Early in the morning the Sister was there, but had to listen to a tirade against the Church, the pope, the priests, the convents. She let them speak, then said: "Well, brothers, this evening please leave your work a quarter of an hour earlier and be so kind as to listen to me as I have to you." At 5:15 almost all were present as she dealt with the value of man in the Gospel. The discussion at the end was so animated that it ran until 8:45. During the meetings following there were still many accusations against the Church and the clergy, but at Mass concluding the Gospel Celebration all solemnly consecrated themselves. The three Communist cell leaders had prepared a final stroke, to contrast the Sisters' convent with the workers' own poor homes. The Sisters led them to the dormitories, huge rooms with 85 beds, beside each only a jug of water. They were also shown the simple refectory and what the Sisters ate. The leader apologized: "They tell us so many lies. I am glad to have found out the truth and want to lay at the feet of the Blessed Virgin my Party membership card."

C. The Bible in Religious Instruction

Today we are returning to the idea of St. Augustine, that the best teacher of religion is God Himself in the Bible. The saint, in his little manual, "On Catechizing the Unlearned," begins with a caution that even those who seem to have unworthy motives should be treated with great kindness in order to change their attitude. "Then," he says, "the instruction should begin at the point where 'God created all things good' and be continued down to the present state of the Church. Do it in such manner as, while relating events and actions, to explain their causes and reasons, and to refer them to that end of charity from which our eyes in speech or action should never be turned away." The key here is to constantly show how what God has done demonstrates His goodness, His love towards us, and invites our appropriate response.

Religious instruction for converts will usually need to be prepared for by a certain amount of "pre-catechism." One begins by trying to build a bridge between people's own religious sense and God's revelation of Himself as the altogether wise, great and good Creator. Father Albert Muthumalai remarks, "If we go around any town or village in India and ask any passer-by whether he would believe whatever God teaches Him; unless he is a militant atheist, he will say yes . . . (but) his mind is prejudiced in favor of his own religion." Almost everywhere I was told that most people take for granted there is a Superior Being and that to try to "prove" God's existence might succeed only in raising doubts. The same holds true for the existence of the soul, for all men believe in a "higher part" of man. Even in "materialist" Japan, one finds both these basic beliefs, shown, for example, by the notions of an after life and of man's responsibility for his acts. I tried a paraphrase of our Lord's words to Nicodemus on some Japanese non-Christians and found it readily understood: "What is born of the body is flesh and will die, what is born of the Spirit is spirit and will live forever."

In following the instruction method of St. Augustine, any catechism may be used, though the best is a simple one that gives the basic framework of doctrine without appearing complicated or difficult. Each lesson is introduced with a Bible story appropriate to the topic. The form of telling should be suitable to the hearers and condensed if necessary, but always as nearly as possible in the concrete terms and vivid style of the Bible itself. A Bible story told in general terms or flat style is not worthy of God's word. The reason for beginning with the Bible story is that God Himself must begin the lesson, He must receive primary emphasis. To start with a man-made story or example and then go to the Bible places

God's word in the secondary position of merely supporting what the teacher says instead of being the primary source. After telling the "events and actions" in the story, explain the "causes and reasons" for what God said and did which show His goodness. It is very bad pedagogy not to explain the "why" as well as the "what" of the Bible narrative.

The teacher is now ready to relate the story with the catechism lesson, and he may begin by reading out one or more of the questions and answers. In order that this may be seen as a natural, not a forced relationship, care must have been taken in the choice of the story. Every doctrine taught in the catechism has its source in the Bible. If this relationship has been sometimes neglected in the books available to us, we may have to give considerable thought and prayer to rediscover it. In relating the Bible story with the catechism and with daily life is where human examples may be used. Comparisons or illustrations from the lives of the students themselves are particularly valuable to help develop incentives. The teacher should always bear in mind that God made us in His own image, that He acts with us according to human psychology and that our human relationships mirror our relationship to God. For example, God is good to us as parents are good to their children, He shares His life with us as parents do with children, love in the family and in human society is an image of the mutual self-giving by the members of the Holy Trinity, the perfect society of Persons.

One chief problem with many present catechisms is that they treat doctrines separately in the different lessons without unity of theme. For example, about the middle of the book is a lesson on love of God and neighbor, but that basic theme is perhaps not mentioned in either previous or later lessons. The central theme of our relationship to God is His goodness. He created angels and men because goodness tends to share itself. Our unifying theme for the catechism is that each doctrine is a gift from God's goodness and shows His great love towards us. The invisible love is shown by the visible gifts. Now when we receive a gift we always respond: we thank the giver and plan to offer a gift in return. The natural human response to God's gifts is by prayer and charity. St. Francis Xavier, after teaching a doctrine, would say, "Let us say a prayer to thank God for what He teaches us and ask His help to practice it." Thus the idea implanted in the mind became an object of faith in the heart. Every article of the Creed, each of the commandments and sacraments, should be taught as a special gift of God's goodness.

What shall we give God in return besides our prayers? He needs nothing of ours, indeed, all we have comes from Him. How does a child make a birthday gift to the parents from whom it receives everything? It sacrifices its own desires in order to please its father or mother, tries to be helpful in the home and towards its brothers and sisters. So as our response to God we use His own gifts of time and talents to please Him and to help His other children on earth in return for the greater gifts of the spiritual order that He bestows on us. While teaching the Creed, for example, the response of mutual love and help towards our fellow man would be emphasized. The commandments would be presented as instructions from our loving Father how to fulfill our relationships to Him, to family and neighbor, including social justice. While teaching the sacraments, by which we share God's life at the highest level, emphasis would be laid on sharing this gift of God's own life with others and helping them pass it on to still others.

The response to God in both prayer and love of others must be learned by practice in order to make these a real part of Christian living. The effective learning method is that of "apprenticeship," in the class, in the family and in the community. The teacher encourages short spontaneous group prayer by the class arising from the matter and from life as well as in turn by members of the class. It is essential not to make prayer life seem limited by certain formulas like morning and evening prayer. The Christian should learn to express his sense of personal relationship to God spontaneously in prayer, not only alone but in family and apostolic groups. Lack of ease in speaking to God may be responsible for much timidity in speaking about God to others as well as for some of our difficulty in meditation. In the apprenticeship of practicing love towards others, the class should decide on helpful practices they will carry out. This group support should be continued as members of some organization for apostolic action, even of the simplest kind.

An idea being recently developed in several dioceses of the United States is to have adult lay Catholics conduct religious discussions based on the Bible for groups of young people in their homes. The original aim was to provide religious formation to students in the higher classes of secondary schools, but young people who are working have equal need of them. The adult leaders receive special preparation, either for each session or in a course beforehand, or a combination of the two. The program fits in excellently with the adult-youth apostolate we have mentioned in a previous chapter. The adult can help young people very much because he has reached the independence in life to which they aspire. He must know how to encourage the young people to discover their own answers to questions by discussion, not act like a teacher who gives the answers. He tries to be a "catalyst" who helps them make a personal response to God and develop practical conclusions for their own lives.

D. The CCD Uses a Bible Method

The Confraternity of Christian Doctrine (CCD) was begun 400 years ago in Italy for teaching religion to poor children. Pope St. Pius X decreed that it should be established in every parish of the world. In his encyclical, *On Teaching Christian Doctrine*, the same Holy Father declared that the chief cause of dechristianization with its attendant evils "is to be found above all in ignorance of divine things." In the United States, the Confraternity is set up as a National Organization, with a program for providing training to volunteer teachers in religion. Others aid them by acting as "fishers" to recruit the classes and as "helpers" for office and similar work. Some 40,000 persons have received the Confraternity diploma after a 30 hours course in method and content. Their chief work in the United States is religious instruction of Catholic children who attend government schools.

The pope in his encyclical quoted the Council of Trent as saying that the most important work of pastors of souls is instruction of the faithful. Sunday sermons on the Gospel are not alone sufficient; there must also be regular catechetical instructions from the pulpit on all Sundays and Holy Days. During Lent and Advent, moreover, they shall be given daily or at least three times a week. There should be an annual "Catechism Day" with all possible solemnity. The day opens with Mass of the Holy Spirit and a talk on the necessity of religious instruction. A contest in catechism is held among the children of each age group who have won in local competitions, with prize giving. Do not neglect the parents as family educators in religion, perhaps offer prizes also to children who best explain their family religious program. The catechizers of the children, both religious and lay, should also be given full public recognition in an appropriate manner.

In the missions it is often necessary to set up the Confraternity in a different form from that of the U.S. When the Maryknoll Fathers began work among the Indians of Guatemala and Peru in the early 1940's, it seemed impossible to find Catholics capable of learning to give religious instruction. Though practically all the people were baptized, they were mostly illiterate and so ignorant of their faith that few received the sacraments except in danger of death. One day I asked a missionary what proportion of the Indians scattered in villages through the mountains could be sufficiently instructed. His estimate was that with the priests and trained catechists available it might be possible to instruct about 10 per cent, chiefly those closer to the parish center. The population was so scattered and so large in proportion to the number of instructors that it did not seem the other 90 per cent could be reached unless some extremely simple method was devised for multiplying catechizers.

That method was discovered a short time later by Auxiliary Bishop Gonsalez of Guatemala City. It is a fascinating story. One day the bishop, himself in charge of a parish with 25,000 Catholics, told a village of 500 that he was visiting, "I note that your children do not know the Our Father and the Hail Mary. Would you like them to learn these prayers?" The reply was unanimous, "Yes, certainly, Your Excellency. We are all Catholics." The bishop spoke to them about the still remembered tradition of village prayer leaders, men appointed by the Spanish friars to lead the people in the recitation of prayers and catechism. During the independence movements the friars were expelled and the practice fell into disuse. Now he asked the village to choose a man and an assistant to teach the prayers to their children. The villagers consulted together, then their spokesman said, "But, Your Excellency, no one in the village remembers the prayers well enough to teach them." The bishop, however, was not nonplussed. "Never mind," he replied, "You choose the men and I will teach them myself, then they can teach the children."

The bishop met the next Sunday with the candidates named by several villages and taught them the prayers. "Now go back and teach the children of five families in your villages. Next Sunday return here and we shall see." Each Sunday the bishop taught them one lesson of the small catechism and during the week each one taught five families what he had learned. Within three months, hundreds were able to receive the sacraments and the catechizers went on to other groups of families. The bishop had discovered the "formula" which brought a dramatic breakthrough in solving the problem of instruction. "Now we can instruct 90 per cent instead of 10," said the missionaries. Before long the bishop had 600 volunteer catechizers at work, all ordinary fathers of families and some unable to read. The catechizers far from the parish gathered at out-stations to be prepared by supervisory catechists. Maryknoll priests carried the plan to Peru, and during Lent of 1955, the first volunteers in the Puno area on Lake Titicaca instructed 400 for Easter Communion in one village, more than made their Easter duty in the whole area one year before.

The equipment of a volunteer catechizer is a Bible history, a small catechism, a wall chart of Bible pictures and an identity card. The training classes which they attend are really "pilot" sessions in which each lesson is demonstrated exactly as it is to be taught. These are held weekly or fortnightly, usually on Sundays. One of the catechizers reads a Bible story related to the lesson, another is asked to tell it as he would to his class, then the rest comment and criticize. The moderator next explains the catechism, one question at a time, relating it to the story and the picture. Several are asked to give it back in their own words and the others comment. At an appropriate moment there is a brief prayer for help to believe and practice what is learned. Those present decide on an application and suggest acts of kindness. The demonstration may be in Spanish, as the *lingua franca,* but the volunteers teach in the language of their people and vernacular hymns are learned. Father Verhoeven, in charge of the Peru program, wrote me, "The Biblical method seems to reach the minds of the Indians, both catechizers and people, and attract them." Already many years ago the famous founder of the White Fathers in Africa had said: "The Africans will learn more dogma and moral from a simple recital of the Gospel story than from any amount of analysis of the catechism."

Choosing and directing the catechizers involves certain psychological factors. At a public meeting in the village or area, the priest or supervisor catechist first elicits general agreement that the children need religious instruction. So do the adults, of course, but that is not mentioned. The parish cannot provide teachers, so the village is reminded of the prayer-leader tradition and asked to choose two men of good character as catechizer and assistant. The public choice by their tribal community constitutes a social mandate that they obey. To apply this method outside tribal communities it is first necessary to set up lay organizations. For example, members of the Legion of Mary do the work assigned them as a social mandate from their group. Moreover, the fact that the community or group gives this mandate makes each member of the group feel a personal interest in the success of the project and causes him to cooperate. The priest confirms the choice for a six-month trial period and a candidate not married in the Church must do so before the end of probation. One who does not prove satisfactory is replaced by his village. I was told that about one in three proves to be good material. The regular assignment of one year is given at a public function before the altar, where each makes a solemn promise of fidelity to his high office and observance of the prescribed social and personal rules of conduct.

Some have thought that the demonstration or practice method of preparing religion teachers is only for ignorant folk, but it is actually a simple form of the method widely used in training institutes for school teachers. With appropriate materials the method is valid at all levels for the multiplication of teachers in general knowledge as well as in religion. It can be used, for example, in underdeveloped areas to prepare volunteer teachers for children who cannot attend school, as well as for teaching religion. In the United States, it could supply the CCD with 60,000 additional religion teachers that are needed. One problem with training religion instructors by giving the full course beforehand is that those who are not professional teachers usually have difficulty in "organizing" a good lesson presentation from their material. By the on-the-job method this is done for them. In the missions it was also discovered that few would be willing to undertake a course beforehand, but the one lesson at a time seems to them relatively easy. In the Maryknoll Mission of Juli, Peru, for example, with 25 priests for 275,000 Catholics, there are 1000 volunteer catechizers after only eight years. This is about four times the proportion to Catholic population of Confraternity teachers in the United States after twenty years. The Peruvian bishops in 1959 praised this modern adaptation of the pioneer method and recommended its extension to all the dioceses of Peru.

The priest and supervisor catechists have maps of each area showing all the homes that have received three months' instruction, those in progress and those waiting their turn. In sparsely settled areas the rule is to instruct five families once a week, but in populous towns and villages the classes number far more. One catechizer in Guatemala said he had no time any more to sleep, for between 6 and 12 at night as many as 100 people would come to his house for instruction. The volunteers make a monthly day of recollection and an annual retreat, have their own Fiesta day. In parish processions they march at the head of their villages. Recently an "Apostolic Bible Hour" of readings and responsorial prayers on the day of recollection has been much appreciated. Those who prove themselves are given an opportunity to go in groups of 40-50 for a 3 to 4 weeks advanced course in doctrine, prayer, Bible, liturgy and teaching methods. From teaching their religion they become anxious to learn more and get the answers to questions or objections put to them.

Among Maryknoll missionaries in Korea and the Philippines, boys and girls in the upper classes of Catholic high schools are trained and guided by a supervisor for giving religious instruction to Catholic children who attend government primary schools. Later those boys and girls will be true religious leaders in their own communities. In New York City, hundreds of Puerto Rican immigrants are being trained by this method to instruct their own people. On Monday evenings they gather at a training center conducted by Catholic Sisters, then on the other evenings of the week teach families and small groups in the apartment houses. Whether in Latin America, with its nearly 200 million Catholics, or elsewhere, this method has proven the most successful for multiplication of religion teachers at the level of the people themselves. Such multiplication is the only way that the Church can have any prospect of coping with the challenge she faces today from the "population explosion" and shortage of clergy. The more simple the method adopted by the Confraternity of Christian Doctrine and the closer it follows God's way of teaching in the Bible, the more successfully can the challenge be met.

10. TOWARDS COMMUNITY OF PERSONS IN CHRIST

Our Lord emphasized constantly that the chief means and method of spreading His kingdom are to be unity and love among Christians. At the solemn moment when He was about to begin His passion, He begged this gift for the Apostles and for us: ". . . that all may be one, even as thou, Father in me and I in thee; that they also may be one in us, that the world may believe that thou hast sent me" (John 17:20-21).

From this prayer of Christ we learn that our model and source of true community on earth is the Holy Trinity itself, the perfect society of Persons. Cardinal Suenens, in *The Theology of the Apostolate* (Mercier Press, 1953), writes: "The Holy Spirit is from the very depths of His own being the gift of self. He is wholly directed towards the Father and the Son, as the Father and the Son turn towards Him . . . This character of openness—a tending towards others—of true personality would deserve a special and more extended study which would be the exact opposite of the philosophy of despair proclaiming that 'Hell is other people'; it would show that 'Heaven is other people.'" The Christian apostle knows that the only remedy for despair as well as the means by which man can reach his highest fulfillment as a person in God's image is to share by grace the community of the Holy Trinity.

Only the wisdom and love of God could devise a means for us to enter into this infinite divine community: the Second Person of the Holy Trinity would become man and open Himself to us at the human level! A French writer, Allo, says in his *Paul, Apostle of Jesus Christ*: "Christianity is not a system, it is a Person . . . It is the presence of another Person in our soul, the hold of another Person on our whole soul . . . Our Christian profession is essentially our entrance into the life of another Person, a Person who is at once human and infinite." From this it is clear how far the "state of grace" is from being a static condition of the soul, it is a living and dynamic relationship with Christ as a Person and through Him with the Holy Trinity. By baptism the three Persons give themselves to the Christian and thus receive him into their own divine community. To share the divine life of God means being one with our Lord and thus related to the Father as the Man Jesus Christ is related to Him, living and growing in this relationship by the action of the Holy Spirit. Our awareness of being related to each Person of the Holy Trinity in a special way helps us dedicate ourselves to enlarge and extend this relationship in our own lives and to share it with our fellow men.

A. Openness to Others as Persons

By showing Himself open to others as persons created in God's image, our Lord gave them a new sense of their human dignity. He brought out in them a goodness and an affinity for the good which they had not dared think they possessed because they had not been shown acceptance as persons having true value in themselves. Here we mention only a few: Matthew, the despised tax-gatherer called to be an Apostle; Mary Magdalen, branded as a public sinner; Zacchaeus, tax-gatherer and usurer; the Samaritan woman who had had five husbands; the woman taken in adultery. The lame, the blind and all that He cured would never forget Him. Yet the effect on their lives could not be greater than on those of the publicans and sinners who would ever after feel lifted up by the remembrance, "He ate with us." Christ received no one merely as an individual in need of help but always as a brother, child of His Father and part of Himself. Throughout Palestine He entered into direct contact with many people, but countless more who never saw Him also felt lifted up by the witness that those who had seen Him bore to His goodness, more than to His miracles.

Now we can readily see why and how every Catholic should be an apostle, to bear witness to the place of Christ in His own life. The missionary task is not simply to tell others about God as if He were a being external to them and to us. The Catholic is Christ visible in the world today. His vocation is to manifest towards all his daily human contacts the personal attitude that Christ showed, so that each one of them may come to understand a little better his own value before God and be led to act in accordance with that value. One reason why religion is often badly presented by apostolic people is that they are not accustomed to speak easily with others about what is personal to them in their hearts. We seem to have a fear of revealing our true selves and so fail to invite the confidences of others who so often desire nothing more than to find Christ in human form today so they may pour out to Him the trouble that weighs them down. Religion, which ought to be considered our most deeply felt relationship with men as well as with God, is so often spoken of as simply a system of beliefs and duties.

The Christian does not have our Lord's power to penetrate directly into men's hearts, but that was not the way He entered them either. He first opened His own heart to receive them and they in turn opened their hearts to Him. To be a representative of Christ today means to speak simply as He did, heart to heart. If we hide our true self and do not enter into communion with our brother, how can he understand what it means to enter into communion with Christ? If a Catholic is unwilling to enter into an "I" and "Thou" communion with his brother, to make the apparent sacrifice it entails which is not really a sacrifice because of the joy it can bring, then he cannot really show forth Christ among men. We associate every day with others in work, business, recreation, but we are unable to show them God in our hearts because we refuse to let them into our hearts. Indeed, from the want of such experience in the deepest part of our being, is there not grave danger that our own relationship with God may remain formal and superficial? Is not this a fundamental problem of religion in today's world?

It is extremely important to remember that our Lord came to insure the happiness of the whole man, not simply to "balance the books" of our sins, as it were. From a purely human point of view, our failure to imitate Him in mutual trust is the greatest single cause of loneliness and insecurity. We have seen how a great gap grows up between adults and youth because the former get so wrapped up in the various masks they seek to wear before the world that they do not know how to manifest mutual trust with their own children. Nay, they may even "use" their children as means to develop these masks. The young are always ready and eager to speak from the heart, but all too soon and too well they learn from their elders to make life one great masked ball. So even well-meaning people are caught up in the web of this diabolical pattern which in the modern context of "getting ahead" has enmeshed mankind.

Herein lies also the crucial evil of social, racial and class injustice. The sweatshop, the slum, the affluence of some while others exist in deep poverty, all are denials of the dignity of the person who is the image of God. As long as the community of which we are a part accepts or condones these denials, then we also are guilty. Equal opportunity of education and social betterment, a living wage, are ways in which the community recognizes the dignity of all men. But individuals also must bring them the message that they are created in God's image and meant to share the life of the Holy Trinity. Those whom our Lord lifted up had been until then without hope, kept down by the self-righteous believers who refused to recognize their human dignity. That is the plight of our under-privileged today. The circumstances of their lives and our indifference have conspired to devalue them often to almost a sub-human level. They need apostles who "care," who will look at them with the eyes of Christ and speak to them with His voice so that they may gain courage to become what they were meant to be.

The encyclical of Pope John XXIII, *Pacem in Terris* (Peace on Earth), is the first in history addressed to the whole world instead of to the Church alone. It constitutes a real "manifesto" on the dignity and rights of the person. The Holy Father's thesis is that the only basis of true peace must be a real concern among the nations that all men be able to live in moral and physical conditions worthy of human dignity. Cardinal Suenens, commenting on the encyclical in *Maryknoll* magazine (February, 1964), quotes the well-known writer St. Exupery, "If respect for man is established in the hearts of men, men will succeed by establishing in return a social, political and economic system that will enshrine that respect."

The Cardinal continues: "This opening up to others, far from contradicting the true personality of man, is an integrating factor. A person who turns inward, who turns away from society, weakens, stifles and ultimately denies himself. This relationship to others is located right in the heart of the true personality and assists its development."

"John XXIII, at the conclusion of his letter, invites us to go forward to the discovery of men beyond the ideologies which oppose them to one another. And what is true for men is true for peoples . . . Every Christian knows that the Christianity which inspires him is worth more than the practical translation which he gives it, due to weakness and egoism in his daily life . . . A first revolution will be made if men learn simply to speak to each other and not only to co-exist side by side. Our century has discovered interplanetary space, but it has hardly explored the space which separates men from each other. Our century has thrown gigantic bridges over rivers, but it does not yet know how to build bridges from people to people and to join the two sides. Our century has discovered nuclear energy, but it has yet to discover the creative energy of peace and of concord which embodies a simple act of love and of mutual understanding."

In order to achieve real and effective collaboration among peoples, states the encyclical, there is required a co-ordinating organ at the highest level, "a public authority whose power, organization and means of action also have worldwide scope and which can take action throughout the whole world." *Pacem in Terris* continues, "It is our earnest wish that the United Nations Organization—in its structure and in its means—may become ever more equal to the magnitude and nobility of its tasks, and that the day may come when every human being will find therein an effective safeguard for the rights which derive directly from his dignity as a person, and which are therefore universal, inviolable and inalienable rights."

Cardinal Suenens quotes further from the encyclical words which underscore the urgency of this need for peace, understanding and mutual aid. "In a world which counts an additional man every second, one has not the right to be an hour behind. Misery does not wait. Two out of every three men suffer from acute hunger. Every year, of sixty million deaths, hunger and its consequences cause thirty to forty million, that is as much as the last war in five years, with all its resources and destruction. It is necessary that this 'unmerited misery' of people cease." The Cardinal stresses the encyclical's statement on armaments that the world's people must either choose the armaments race with, at the end of this rivalry, the permanent risk of collective nuclear suicide; or select the growth in trust which alone can create the climate necessary to the stability of peace. Only if this nightmare of the armaments race disappears from the horizon, can we begin to solve, by the universal collaboration which alone accords to the scale of our needs, the principal social problems which bring such misery to so many of mankind.

Now this growth in trust must begin for each one on his own street, with the people around him; from there it can encircle the world. The boy-hero of the Dondi comic-strip expresses perfectly the kind of openness to others that should animate the Christian who is Christ visible today. Dondi has given up his most prized possessions to a very selfish boy and one of the others asks, "Why does he take your things if you are best friends?" Dondi replies, "He's my best friend but I am not his best friend—yet."

B. Some Problems of Communication

The mass of men are practical existentialists. Their lives are lived in concrete situations of family, neighborhood, clan, work, education, recreation. The ordinary man's attitude towards religious values is due very little to books. It is deeply influenced by the reaction of his whole being to the environmental experiences of his daily life. As their life situations differ, so do their religious reactions: the farmer, the factory worker, the merchant, the slum dweller. The apostle must try to present Catholic ideas in the concrete terms of his contact's daily life, show life's significance to him in those terms. Why, for example, is religion looked upon in Latin America and other parts of the world as for women and children? Chiefly because it has been presented in terms of devotion which appeal rather to women than to the active nature of men. God made man to be a builder of social, economic and political structures. Work is the concrete reality in his life. It is an expression of his love for his family. Religion becomes real for him if related to these realities, if he sees himself as God's co-creator to build a new world for those God gave him to love.

In a lecture, "The Crisis of the World" *(Dublin Review,*

Winter, 1957), Donald Nicholl stated, "Adherence to certain social groups renders their members incapable of expressing or of being moved by various human experiences." He gave the example of resident professors in an institution of learning, his own occupation. "They are," he continued, "largely insulated against danger and poverty and are incapable of being affected by the evidences of poverty all about them or of communicating to those who suffer any vital religious truth and the values which depend on that truth." The present writer visited Catholic colleges both for men and women in various parts of the world, yet found few teachers personally interested in the problems of the masses in their area. I recall several which even had immense slums at their very door. In one case a group of nuns who had a large school for upper-class girls said, "The people of the slums do not wish to be helped. We started sewing classes but practically no one came." They had failed in the first step of the apostolate, the out-going personal contact to show that they regarded the others as having value.

Throughout Latin America the number one problem, both religious and social, is that the small minority of well-to-do are incapable of feeling with the great masses of the poor. It is also the problem of dealing with social and racial injustice everywhere. It is the problem of how the apostle who enjoys a certain social standing and certain comforts of life can establish some sense of shared experience with those whose daily existence is ever on the uncertain edge of want or who suffer the sharp sting of such epithets as "shiftless" or "hopeless." Otherwise, when the apostle speaks of the compassion of Christ, how can his hearers know that it comes from the depths of his own being? Perhaps there should be a campaign for more Catholics to spend their vacations in the slums, rather than at the seashore or in the mountains!

The August, 1960, issue of *Jubilee* has extracts from a book, *I Looked for God's Absence* (Sheed & Ward, 1960). The author is Father Iraeneus Rosier, who spent a month as an ordinary worker in an iron mine of northern France. His experiences and conclusions among the "dechristianized" masses are very illuminating. "The workers," he writes, "do not doubt the existence of God. Yet there is a kind of negative scepticism, because life, the reality about them, has a stronger impact on them than the reality of God—in fact, than any other reality as well that does not lie on the surface of experience. In this superficial agnosticism there is still an underlying faith in God, in Christ, and even in the Church. At least, they are still waiting to be taught how God manifests Himself in the world.

"In the working world is found an elemental simplicity. The workers hate formalism, the facade of hypocrisy . . . They accuse of hypocrisy those who practice because they identify practicing with the belief that one can save himself by complying with formalities—and also, most of the time, because the churchgoers are capitalists, or the well-to-do . . . They tend to be bitter towards the clergy, whom they believe to encourage such people and such formality . . . The working world suffers more or less from the formalistic culture and from the facades of a religiosity in which it does not participate. Their "betters"—the capitalists—who represent this culture and this religiosity, have thought of the worker as a 'force' which is used for gain. The worker is not valued primarily as a man, but rather for his contribution to this gain.

"The social organizations have improved the conditions of the worker's life, but not the structure of the work itself. To be more precise, they still suffer the injustice to be used like an inanimate force. All this has created an inferiority complex in the working world. This sense of inferiority shows itself in the great responsiveness of the workers to every attention and sign of regard shown them. The same sense of inferiority seeks compensation in boasting among fellow workers and in explosions of revolt; or it dulls itself with alcohol or in the satisfaction of the passions." Father Rosier's statement about "the great responsiveness of the workers to every attention and sign of regard shown them" indicates what should be our apostolic approach to the masses. It also helps explain the great influence among them of the Communists.

Michele Aumont, a French school teacher, became a worker in 1949 in order to devote herself to the apostolate among factory workers. In *Christ to the World* (1958, No. 1), extracts were published from her work, *The Unknown Working World*. Under the heading of "Factory Notes" Miss Aumont wrote: "Great distrust of words and talk . . . The believer and the priest have the reputation of being talkers . . . 'You should have been a priest' they say to the young man who talks glibly . . . Living in a domain of concrete and material in their work, the workers, more than any others, need to be sure, to see and touch . . . The manual worker needs an incarnation of the idea of truth." This need of the worker noted by Miss Aumont was anticipated by the Incarnation of God's Son, revealing divine goodness in human form. Today it is the Christian, the other Christ of our time, who must incarnate the idea of truth and goodness for the worker.

The men and women of Palestine, even the most lowly and neglected, could see our Lord's smile of welcome at their presence, hear His voice of compassion in their difficulties, feel the touch of His hands as He healed them. Today's apostle to the masses must be Christ for them, by his approach, his politeness, his tone of voice, his respect for them and their ideas. Discussion on religion must avoid like the plague any suggestion of glibness or a lesson learned by heart that would brand the apostle as "a talker." Christ always used concrete human relationships to illustrate our relationship to God. When asked, "Who is my neighbor?" He did not give the perfect definition He could have, but told the story of the man who fell among thieves on a road of Palestine notorious for robberies. The lesson of the Good Samaritan was one of action, not theory, and equally clear to both the unlettered masses and the cynical lawyer who had asked the question.

C. Apostolate to the Dechristianized

According to Canon Gravis, in *Christ to the World* (1955, No. 1), dialogue carried out in a spirit of mutual respect is the means par excellence to at least make a start towards the restoration of understanding and good relations. This dialogue must manifest on our part full respect for the autonomy and the opinions of others. Canon Gravis warns that it is often unwise to speak first about people's religious situation. He says, "Feeling itself pursued, the soul shuts up and rebels. Self-esteem spontaneously refuses all attempts at penetration." He found that some, especially those with a more recent background of religion, were pleased to get in touch with a priest, but paralyzed by the irreligious environment in which they lived, had been psychologically unable to take the first step.

Abbe Michonneau is quoted in *Christ to the World* (1957, No. 2): "When I first came to this parish, 2 per cent practicing Christians, Catholics said to me, 'Father, people will come to Mass in proportion as they know you.' We must go to our parishioners to destroy their prejudices about priests. Let us repeat here a remark that is often heard during or after a visit, 'We didn't know a priest was like that, or that we could talk to one so easily.'" Michonneau adds, however, that to "flutter about" paying innumerable visits with the hope that they will add up to something worth while, accomplishes little. As isolated families, these people cannot feel at home in the parish because they have an inferiority complex, as Father Rosier points out. To compensate for that complex, they have developed a strong group mentality, and must be contacted as groups. The same inferiority complex exists in slum areas; the people feel unable to cope alone with the world outside. Now the natural group is of neighbors, and Abbe Michonneau always made it a point in his home visits to bring some neighbors together.

The dechristianized and the lax will begin to return only when they perform some simple Christian acts in groups. The unchurched masses are most easily brought to God in the same way. The dechristianized are anti-clerical because they identify the clergy with the practicing Catholic employers who exploit them. They must be made to feel that they also have standing before God and the Church by getting them to do simple things which have religious value, such as works of mercy. Lay apostles as well as priests can suggest simple acts of neighborly helpfulness. For example, "I just came from the home of so-and-so, the mother is sick. I thought at once of you. Could you ask some of the neighbors to help clean up the house and care for the children?" If the lay apostle will help also, so much the better. We praise them for what they do, and their lives become lighted up with a sense of value which had been lacking before. Both the dechristianized and the unchurched masses will have a new attitude towards the priest or layman who does this for them and feel more drawn to God and the Church.

Try to get the more intelligent and cooperative mothers to take the lead in promoting better family life, harmony between parents and good example to children. Their husbands will notice the difference and become interested. Get them together in little groups, Mother's Clubs, to discuss and plan action along these lines; make them feel that they are doing it. Tell them: "All fathers and mothers wish their children to become men and women of whom they can be proud. But they must train their children now; it won't happen just by wishing it. God our Father desires exactly the same of us, that by our lives we give Him honor before men. In fact, it was God who gave human parents this same desire of being honored by their children that He has. God is all-good, but people cannot know that unless we show it by our own goodness in our family and neighborhood, show by our lives the example of how God wishes mankind to honor Him."

To neglect the "non-practicing" or other groups within the parish boundaries on the ground that they will not be receptive to our message inflicts untold harm on the Church. The separation of people by indifference turns so easily into hatred. We can at least go to them in a friendly way, show that we respect them as human persons, and already many obstacles are cleared away—on both sides. And who can say what fruit it may not bear in the future though not at once apparent, as did our Lord's apostolate in Palestine? In many parishes the "better classes" practice the faith better than the uninstructed poor, so the clergy tend naturally to be in closer touch with them. Even in certain lay apostolate movements, the priest may come more into contact with the upper and middle classes than with the poor. The result is obvious. The poor feel that the priest, and therefore the Church, is not interested in them. What a terrible situation for them, to feel abandoned by God's own representative—and terrible for him! It was by giving recognition to the "non-practicing" of His time, the despised and ignored, that our Lord rescued them from their frustration of not being shown value.

A recent Protestant study on the suburban church in the United States emphasizes the importance of the apostolate to the masses. The report draws this conclusion: "Whenever Christianity has become identified with the upper-class elite, it has lacked a substantial base in the working population and has been unable to weather social change." Such an inbalance may come about very easily in the average parish. The better educated meet the priest, who is also educated, than do the poor with their shyness and the results become cumulative in both groups. The former keep up their contact with the Church while the others may gradually grow alienated. It is quite noticeable on the street and in public gatherings that the poor are inclined to wait for the priest to speak to them first, unless he has been in close contact with them through neighborhood groups and home visits. The priest must keep in touch with social changes within the parish. A sociological survey in one typical American parish showed that the priests had far more contacts with the Catholics of an older section than with those of a newly developed industrial area. These considerations make clear that a fundamental aspect of the Church's mission is to help every person feel valued in God's sight from being shown value by God's representatives, both clergy and laity.

D. The Little Courses in Christianity

It is clear that the source of much laxity and unbelief today lies in the self-centered individualism of modern society. One who has developed little capacity for communion with others as persons finds it difficult to have a strong sense of personal relationship to God or to Christ as Man. One very promising movement aimed at remedying this situation is the "Little Courses in Christianity," founded by Bishop Juan Hervas of Ciudad Real, Spain, with a team of priests and laymen under the title *Cursillos de Cristianidad.* The motto of the Cursillos is: Contact with Christ and with my brothers. At a Cursillo made by the present writer, one of the lay "professors" who spoke on the Mystical Body in daily life expressed it this way: "We stay in contact with Christ by staying in contact with our brothers. This is extremely important. Left to ourselves, we'll drift back into indifference towards the cause of Christ. This contact will maintain us in our weakness and raise us in charity."

A Cursillo consists of 20-40 men (they are held also for women) who spend three days living together in study, discussion and prayer about this relationship to Christ and their fellow man. A retreat house is fine, but not essential. Cursillos have been held in a gymnasium, and in a church basement with cooking facilities. Cots and wash basins were borrowed, the men brought blankets and towels. The Cursillo is neither a retreat nor a course in doctrine, yet it has elements of both. The exercises of the opening "long night" are in retreat form, including Stations of the Cross offered for the success of the Cursillo. The talks during the three days are all doctrinal, with chief emphasis on the life of grace we have in Christ, our Brother, lived in the Church by the Holy Spirit with and for our brothers. "Now I see," said one participant, "that to live this life with Christ more fully I've got to get to know more people. If I pass up the opportunity to know someone, I miss an aspect of Christ and His personality which only that person expresses."

The "Cursillistas" include every walk of life, from government officials and university professors to ordinary workers. When they gather on Thursday evening, some are friends or acquaintances but most are total strangers, all with many questions and considerable uncertainty, some with reservations or even antagonism. In three days they discover one another as persons in Christ and leave as brothers, committed wholly to Christ. The Cursillo is conducted by one or two priests and 5-6 specially trained laymen, of whom one is the "rector" and the others "professors." They are not all of the same social level and may include, for example, two professional men, a businessman, an office worker, a workingman. The priest gives a daily meditation and two doctrinal instructions; the professors give three conferences daily on their application in lay life. The participants are divided into teams seated at 4-5 tables with a professor at each as guide. One of each team is named leader and another secretary for the discussions and a summary after each talk. Each table also prepares a poster to visualize the key idea of the talk. The summaries and posters are presented at the end of the day.

The exercises of piety are not very numerous but are geared directly to the purpose of the Cursillo to overcome human respect and promote brotherhood. In the evening one of the professors leads public rosary in the chapel for the most important intentions of the Cursillo, everyone kneeling and some decades with arms outstretched in the form of a cross. The priests are present in the confessional to make it easy for all who wish to go. The first day sees the teams organized at their tables. The second day, each team visits the Blessed Sacrament with its professor guide and each one prays aloud before the tabernacle in his own words according to a model suggested by the guide. The men are frequently reminded during the day to return alone to pray before Christ in the Eucharist. The third day there is an "Apostolic Holy Hour," in choral recitation form before the Blessed Sacrament exposed, with the rector presiding. Then the chaplain returns to each participant the sheet of resolutions he had previously signed and laid on the altar. Some promise a great deal, or a simple worker who has not been practicing may resolve to attend Sunday Mass and receive the sacraments. A final blessing closes the *Cursillo de Cristianidad.*

The results of the Cursillos have been literally miraculous. In Bishop Hervas' own Ciudad Real, such key men as the mayor, the prefect, top men in education and the professions, leaders in the business and labor fields, have passed through the more than 100 Cursillos already held and give the city a new Christian stamp. Few of them had before been really faithful to their religious duties. A similar report comes from the Maryknoll Bishop of Juli, on Lake Titicaca in Peru, where the movement is still young. Men have returned to the sacraments after an absence of 30 to 40 years. Priests in Caracas told me of the "miracle" that so many men were now seen at Mass and the sacraments, even daily. One served my Mass. During three years, since the Cursillos began in Venezuela, some 250 university professors and 1500 students (a third of them from the Communist-ridden Central University at Caracas) and 10,000 from all walks of life have made the Cursillos. Stories of amazing conversions come from all over the world. A Spanish Communist worker became an apostle of Christ in his factory. One had frequented the red light district and his wife marveled how he had become a devoted husband and father. A habitual drunkard became a frequent communicant and an apostle among alcoholics. One man, already a daily communicant, said that he had never before really understood the meaning of Christ in his life.

Two Spanish airmen at a training base in Texas introduced the movement to the United States in 1957. Writing in *Ultreya,* national organ for the Christianity Courses in the U.S., one priest of the southwest states: "Again and again I saw instances of enemies becoming friends, deadly hate melt into Christlike forgiveness, hypocrisy give way to sincerity, to a fearless practice of the faith . . . Men, now real lay apostles, dedicate themselves to the salvation of souls." Another priest writes, "Our adult instruction class is full to overflowing and so are the catechetical classes for the children . . . Since the Cursillistas have lost their fear, now it is we who are visiting the Pentecostals and Jehovah's Witnesses, as well as the cold or fallen-away Catholics.

A very usual question is: How can a man's life be changed in only three days? Bishop Hervas replies that the Cursillo does not profess to do that, but simply to change its direction by concentrating on man's true relation to Christ. He is God, but He is also our Brother who died for us! During the three days each one is involved with Christ in his whole being: mind, will and emotions, through eyes, ears, hands and voice; by self-expression in discussion, writing and sketching, by jokes, laughter and song, by silence and prayer. He learns that to see the Christian life in gray is heresy. God made creation shining with His glory and full of every color, "and so must all love be." When the Cursillos were first given in English, an "adaptation" was tried, but it did not succeed. Then exactly the same method was used as in Spanish and everything went fine. At the end of the three days the participants are owners of an ideal, an impelling ideal—to get grace, to keep grace, to make grace grow in themselves and in all around them. What is grace? Why, it is the Holy Trinity entering into us through Christ to share their mutual life with us. Its action in us may be illustrated by the story about the contest between the wind and the sun to make a man take off his coat. The sun entered into him with its warmth and caused him to act accordingly, so we are changed by the Holy Trinity within us.

To give the Cursillistas maximum help in living this life of grace, there is a twofold follow-up, one for a short period and the other long-range. The first is the *Ultreya* ("beyond"—the Cursillo), a once or twice weekly session for six months at which a 'Cursillo priest', one who has made the course, gives continuing instruction in doctrine and the Cursillistas discuss how to apply it to life. All who made the Cursillo together are thus kept united in a common atmosphere: serious yet joyful, prayerful, self-sacrificing. On the third day of the Cursillo itself is explained the long-range program for the "Fourth Day"—all the rest of one's life. The talks emphasize how to live the full life of grace together in their environments and the cell meeting is explained. A group of 4-6 Cursillistas make together a weekly open examination of conscience on the external observance of their duties of piety and on their success or failure in one or another apostolic work of the past week, with their plan of action for the week to follow. It is the key of perseverance by Cursillistas.

From the very first day of the Cursillo the participants receive a concrete demonstration of the spirit of brotherhood and sacrifice which pervades the movement. Everyone is impressed as the lay rector begins to read out letters and telegrams of *palanca* (leverage) which have been received in response to the announcement that the Cursillo is to be held. Some are sleeping on the floor for us, or recite the rosary with arms outstretched; here a whole family is fasting for us; others spend hours before the Blessed Sacrament. A nun dying of cancer gives up one day's sedation; a football player in hospital with a spine injury offers his pain. At our Cursillo the *palanca* was laid on the altar during morning Mass. Still, these our brothers were simply names until we saw them come to life when they arrived to celebrate the Cursillo closing. These were they who had made such sacrifices for men they had never seen to help them come close to Christ and gain the graces for a new way of life!

A typical Cursillo ending is most difficult to describe. Sunday evening supper has ended and someone is telling a joke, as is done after every meal before going to the chapel, but he stops short at the sound of guitars outside. The musicians march in sedately enough, then suddenly the room erupts with Cursillistas, perhaps hundreds of them, singing the Cursillos theme song "*De Colores*" until it would seem their lungs must burst. They have come to give the new group some taste of the "fourth day," its joy and comradeship. Our Cursillo in Boston was conducted by a team from Saginaw, Michigan, and Cursillistas from there came to the closing by chartered plane. As the old Cursillistas embraced the new, all strangeness was washed away. The Cursillo has brought us together as brothers and made us realize how many are willing to pray and fast for us, keep night vigils, sacrifice themselves for us.

What do the Cursillistas do afterwards? Of 98 who made the first ones in an American city, 28 joined the Legion of Mary, 35 other societies; more than half became members of the Nocturnal Adoration Society; 31 belonged to discussion clubs in their parishes; 60 went in pairs once a week to teach or review catechism in homes and secured the validation of 58 marriages. Three years later the Cursillistas numbered 1500, with a proportionate increase in activities. For example, they now had nearly 3000 children and adults under instruction. Some priests are saying that new outlets should be provided for the awakening zeal of this vast force who for the first time are really aware of what it means to be militants for Christ. One of these outlets may well be to put the social teachings of the Church into practice. In fact, the Cursillos have been called "the most important social movement that Catholicism has produced in these latter days." Until now, the social aspect of the lay apostolate has been much less stressed than the directly religious one.

One recommendation I heard in Latin America was that the cells of 4-6 members should be engaged in the same apostolic activity in order to make it easier for them to hold the all-important weekly cell meeting. Another suggestion was not to expect all who are brought back to the faith by the Cursillo to take part in a directly religious apostolate. Many must remain in an anti-clerical environment by reason of their livelihood and they would be ridiculed as "the priest's boys." But they could do a great deal of good in promoting the Church's social doctrine. Above all, when the movement is beginning one should accept as candidates only good Catholics who have leadership qualities. A priest in Peru told me he made the mistake of inviting a Communist to go and now he does great harm by saying he knows from experience that this is a trick of the priests to dominate people's minds. It is the Cursillistas themselves who should work on and sponsor careless Catholics as their personal responsibility. The priest himself must make one of the first Cursillos in order to be able to guide the Cursillistas afterwards.

11. SOME APOSTOLIC APPROACHES FOR TODAY

As we reflect on the question of how to make the faith truly operative in human life, it becomes clear that this is not alone a matter of knowing it by study. The faith can become an activating force in the world only as lived by the People of God in every aspect of family, community, educational, economic and political life. There is a distinct Christian way of life, a Christian culture, and the faith will penetrate human cultures only if it is seen to satisfy certain needs of man that they do not.

The faith was not accepted by the barbarian tribes of Europe solely because their leaders did; it was also regarded as conferring a desirable new identity. During the Middle Ages, before the invention of printing and the spread of education, religious formation was passed on very simply as part of a traditional Christian culture that had developed. It was a rather static society where few could read and one was not involved in serious problems of culture change, so that simple verbal instruction by the priest on Sunday could supplement quite well the cultural transmission. But with the rise of cities and the development of education, such a system was no longer adequate, and the decay of religion in Europe may be traced to failure of Christian culture to provide for men's new needs. Today in Latin America one is amazed to see how the culture of the masses remains basically Catholic, in spite of vast religious ignorance due to lack of priests and very slow adjustment of parish methods to the social changes now taking place. The present moment, however, marks the point of crisis for the faith in Latin America and if means are not quickly found to meet it, we shall witness a wide de-christianization of the culture as in Europe.

In previous chapters we have discussed some of the problems involved in transmitting desirable values, including those of the faith, when social change is occurring at so rapid a pace as today. All life tends to become fragmented, lacking unity of its parts, and so is no longer a good vehicle for transmitting accepted values. Religion also tends to suffer from the same lack of cultural unity. It is often regarded, for example, even by otherwise highly intelligent people, as a formal service of God on Sunday morning only, not as an integral part of life. More religious instruction cannot of itself solve the problem, whether here where we are or in Latin America, if religion be still assigned chiefly to an internal and spiritual segment of life. A Christian culture that is not a complete whole for all of life cannot stand against the full material organization of life that Communism takes from technology. "You cannot serve two masters." When man's heart is divided, he is already defeated.

A. Religious Approach in Mission Lands

Among most non-Christians, religious ideas run chiefly along the line of the flow of life: God, ancestors, the living. Life is the great reality which integrates human existence and to pass it on worthily is the great human responsibility. Since they lack the revelation of Christ as Redeemer, the ancestor is regarded as man's chief link with God, for he lived on earth and is now in the spirit realm. Whether in modern Japan, in China, India or Africa, the fundamental religious ideas are transmitted in the family, the obvious center of ancestor "worship," and this link with their own flow of life keeps these ideas real and concrete. Such religious philosophies as Buddhism, Taoism, Hinduism have been rather an overlay which changed the

"You know that God is far above all living things, greater than the greatest paramount chief in the world. God made all the people, He made all the chiefs in the world and placed them over us. God gave all mankind the human life force that makes us superior to animals. This life force comes to us from God through our ancestors. God gave men and women power to have children in order to pass on this vital force to their descendants. God gave men and women intelligence to use the power to have children in the proper way. If they use this power only for their own pleasure, then they waste the vital life force and cannot hand it down to their descendants in strong condition. People are not like animals that do not know what is right. If they use the great gift of God in a bad way they sin against Him and cannot receive His blessing. The thoughts and imaginations of such people are so filled with the pleasures they have had or plan to have that they cannot give their full attention to care of their family and work for the development of their country.

"You also learned from your parents and elders to help other people. If one of the clan is sick, you cultivate his field. If a mother is sick, the other women come to cook and take care of the children. If a traveler comes to your house at night, you arrange for him to have food and shelter. A man who has a bicycle will give his neighbor a ride to the market. There are many kind deeds that you do every day for others and God is most pleased with them as a father is when his children help one another. You have always helped mostly those of your own clan, because you have the same father-ancestor. But when you are Catholics you help everybody in need, even if they do not belong to your clan or tribe. That is because God is the first and great Father-Ancestor of all the people in the world—in Africa, in America and all countries. People of every tribe and in all countries of the world are truly our brothers and sisters because God is our Father.

"If your friends and neighbors ask you why you came to

study the Catholic religion, you can tell them what I have said. All of you fathers and mothers desire above everything else to have good children that you can be proud of. Then people will say: 'That is the son, or daughter, of So-and-so; see how well-behaved he is.' Now God, our great Father in heaven, wishes to be proud of us before mankind. When people see Catholics live as God's good children, they will give honor to God and say that the Catholic religion is good and true. Moreover, in the Catholic Church, God gives us another gift besides our human life force. He gives us a share in His own divine life force so that we can truly live on earth as His children and after we die go to live with Him in heaven."

The African idea of the vital life force in man is described in a book, *Bantu Philosophy,* by Father Placid Tempels, O.F.M., a missionary in Katanga, in the Congo. The Catholics of his area have developed a family movement based on the doctrine that husband and wife in Christian marriage share the gracelife of the Holy Trinity. In the African conception, the transmission and nurture of spiritual life implies parenthood as in human life. The husband is spiritual father of his wife and she his daughter in Christ, while the wife is mother of her husband and he her child whom she nourishes with the grace of matrimony. One is reminded of the mystery that the Church is the bride of Christ born from His side. This conception of how spiritual vital force is augmented through Christian matrimony has had profound effect in elevating the African view of marriage. One man said, "I have been married fifteen years, but only now do I feel a true unity with my wife." Many Catholics who fell into polygamy have been led to regularize their marriages.

B. A Filipino Parish Community Apostolate

This apostolate, known as the "Barangay of the Virgin," was founded in 1949 by Antonio Gaston, a Filipino layman. While convalescing from a long illness he gave much thought to the situation of the Church in his country: extreme shortage of clergy, immense parishes of as many as 200,000 faithful, great religious laxity especially among the men. The term "barangay" (a Tagalog word meaning clan) was an inspired choice, for to a Filipino it conveys the idea of united action for the welfare of all. Antonio began by inviting several men who had been long away from the sacraments to visit him. He told them that the Church in the Islands depended on them and that it was just as necessary for them to assume their responsibilities in Catholic life as they did in other areas. This appeal to them as men struck home as no other argument would. Within six months all had returned to their duties. Before long so many groups were meeting that there were not enough trained men to lead them. Then someone suggested, "Let us plan meetings that the people everywhere can hold by themselves." Already one essential fact had been demonstrated. It was possible to interest Filipino men in the Church and the key was to give them responsibility.

All the leaders in the Barangay of the Virgin are men, even though they may not be able to lead the meetings. The basic unit is the Rosary Group of fifteen families, headed by a man called the *mayor*. The requirements are simple, that each family send a representative every evening to the rosary meeting at one of the homes. It is not simply a form of the block rosary, however, for each meeting has a ten-minute religious instruction and the groups are united at parish, diocesan and national levels. It was largely the rosary that preserved the faith after the expulsion of the Spanish friars. When anyone died, a novena of rosaries was recited; the rosary was said also after a month and on the anniversary. Services on Sundays, feast days and other occasions consisted mostly of the rosary. In the Barangay, each household is dedicated to a rosary mystery, and those of the joyful, sorrowful and glorious mysteries form three sub-groups, each with a man as head, the *cabeza*. Three 15-family groups form a Trinity, 45 families, with a *cabeza-mayor* at the head. Usually the *mayors* and *cabeza-mayors* are also *cabezas* at the head of sub-groups, so that a Trinity has at least nine men directly involved as leaders.

As the Barangay began to spread, a serious difficulty arose. It was agreed on all sides that the idea of having men as leaders was essential if the movement was to secure their participation and be really able to vitalise Catholic life in the Philippines. Yet so many men were practically religious illiterates that they often could not even lead the rosary, let alone give the religious instruction. Then came the second inspired suggestion: The officers of the Barangay will continue to be men, but anyone capable may act as a "Barangay teacher" to give the instructions. By 1955 the Barangay had about 15,000 members, mostly in the Bacolod diocese where it began. In that year the bishops approved the movement for the entire country and within two years it spread to almost every diocese, bringing community prayer and religious instruction to 2,000,000 persons. It reached even to remote villages which had been without religious care since the expulsion of the friars two generations before had left the country so short of priests.

The formation of Barangay leaders and teachers is carried out at weekly meetings in parish and diocesan "Barangay Centers." In country areas there may also be sub-centers where groups too far from the center meet with someone assigned to act as moderator. The purpose of the meeting, held usually on Sunday, is reports by the officers and discussion on how to promote the Barangay and foster its spirit. In large city parishes, which may have 40 or more Trinities, it is best to have a separate meeting for the officers of each 10 Trinities. The diocesan center usually sets the program for all parishes and may also have special training courses for Barangay teachers. The "teachers" for the rosary group meetings may be men or women, perhaps a school teacher in the area or a Legion of Mary member. Gradually more and more of the leaders themselves, especially younger ones, are undertaking the task.

Official organization of Barangay units is always done by men, but women are active in gaining new members. Many young women make it an apostolate to go from house to house after their day's work asking the families to join a rosary group. Even one baptized Catholic in a household or a single Catholic servant in a Moslem home counts as a family and the rosary is said there in turn if permitted. The devotion of the Filipinos to Mary and her rosary makes the Barangay of the Virgin sound attractive. Once established, it provides a rich field for the development of the lay apostolate. Many homes, often whole areas that even the Legion of Mary had not penetrated, are now thrown wide open to welcome Mary. "The Barangay and the Legion of Mary" one priest told me, "are made for each other. The Barangay gets everyone into the active participation that is so important for their development while the Legion helps insure discipline and perseverance."

The Barangay of the Virgin is a true product of Filipino culture with its roots deep in Filipino life. Every rosary group has its banner, with fifteen ribbons on which are inscribed the parents' names. There are five each of white, gold and blue ribbons for the joyful, sorrowful and glorious mysteries. When a death occurs in the group, the ribbons are changed to black until the rosary has been said once in all the homes. Every evening after the rosary, one sees banners being carried with lights and hymns to be set up outside the next house. Some streets display so many banners that every day looks like a fiesta. Each decade of the rosary is offered for intentions important to the members, such as for those who are sick or for good weather, and the last decade is always for the intentions of the host family. No refreshments are served, which avoids the danger of competition and needless expense.

Priests everywhere are astonished at the results, especially the changed attitude of men towards the clergy. Formerly they avoided the priest; now he is greeted as friend and father, particularly if he works with the Barangay. One Filipino priest stated that he formerly had many parish organizations, but was in contact with only two percent of his people for none were able to bring the masses to him. After one year of the Barangay, he was in touch with most of the families. In city worker districts where the faith seemed dead, prayer and instruction by the lay community have renewed Catholic life. Men from areas where a few years ago the priest and even the Legion did not dare enter are now proud of the part they play in the parish. Antonio Gaston told me that it makes one aware of how the apparently indifferent masses really thirst for religion at heart. The obstacle for them is very rarely real unbelief. It is often psychological, a sense of having no vital or needful part to play in the Church, that it is not in a felt way "their" Church.

One priest said, "I am almost frightened at the power the Barangay gives us!" At a parish Center meeting of officers I suggested that it would greatly honor Mary if people received the sacraments on the approaching feast of the Miraculous Medal. Nearly 15 per cent of the parish came to that weekday Mass and most received Holy Communion. A bishop related: "We used to have great difficulty getting people, especially men, to take part in Processions of the Blessed Sacrament, so timid and cold had they become in anything organized by the priest. But at a recent diocesan Eucharistic Congress it was announced that the Barangay banners of the three city parishes would join in the procession. There were 300 banners in the march past, carried by men, and all followed by members of their fifteen families. Few were left to be spectators!" The Barangay is credited with helping to bring about a marked increase in vocations, as the men who are officers identify themselves with the Church they become proud to have their sons think of being priests.

Some observers have thought that the Barangay of the Virgin was kept at too popular a level; it should, they say, aim higher. But when any change is suggested, Antonio always asks, "Will that keep anyone out?" One parish with a successful Barangay tried to introduce discussion on the admittedly serious economic problems of the people, but so many lost interest in the meetings that the idea had to be abandoned. The Barangay provides for such discussions by special committees apart from the rosary meetings. Some quote the saying, "You cannot teach religion to a man with an empty stomach." Antonio sees a fallacy here, feeling that many are hungry from failure to apply religion in daily life. "So often," he says, "we see men blame on lack of money their vices that show obvious loss of religious values, such as gambling, drinking, women, family disunity, juvenile delinquency." He holds that if people do not acquire a sense of mutual responsibility and willingness to work together for the common good, then there is no way to solve their economic problem except by imposing discipline from above as the Communists do.

As vindication of his belief that the spirit of co-operation based on religion is the best preparation for solving Filipino economic problems, Antonio points out that the Barangay has launched the first successful credit unions, even producers and consumers cooperatives, in a number of areas. These are increasing as the movement strikes deeper roots. The sense of mutual responsibility had previously been lacking. Sports are especially encouraged by the Barangay to help overcome dissipation of wages in gambling and drinking, which are so often a compensation for lack of active interests and healthy outlets. One town mayor praised the Barangay publicly for emptying the local jail. At every Barangay gathering the national anthem is sung, and no civic or other organization sings it more often than does the Barangay.

C. Every Catholic an Apostolic Task

In 1960 I visited a diocese on the island of Java, Indonesia, where stress is laid on the principle that being baptized confers apostolic responsibility to share with others the gifts one has received from God. The priests tell their people, "You are a member of the Christian Farmers' Union. Show charity by sharing with your neighbor the ways the Union has helped you and at the same time tell him about the Christian motive of brotherhood. Do you work in a factory, on a construction job? Apply what you have been taught in the Catholic Workers' Union. Help young workers find decent quarters and introduce them to good friends; unite with other decent men to protect the young workers from the evil influences of some older men. Don't be a member of the Credit Union simply to get loans at cheap interest, but look on fellow members as your brothers whom you wish to help in every way possible. We must not merely seek the help of these organizations for ourselves but also how through them we can help others."

Formation in the spirit of apostolic co-operation is given by means of emphasis in every sermon, every lay retreat, in Sodality meetings and in the various actions undertaken. Leader training is basically acquired by an apprenticeship of working with those already experienced. Further development takes place in periodic Study Days and Study Weeks for the various apostolic fields. The co-ordinating body for all these activities is a Parish Council with representatives from the various fields. It also recommends the persons to direct each activity and calls on others to assist them. Temporary committees are set up to study special questions. To lighten the parish priest's burden, the Secretary of the Parish Council is a paid member of the parish staff and all apostolic works are first referred to him. The Parish Council's work is greatly facilitated by close cooperation from the leaders of the neighborhoods into which the parish is divided. These neighborhood groups have particular responsibility for works of mercy and apostolic activities at the local level.

The compound of the cathedral parish, where I stayed, buzzed with activity all day and until late at night. As I went over for Mass a number of women who had been at the previous one sat on the cathedral steps eating their breakfast of either cold rice wrapped in leaves or a couple of sweet potatoes. They had left home long before daylight as the day's representatives of their villages in the weekday Mass chain. After Mass and breakfast I visited a class of about twenty girls, 15-17 years old, who had finished lower middle school and were being trained to become leaders among the village women and at the same time for their own Catholic marriage. They were at the moment engaged in a Gospel discussion study on its social message for their lives. The girls have lessons in sewing, domestic science, baby care, Catholic family life. The very capable business woman who gives many hours a week to the class permits no nonsense. It is a hard schedule that ends at 11:00 p.m., but so will be their day as village wives and mothers. The course is for three months, then another group comes. Each year they have a retreat, which helps to unite the members of different courses and villages.

All during the day people were coming into the Secretary's office with regard to one or another aspect of the parish apostolate: catechists, neighborhood leaders, officers of co-operatives, leaders of the Catholic Workers' and Catholic Farmers' Unions. I was introduced to the head of the Catholic Farmers' Union, an outstanding leader at thirty-five. Though the Union is comparatively new, the members are being formed in responsible community action and capability of leadership in an expanding sphere. There were classes of housewives being taught the faith by other housewives, in the simple way of explaining what a Catholic mother does and why. After school several groups of school children trooped in for religious instruction given by high school girls and other volunteers were doing the same in many neighborhoods of the city and villages. All those who teach religion are briefed beforehand by a demonstration method similar to that used in Latin America to train voluntary catechizers. A nurse from the Catholic Nurses' Guild conducted a class in midwifery.

In the evening there seemed to be something going on in every room of the parish building and even in corners of the same room. Several classes of English and arithmetic were being taught by volunteers. The leaders of the Catholic Workers' Union were making final arrangements for a trip next day to explain their movement in another diocese at the invitation of its bishop. One priest had a meeting with the neighborhood leaders from one section of the parish. A doctrine class for men was in progress, conducted by a business man who was explaining the Fourth Commandment in terms of good Catholic family life. I watched the employment bureau of three men at a table on the veranda with a priest of the parish sitting in, while about twenty job-seekers waited nearby. The priest told me that they were mostly pagans and it made the Catholics particularly happy to be able to show them how the Church has a care for all. About five received job assignments; the others must wait while the bureau checked their credentials and looked for openings.

The priest director of the Parish Council introduced me to a young teacher who was neighborhood Catholic leader in a *kampong* (village) at the edge of the city where his school was located. He spoke understandable English, and in half an hour with him I learned facts about conditions among the people that no one else had given me. The young man said that all the ninety families in the village were casual farm workers living in poor huts. The island is so heavily populated that 42 per cent even of the rural people have no land to cultivate and can average only about 250 days or less of work a year. Twenty years ago, with the population of Java at 40 million, there was sufficient rice and a day's wages would buy 8-10 pounds. Now the population has reached more than 60 million with no greater production of rice, the staple food, and a day's wages will buy only 3 pounds! The village had six Catholic families and nine following the Muslim religion of the country, but the remainder, formerly Muslims, had become Communists.

The young man asked what I would advise. The only course I could suggest on the spur of the moment was that he make the situation clearly known to the Parish Council if they were not already aware of it. His little group would seem to need first of all the encouragement that would come from a demonstration of solidarity and assistance by stronger units, as many others obviously were. The lay apostolate implies not only mutual assistance among stronger and weaker families in the same neighborhood, but also cooperation by stronger groups to help weaker ones. Without such assistance and encouragement the weaker neighborhoods cannot gain the strength to fulfill their proper function of mutual assistance internally, not to mention action in the parish apostolate externally. I had not yet met Mother Theresa, in India, or I would have suggested also that the Catholics, poor as they were, take every occasion to say to their neighbors, "Come, let us do something good for God." Probably most of those families had become Communists from discouragement and still had a religious sense. The frustration that drives people into the arms of the Communists is not alone due to economic conditions, but also to the loss of a feeling of self-value. The satisfaction of doing good helps to make a person feel that he does have value.

D. The Apostolate by Whole Dioceses

It is clear that, to reach a significant number of people with the faith's message of life, the principle of friendly contacts by Catholics must be applied on a large, even massive, scale.

Is it possible to organize the laity of a parish, a diocese or several dioceses in an effective campaign to bring the faith to the maximum number of people? The basic difficulty with most convert-making programs is that they have too few persons doing the preliminary work of contacting potential converts. The key is to multiply the number of those working at the level of making contacts of welcome and this is just what ordinary Catholics can do if organized and briefed for it. Father John A. O'Brien of Notre Dame University tells in *Christ to the World* (1959, No. 3), how the bishops of all five dioceses in the State of Wisconsin organized a contact campaign in which 26,000 husband-wife teams took part. During one week they paid a friendly call to everyone of the 426,524 non-Catholic families in the 819 parishes of the State as well as to lax Catholics.

They had a simple yet nonetheless essential task. It was to introduce themselves in a friendly way as neighbors living at such and such an address. They gave each family a written invitation from the parish priest to an Open House at the parish on the following Sunday. They contacted more than 2 million persons in the State's population of 3.5 million, the other 1.5 million being Catholics. As a result of this single week's concerted action, 2137 converts were afterwards instructed and baptized. Almost 200,000 lapsed Catholics were discovered that no census had revealed! Some 10,000 returned to the sacraments at once and the Legion of Mary began work to bring back the others. One most agreeable finding was that most families received the visitors well and only 1.8 per cent showed outward antagonism. Some others were rather indifferent, but 82.8 per cent of the 426,524 families expressed pleasure at the visit! More than one said, "We had often felt that the Catholics seemed clannish."

The bishops of Wisconsin had previously issued a joint pastoral letter announcing the "Crusade for Souls" campaign in which they pointed out that relatively few Catholics were sharing the treasures of their faith with non-Catholic friends and neighbors. They stated that 40 per cent of the converts in the United States during the previous year had been in the 5 per cent of dioceses which held such campaigns. The bishops called first for a crusade of prayer After every Mass a special prayer was to be said. All families were urged to say the rosary daily and the sick to offer their sufferings for the success of the campaign. Not a few who died during that period offered up their lives in union with our Lord's to gain grace for souls. On four consecutive Sundays the sermons at all the Masses explained the responsibility of every Catholic to share the Faith in the ways he was able. The campaign was not a mere promotion technique to win converts. It was the first step to get people thinking about the Catholic faith; then grace would do the rest.

The parishes were divided into sections, each with a captain and lieutenant, and the officers from all the sections comprised the Parish Campaign Committee. They worked out with the parish priests a statement of the campaign's purpose, its methods, and how to make a tactful approach. The section leaders briefed the husband-wife teams of their areas. They had never directed such a campaign before, but as laymen in various occupations they had developed a sense of initiative and responsibility which they now gladly put at the service of the parish. Cards of different colors, filled in after leaving a house, indicated if the family were church-goers or not, whether interested in learning more about the faith, or if they were lapsed Catholics. Pamphlets suited to each type were left at the homes. The teams agreed that to give one week was not too much, and the visits to nearly 500,000 families took place during the week of Sunday, September 22, 1957.

On the next Sunday every parish held Open House from 3-5 p.m. Light refreshments were served and the teams were on hand to welcome those they had visited. They had offered to arrange for Catholics to bring those who had no transportation, so that those who did no visiting also had a part in the campaign. After a short social hour, there was a tour of the church, school and convent. Lay people acted as guides, explained everything in the church and introduced the guests to the priests and nuns. It is extremely important that the guides be laity in order to establish in the minds of the guests an association of things Catholic with lay people like themselves and not only with the priests. Each guest received a leaflet announcing that they could get further explanations at Information Forums to be held on two nights a week and offering to have Catholics accompany those who wished to come. They would often ask for the visitor team or someone they met at the Open House to come with them. Experience has shown that the Open House brings a far greater attendance at the Information Forum because of the closer contact it develops.

One great value of such a wide campaign is that it contacts so many who are positively interested in learning more about the faith and these form a backlog of prospective converts. In Wisconsin they numbered 19,000 families, nearly 5 per cent of those contacted. The diocese of San Diego, California, which held the first doorbell ringing campaign in 1951 capitalized on this "backlog" by repeating the campaign each year. In 1951 about 1000 converts were baptized, the next year 1500. Annually the number of converts rose until in 1957 more than 5000 were baptized. The average number of converts per priest each year rose from 4.6 to 21.4 persons. During six years of annual campaigns in the San Diego diocese which had 150,000 Catholics in 1951, there were 23,439 conversions and 35,000 lapsed Catholics returned. Such results rival even the best of the mission fields abroad. There are over 2000 dioceses or vicariates in the world. If each year they all held such a crusade for perhaps one month, what a harvest there would be of conversions and return of lapsed Catholics.

Father F. Zubeldia of North India tells us in *Christ to the*

World (1962, No. 1), how he used the open house method in his parish of 320 Catholics in a district of 300,000 inhabitants. Knowing that the people were really curious to know what Catholics believed, he placed a sign on the street inviting them to visit the chapel to see what it was like and hear explanations. But the mission stood on a side street, so another sign was set up not far away on the main street, at the entrance to a bridge. On some Sundays during the hours allotted, 6.30 to 8.30 p.m., as many as 200 came, both Hindus and Moslems. At the chapel entrance were a number of Gospel pictures, which gave a good opportunity to explain the goodness of our Lord and how He taught us that God is our Father. The chapel is God's house where we come every Sunday to render Him homage. Many expressed appreciation and gratitude for being given the opportunity of learning about the Church and a good number enrolled in the Correspondence Course conducted by the Mission. A good indication of the interest aroused was shown by many returning later with friends and relatives.

"Another noteworthy fruit," writes Father Zubeldia, "is the training my promoters receive while carrying out this apostolate and the spiritual joy they experience as a result of spending those Sunday evenings so fruitfully. Experience has taught me that this simple method of making Christ known to the non-Catholics is really effective. My chapel is small; it is a hall on the ground floor of my bungalow; however it has attracted a good number of persons. Consequently I believe that wonderful results can be expected in other towns and cities of mission countries, where there is a large church on one of the main streets. Every church and chapel is a treasure of the apostolate for us in which we may reach our non-Catholic brethren. For them, it is like a holy exhibition. That natural curiosity of people to see exhibitions gives us a good means of conveying the message of Christ to them."

12. THE PRIEST'S ROLE IN APOSTOLIC TEAMWORK

The Catholics of a parish have a natural confidence in their priest. They look on him as a spiritual father who for them has sacrificed the human satisfaction of having his own family. But the father of his people, like the father of a family, must understand what his children have a right to from him. "Man does not live by bread alone." The People of God have also other needs besides being given the spiritual bread of the sacraments and the word of God.

Everyone knows, for example, that children will grow up immature if a father sees their needs only in terms of physical and intellectual nourishment. He fails miserably in a father's essential duty if, as children develop, he does not gradually initiate them into the sense of both individual and social responsibility they will need as adults. Moreover, if he simply does things "for" them but not "with" them, the children feel themselves of less value to him than the other interests in which he immerses himself and an emotional block arises between them. The chief cause of delinquency is the child's feeling of not being valued for himself, and hence it may occur at all social levels. The extreme actions of the delinquent are an attempt to prove that he is a "somebody," that he does have value. They are usually anti-social acts because he rebels against the father who fails to share his own life with his son, and hence against the standards of the adult world represented by his father.

The parish priest as father of his people has a similar responsibility in the life of the Church. By the sacrament of confirmation they receive the responsibilities of Christian adulthood at every level of life. The powers conferred by the sacrament are complete in themselves, but the persons to whom they are given must be trained to exercise these powers properly in order to enjoy the full life of Christ. And as parents should train their children especially for assuming the responsibilities of parenthood in their turn, so the priest must train His spiritual children to fulfill their adult role as Christians responsible for transmitting and developing divine life. Otherwise they do not reach the full Christian stature that is their right and cannot play their proper part in the Church's growth and welfare in their various areas of human life. The priest must do more than simply instruct his people about their responsibility to put the powers of confirmation to full use. That he must do, but he can achieve the fullest transmission to them of his own ideas and values only by participating with them in appropriate activities as a good father shares daily living with his children.

A. Cooperation of Priest and Laity

Modern business has done much research in the factors that help the worker identify himself with the enterprise in which he is engaged. A weak sense of such identification and loss of interest in his work go together. Now in religion the same tends to hold true. The Church is faced today with a serious problem of drift away from the faith, especially among young men. And in many of the homes that they will set up when they marry, Catholic family life will be weak or even non-existent. As every priest knows, simple exhortation has changed the lives of very few. That is the weakness of any lay apostolate which works "on" people by urging them instead of "with" them so that they also have something to do. The essential means of developing a sense of identification with the Church among the members of a parish is to get them engaged in action that makes them feel they have an important part to play. Otherwise, as religious indifference creeps in from lack of identification, there will be also a noticeable increase of anti-clericalism and criticism of the Church.

Father George Maertens, director of the Center for Pastoral Studies which I visited in Leopoldville, writes in *Christ to the World* (1958, No. 4), of his observations in the Congo. He points out that the first missionaries who came during the last century had to do everything themselves because they started from nothing. Now there is a large number of Christians, but still "the priest does everything, controls everything, judges everything." The Christians themselves, says Father Maertens, "rarely have a responsibility or a decision to make; they have not become adult Christians." He states that every village, for example, has a school, but it is "the Father's school" and the people feel absolutely no responsibility for its upkeep or its program. They do not feel responsible either for making or instructing converts; that belongs to the teacher-catechist sent by the Father. During my visit to the Congo I was told that many had stopped practicing their religion and were being drawn into local politics, which gave a sense of participation that the missions had not developed in the service of the Faith.

One of the most common topics of discussion among missionaries is, "What constitutes the founding of the Church in an area?" An answer commonly given is that it consists in establishing a native clergy and hierarchy. This, however, tends to emphasize only the institutional aspect of the Church, since it says nothing about the assembly of the faithful. If we look, however, at St. Paul's method of founding the Church, we note that from the very first he presented the faith as the work of the Holy Spirit more than of the Church as such. If the missionary in his teaching seems to stress chiefly obedience to the laws of the Church, then converts look for strength to him as representative of the Church and not to

Christ and the Holy Spirit. Such an outlook not only hinders the growth of converts towards spiritual adulthood, but actually robs them of the inner resources they naturally possess and would naturally use. Another seriously bad effect from too much emphasis on the institutional aspect of the Church is that even the native clergy tend to have an authoritarian rather than a co-operative attitude towards their people.

In his book, *Missionary Methods: St. Paul's or Ours* (Eerdmans, 1960), Roland Allen points out that when St. Paul set up an indigenous "church" it was whole and entire. It had not only a responsible clergy but also laity, and was capable of growth and expansion by its own spiritual resources. That is how St. Paul could found so many churches after only a short time in each place. He makes clear in his epistles that he still has authority over them, but he invokes it sparingly and not so much to command them as to point out the right course of action and leave to the local assembly how to carry it out. For example, he had been away from Corinth perhaps two and a half years when he wrote the First Epistle to the Corinthians on hearing that incest had been committed, though it is clear from his letter that fornication was a common offense. Yet he does not mention that fornication is contrary to the Ten Commandments and had been condemned by the Jerusalem Council. He simply shows his detestation of the crime reported to him and directs the Christians themselves to meet and take appropriate action. The offender's excommunication by his neighbors would be good both for him and the Church. Only the congregation itself could clear the good name of the church which had been sullied by the act of one of its members.

Here we quote, from the many given by the author, some examples of modern missionary efforts to apply the methods of St. Paul. In one district there had previously been severe persecutions and some of the Christians had fallen away, though did not apostatize. The missionary did not search out these people, but addressed himself to the congregation. He explained how vital to them was the welfare of the Church as well as the sad state of the lapsed Christians. He asked them what steps they proposed to take, but left to them to decide what they would do. They appointed some of their number to visit the fallen-aways, to set before them the dangers of their situation and ask them on which side they would stand: with the Church for Christ or with the pagans. "They sent out their representatives with prayer and received their reports with thanksgiving." In a few days most of the lapsed were restored to the Church. When a poor man died, they collected money to bury him and the missionary added his contribution as also a member of the church. Or they wanted a school? "How do your pagan neighbors get their children taught? They subscribe together and invite a teacher." The missionary told them to talk it over and see what they could do; he would perhaps help a little if they were in difficulties. At the end it cost him only a fraction of what it would otherwise and they ran their own school, proudly.

In another case, a prominent member of the church had driven away his son's wife during the persecution and contracted for him a marriage with the daughter of a leader in the persecuting society. The missionary presented the matter to the assembly. Soon after he met the offender and told him the church thought he should be excommunicated. "Why do you make things unbearable for me by stirring up the Christians?" said the man. "What do they expect me to do?" The missionary replied he did not know, but he thought if the man was truly penitent and made a public confession in the church, and then published his confession in the city, so that the name of the Church would be cleared, then the Christians might accept him back as a penitent. When the missionary saw the catechist and asked him if he thought the Christians would be satisfied with such an act of penitence, he replied, "It is not important. Whatever he may do, he will never do that." Yet he did. It is one thing to be excommunicated by the bishop far away, it is quite another to be excommunicated by one's neighbors. The man read out in the church an open confession, then went with two or three leaders of the church and posted that confession on the four gates of the city.

A further instance presents a problem that is far from uncommon in missionary life. A man came one day with a tale of persecution and begged the missionary's assistance. His pagan neighbor, he said, had moved his landmark and threatened to accuse him in court as the offender. The only answer he received was, "Tell it to the Church." Eventually, one Sunday morning after service, he rose and said, "I have business for the Church." All listened patiently to his story, then an old farmer arose and said, "I propose that we adjourn this matter until your adversary carries it to court." Some weeks later the man came to say that his enemy had now gone to the court. Again, an old man arose: "I think we had better not consider this matter any more." No one said a word, and in that silence the whole church condemned their brother. They all knew every detail of the case, but they would not have dared tell the missionary even to prevent his making a serious mistake. But none was ready to uphold the evil himself. The author concludes, "The aged, respectable leader, illiterate, ignorant in many ways, dull though he might be, in the council of the Church found his voice and fulfilled a duty which would have tried the wisdom of the best educated and best instructed teachers."

B. All Mutually Growing in Christ

"It is so much easier to do something *for* another than to do it *with* him," writes Cardinal Suenens in *The Gospel to Every Creature,* "to solve a problem for him than to make him discover the solution for himself and to work with him at applying the result. It is essential for a priest not to assume an authoritarian attitude, he must trust the resources of the laity. He must resist the temptation to do everything himself, on the plea that all will be better and more quickly done; he must learn how to inspire others and efface himself; in a word, to be all and to be nothing . . . Control is no doubt indispensable; control, however, does not mean repression; but rather stimulation, guidance, encouragement. To control is not to take the place of the workers; on the contrary, it is the art of getting work done by others, rather than doing it oneself, of provoking life and growth, instead of stifling or quenching energy. If work undertaken in common is to be successful, each worker must feel himself pledged, responsible, fully active, and sharing from within in the task of all" (Newman, 1957).

Father Joseph Sellmair, in his book *Priest in the World,* states: "The lay apostolate properly understood is the best preventive of anti-clericalism . . . It is in the lay apostolate that the layman finds his true position in the Mystical Body of Christ . . . As a true disciple of Christ, as a living member of the Church which is a leaven, he must be a leaven himself; he must be the salt of the earth, the light of the world" (Burns & Oates, 1957). The priest's work among his people must be not only as service to individuals but also have social meaning to make them aware of themselves as a leaven. While he leads them to praise the Holy Trinity he has also to lead them in sharing the Trinitarian life of grace with others. They both share by baptism and confirmation in the same priesthood of Christ. They have different functions in that priesthood, but each completes the other for carrying out Christ's mission. They have therefore mutual obligations of active obedience to one another in that relationship according to their functions. This means to share in consultation and planning, each making the contribution for which his own background fits him. It means intelligent acceptance of each other's contribution to the common decisions and working out together the best way to put the decisions into practice.

The bond of "member with member" between priest and layman is much more strongly felt in the apostolic relationship than in the usual religious ministrations. In the latter the priest is God's instrument in a formal action, which tends toward a certain impersonal quality. In the former there arise love and respect in the mutual exchange between persons working together for and with Christ like the bond between Christ and His Apostles. Father Sellmair speaks with eloquence of this relationship: "The layman desires that the priest should frankly and without embarrassment lay bare and discuss his sorrows, his anxieties, longing and sufferings, and all the problems arising from his being himself a man signed, as well as those of his actual work. For the layman is only too anxious to himself feel something of the priest's burden. As against this, he also desires that the priest should know something of his own necessities, should sympathize with them and help bear them. What is more, he desires that the priest should lead him even further into that wonderful land of religious knowledge, that he should teach him to penetrate more deeply into the nature of the sacrifice, so that strengthened in faith and love, he may be able to carry the name of Christ into every home and workshop, in places to which the priest himself is often denied access." These words open up to priest and layman the vast potential that exists for both in their relationship.

As the priest comes to share with lay groups more of the burdens that he formerly tried to carry alone, he discovers in them human resources and hidden potential that he would never have believed were there. With his encouragement and interest, many develop and flower into what seem like different people. Unimagined reserves of zeal, devotedness and self-sacrifice are tapped which challenge him to match. No longer do they all hang upon him in every spiritual need, but help one another. They become an inspiration for him and not he alone for them, in a way that makes his sermons and conferences come alive in a true sense. Gradually a holy intimacy develops between priest and congregation which helps solve the problem of spiritual isolation for both and lifts both out of the dangerous routine performance of their respective religious roles. The priest comes to know the problems and needs of his people with a personal understanding that he could not have in any other manner. The virtues of priestly and married chastity are no longer seen as separate burdens but as supporting each other in a mutual spirit of sacrifice. The sense of the Mystical Body becomes a reality for both in a way that no sermon, no retreat, could convey because being member of member is experienced in actual life between the spiritual father and his children. And each is spurred by a strongly felt desire to prove himself worthy of the other's confidence in him.

Then religion, so often in danger of being regarded chiefly as comprising certain duties for certain times that one dare not neglect for fear of sin, is seen as a work, a life, of love among men as well as with God. In place of being a set of obligations, and therefore a burden, it becomes a motive of apostolic action at all times and in all the daily circumstances of life. The good of religion in the community becomes to our laity a personal concern from their identification of themselves with the parish and the Church. It forms a natural topic of conversation among them and they can thus speak of it more readily to others. There can be no mass religious influence anywhere except by making the faith in its relation to life the topic of mass conversation. Young people are caught up by the interest on the part of their elders and tend to acquire a positive Christian mentality which makes them far less likely to be led astray in today's secularist environment.

One young man expressed it this way: "In church the priest tells us what we 'ought' to do as Catholics and in some things, at least, this is hard for modern youth to take. In the lay apostolate he works with us to discover how to live Catholic life in its fullness. Then we see that God in reality gives us freedom to choose and asks us for a free consent." Such results do not come from merely exhorting our people to be apostolic. They come from the priest sharing with them his own apostolic motivations in relation to specific and concrete life situations. The laity whose life he thus shares then come to feel that they have a part with him in the common cause of Christ, a part which befits them as free and intelligent beings. They are not being treated either as merely passive recipients of the priest's ministrations or as his errand boys in parish activities. Someone has described the role of the priest in the lay apostolate as to help the Christian multiply free acts of generosity towards God in union with Christ.

C. Inter-Parish Teamwork of Priests

The individualist priest in parish work has few with whom to share his burdens. Moreover, when a man plans alone, his ideas often do not become fully developed from lack of mutual stimulation through discussion and some vital aspect of a question may escape his notice. It is a common human experience that, when a certain trend of thought absorbs our attention, some simple yet important factor may easily be overlooked. The man who works alone may have fundamentally excellent ideas, but his field of vision and his perspective in depth are naturally restricted by the limited view of one person. To see all aspects of a matter in order to form as objective a judgment about it as possible, we need to see it from the point of view of others as well as our own. One great value of group discussion is to "mill ideas" into a practical and usable form. The act of trying to put our own germinal ideas into words for others helps to develop them even in our own mind. Then the reactions and suggestions of others carry forward our own thought to a new position and our statement of this affects their thinking in turn. It is thus that clearer and even new conceptions are produced, usually much superior to the original idea.

The first level of co-ordinating apostolic work is, therefore, group study and research by priests themselves to discover the needs in their own field of work. An informal "working group" of neighboring priests could not only share ideas for their own parishes, but could be of great assistance in making diocesan conferences more fruitful. Since few are experts, they must go back to sources, search books and current literature. One priest of long experience told me that no one could have a real understanding of pastoral and apostolic work unless he did continual serious reading on those matters. In everyday life it is recognized that those who do not keep in touch with new developments and ideas in their field will be left behind. Why should it be any the less true in the priest's work? True, he deals with eternal and unchangeable verities, but the living Holy Spirit in the Church gives constantly new insights into those truths as man grows in understanding about the world and himself. The priest faces no greater handicap in his ministry than to be out of touch with those developments. The fundamental reason why so many today abandon religion is that they have not been instructed in its relevance to modern life.

For the research to be effective, it needs as wide a frame of reference as possible. This means not only the relevant sciences, but also a study of practical methods that have been successful elsewhere. Once we understand why they succeeded there, we can adapt them to our own circumstances. In spite of cultural differences, men everywhere have the same fundamental religious needs and aspirations. A different culture would simply guide the local adaptation of basic methods. All peoples have the same desire for true happiness, the same reaction when told that they are created in God's image and that He is their Father. They are all moved by the story of our Lord and by the marks of true friendship which lay apostles offer them. The missionaries know that, no matter what the local forms of worship, all men lift their hands and hearts to heaven to make contact with God and seek his blessings. And because they are all the image of God, they all respond to Christian goodness when demonstrated in such a way that God's goodness shines out.

Possible research subjects are innumerable. Do we tend, unconsciously perhaps, to think of education as chiefly schooling? How do we train families to accept their responsibility as educators? Lay responsibility must today be everywhere the bulwark of the Faith, not only where unfriendly forces are in control, but also in our pluralist society. What is the value of student hostels? In number of Catholics reached? In permitting Catholics to attend various schools more suited to their scholastic ability? Have hostels any special value in training young leaders to contact non-Catholics in their schools? Would it be useful to have lay teams from the center visit out-stations to prepare for the priest's coming? How much time should the priest spend there: visit with the people, hold a public meeting with them? Has "putting the priest on wheels" tended to decrease his "walking" his area to meet the people? How do results in one-priest parishes compare with others? Can he tend as many parish societies and apostolic groups? Could two small parishes increase *esprit de corps* by holding some joint meetings?

Could a Press Group of young men help inform the public about the Church and become Catholic leaders in the process? They would prepare brief, informative items for the secular press on the Church's teaching, her history, her great men. This would form part of a public information program aimed at showing how the Church contributes to human development. If lay Catholics cultivate the acquaintance of editors it will be easier to get such articles accepted. If radio time were available, it would be used in a similar way. What opportunities in our area for Catholic credit unions to rescue people from the clutches of money lenders? How can we train the officers to have a sense of responsibility? Usually the best plan is to build socio-economic action on religio-social action to make use of religious motivation. One priest should make a special study of this field before anything is begun, it has many traps for the uninformed. How about a priest-lay team to promote education in the Church's social teaching? Another to take the lead in work for the family, such as Cana Conferences, neighborhood discussions on Catholic family life? What helps does the family need to carry out its role of preparing children for their place in the modern world?

A research team might well list things to be done in order of urgency as a basis for general discussion. Does our work tend at present to depend too much on institutions such as schools which Communism would destroy or nationalism take over? Does it depend too much on the priest and a few helpers with little formation of the laity in responsibility? Parish surveys would be very useful hree. Questionnaires could be addressed to the Catholics: Did you speak of the faith and how often? Did you introduce anyone to an apostolic leader? The Catholics could distribute questionnaires to non-Catholics in order to discover their attitudes towards religion and the faith. A few questions like the following could be included: Did any Catholic ever tell you that man is made in the image of God and therefore has a great human dignity as God's co-creator? What do you think of this idea? Have you read or heard anything about Jesus Christ? What do you think of His saying that all men should love one another as brothers? Have you heard His saying that all men will be judged according as they have helped others, even the least? What is your opinion?

Some priests may feel that they do not have time to take part in such groups with fellow-priests, but with today's ease of travel the majority of priests do visit one another fairly often, even in the mission field. We do not mean to say that a friendly visit for recreation should be devoted to "talking shop," but why not take advantage of the occasion to also hold some serious discussion? Where travel may be an obstacle, meetings of several days could be held a few times a year with further communication by letter. In the western United States, some priests drive 200-300 miles to attend a priests' team meeting every three months. In city parishes, the telephone enables busy priests to arrange meetings on short notice at a time convenient for all. The chief hurdle is often one of decision to begin, to be convinced of its importance. Once a program is under way, there will naturally be a useful exchange of ideas on every occasion that two or three of the group do meet one another.

The Diocesan Apostolate of Buffalo, New York, for young priests is a form of the "working group." It was founded by Father, now Bishop, Navagh, as a one-year's training course for those newly ordained. They are assigned to start parishes in a "priestless" area of the diocese and come in every Monday to the Apostolate Center, which is in charge of an experienced priest director. Here they discuss and plan their work, then go back on Wednesday to work with the people in their parishes. If they lived at the Center and worked out from there, the people would look on them as temporary chaplains instead of as "our priest." Of course, the Buffalo situation is special and the periodic meetings of "working groups" that we have been describing would not require an Apostolate Center. The idea of a diocesan director to promote small groups for study and discussion of the pastoral apostolate would seem, however, an excellent one calculated to extend the program to include many more priests.

D. Teamwork of Priests Within a Parish

In many parts of the world the young priest at ordination faces a long period as parish assistant, up to 10 and even 20-30 years before becoming pastor of a parish. His assignment as assistant is not simply to help with the priestly work but also that he may be trained in the pastoral apostolate. This training is not well done, however, if he is treated as a sort of "ecclesiastical handyman" who simply carries out assigned duties or is kept during his best years in charge of less important activities. The young priest should be welcomed from the beginning as a full partner in the parish. He needs to learn how the whole pastoral operation of a parish is planned and fitted together to prepare him for becoming himself a parish priest. He needs especially the personal experience of taking part in the planning of the pastoral program so that he may grow through the years. Sometimes he is looked on as too young to take part in such planning, but that is precisely his best time of learning how to do it. Someone has characterized as a common attitude of older men towards the younger: "They expect too much in the way of experience and give too little credit for intelligence."

Various methods have been used to organize the priests of a parish as a team so that all of them may have part in both pastoral responsibility and parish planning. One simple method is to give each priest charge, under the parish priest, of all work in a certain sector of the parish. He makes the pastoral visits to the Catholics, takes the sick calls and arranges for funerals, handles marriage inquiries and arrangements, gives religious instruction and examines in doctrine, admits to baptism and the other sacraments. He receives those who come from his sector for advice or help and dispenses charity from parish funds in case of immediate need. If a priest must be absent, the team arranges to carry on his work.

All the priests of the parish meet once a week with the pastor or one named by him presiding. If the meeting cannot take place at the time set, it is held at the first subsequent free hour, but never canceled. Each one reports, beginning from the senior present, on the week's work in his sector and whatever special task he had in the parish as a whole. Some time is given to planning work for the period until the next team meeting. Each one may propose questions, suggestions or new business. A certain part of the meeting is devoted to discussion study of a special topic connected with parish work, perhaps introduced with a short paper by one of the priests. It may sometimes be found useful in a parish organized on this plan not to divide all parish societies according to sectors but certain groups may cover two or more sectors. This would avoid too great multiplication of parish society meetings to be attended by the priests.

When the Abbe Michonneau was parish priest of Colombes, Paris, he described in *Revolution in a City Parish* (Newman, 1950), the purpose and results when the priests of a parish work as a team. "In this way," he wrote, "the isolation that most of us have known in our priesthood is eliminated. We do not have to plan alone, and wonder whether we are right or not; we do not have to be afraid to approach other priests for ideas. Most important of all, there can be no cleavage between our assigned activity and the advance of the whole parish. Even when things go wrong in our part of the work we are not obliged to face the difficulty alone. The others notice our downcast look, and bring us out of it either by their joking or by their actual help. Before long we really begin to think and act as a team, so much so that we instinctively lean on and support one another . . . Honestly, it has reached the stage where we hesitate, in a sense, to act without consulting our *confreres.* By this time a parishioner no longer shows surprise when the parish priest says that he wants to talk over the proposal of the parishioner with one of the assistants before deciding it.

"At first glance such an attitude on the part of the priest may seem harmful to good order, to authority and obedience. Somehow it does not work out that way. Everyone realizes that the parish priest has a better knowledge of the needs and capabilities of the parish, and that his experience in the priesthood is fuller. Quite naturally it devolves upon him to decide the general directives, and his position and experience are enough to settle any discussions which threaten to become interminable. Obedience to him, too, is all the easier because it is free and not forced; it is given to him willingly because of the sacred task of all the priests in the parish. He is not a dictator, but a leader. He himself is bound to obey and submit to the demands that the common good lays upon all. Consequently, obedience becomes not a burden but a joy. No one is asked to be a slave, but all are asked to make a complete consecration of themselves. Parish priest and assistants alike are involved in this . . . If the emphasis is placed on authority, the teamwork comes to a full stop; instead of developing and building apostles, we shall have discouraged and cynical priests. Even if this solidarity did no more than this, it would be worth while; merely ridding rectories of rivalry and ill-temper is a glorious result.

"But over and above this, it touches and transforms our apostolicity with the lighthearted zeal most of us have not known since seminary days. (This was very evident during a meal the writer had at the Colombes rectory in 1961). Passing beyond the walls of the rectory, it reaches out to the people, and infects them too. Some readers may smile at this, but a member of the parish actually told one of us that he enjoyed visiting the priests' house, simply because it was such a pleasure to see how well the priests got on with one another. There must be some reason too for the increase of vocations from the parish; and, since we have abolished most of the traditional parish activities, the reason must be found in the evident spiritual joy of the priests . . . Nor was Christ joking when He told us that wherever two or three are gathered together in His name he would be in the midst of them. We live and work, held together 'in the Name of Christ,' and that unity is the source of both efficiency and grace for us, and for the whole parish. We know that the faithful notice scandal and discord in their clergy, but we seem to forget that they also notice and imitate our singleminded spirituality.

"The priestly team must be no more than the nucleus of the parochial one. The latter could not exist without the previous priestly formation; but this in turn must include all the active elements of the parish from every corner of it. After all, why not get the parish interested in its own welfare? When we talk about a parish we certainly mean the people more than the priests; they were here before we were and will, no doubt, be here long after we have been sent to some other post . . . What a pity, when the faithful confuse the parish with the priests that direct it. Because of this attitude they no longer think that it is their affair too, and that they ought to be interested in it . . . To join priests and people in one team means more than simply calling meetings and setting up committees with no more results than a vague feeling of accomplishment. We must so act towards our people that they may be really and completely united to the life and progress of their parish. We have lay-movements; let lay-people take charge of them! Let them realize that this is *their* movement . . . outside of questions of faith, morals, or things touching the welfare of the entire parish, they themselves should be capable judges."

In the view of Abbe Michonneau, the dedication of priests to parish life implies a pastoral community focus also in their own spirituality. At the annual clergy retreat, for example, they should make it a serious subject of self-examination whether they demonstrate the spirit of community at least as well as they ask of the laity. It may also occasionally form in one or other aspect the subject of a recollection day conference. Do they give an equal welcome to all and play no favorites? How can true community flourish in a parish if some priests keep visiting certain families, or seem to prefer the company of the well-to-do or certain nationalities? In the lay apostolate we ask people to make many sacrifices of their time and personal inclinations to "do good things for God." Shall we priests ask less of ourselves? People do not blame a priest if he is not eloquent or intellectual, so long as he is single-minded in his vocation. But any signs of inconsiderateness, self-indulgence, laziness, inconsistency in decisions or relationships, are bound to weaken the bond of confidence that is the first requisite for an effective priest-lay team.

13. THE INTEGRATED PARISH COMMUNITY APOSTOLATE

Our Lord, by becoming Man, entered into human society that He might associate it and its life with the Holy Trinity. He still enters into society through every member of the Mystical Body. That is the new society which Christ founded in order, by the ministry of His members, to elevate all human institutions to share the mutual self-giving of the Holy Trinity. To enter into the infinitely perfect Society of divine Persons is the inheritance that Christ their King brought to the People of God and begs them to share with all mankind.

The term "Mystical Body" is familiar to every Catholic. Yet the lay apostolate does not develop as it should from our failure to think through the real significance of the Mystical Body as the model for a new human society of mutual love, the society that man needs for his highest development. The good-living pagan, guided by the inner sense of religion which he has from being God's image, lives in an attitude of religion to the degree of which he is capable. But modern man can no longer live by the pagan's conception of life and can find his true relationship to God only in Christ's Mystical Body, the new society that restores the true order of human values at the highest level. How could any Christian, therefore, honestly attempt to help the newly emerging peoples attain a modern social level without at the same time seeking to bring about their incorporation into the model human society of the Mystical Body? Indeed, the means par excellence to lift up mankind all over the world is to make the Mystical Body visibly seen in the People of God as such a model of human society.

The Mystical Body, set up by Christ to incorporate us into the Society of the three Persons in the Holy Trinity, is the society for which God destined all men when He created them. Man in his human nature as an individual, in his intellect and will, is created in the image of God's nature. This answers the question: What is man? But we must also ask: Who is man? As a person, as John or Susan living in the relationships of the family and of society, man is the image of the divine Society of three Persons. He was created in the image of God's nature and also in the social image of God in view of being elevated into relationship with the Holy Trinity: as son of God the Father, brother of God the Son, living temple of God the Holy Spirit. When a Catholic enters into apostolic contact with another person there begins to form a cell of the new human society sharing through him in the mutual life of the Holy Trinity. It is clear that such cells must be formed in every part of existing society by division and multiplication "until the whole is leavened."

A. Group Dynamics and the Apostolate

The cell idea has been widely accepted as basic to the lay apostolate. When Pope Pius XI a generation ago sent out his clarion call for the apostolate of the laity, he emphasized that both formation and action should be in small groups. The principle of group dynamics operates here, that the personalized face-to-face relations which obtain within a small circle of persons with a common purpose is important for the discovery of self with relation to others that is then to be applied in apostolic action. The small group helps develop a respect for the autonomy and value of others which is essential in the apostolic approach. These formation groups are calculated to produce an apostolic elite—alert, devoted, disciplined. In view of cell multiplication they seek to associate others with themselves, perhaps formed into "action groups" but with less intense formation. Now, after thirty years, students of the lay apostolate are trying to analyze how successful these groups of elite have been in the task they set for themselves, to transform their environment in the likeness of Christ.

The chief form taken by these groups is known as Specialized Catholic Action, but as we look at the average parish, it is seen that they include no more than 3-5 per cent of the adults. Of the others, many lack the ability to undergo the required training or to do the special work; a large number are impeded by obligations of family or occupation. (In a number of areas I was told that few of their people could follow the rather formal inquiry method commonly adopted by Specialized Catholic Action.) How, then, shall the ordinary people of the parish, who form the vast majority, take part in the apostolate as the popes say they should do? How shall the Catholic masses, such as the vast majority of workers in industry or farmers who so often have a low educational level, find the fulfillment in Christ which comes from sharing His mission through being apostles to their fellows? How are the Catholic masses to give one another the mutual support they ought against the influence of today's world, so depersonalizing, isolating, secularizing? Against moral evils of wide acceptance, such as birth control or sexual laxity? How are they to make practice conform to belief as something dynamic in the world? It becomes evident that a relatively few elite apostles cannot personally support the morale of the Catholic community and at the same time undertake the vast apostolate to the masses outside the Church. Both these tasks must be the work of the whole Catholic community.

At the same time that Pius XI issued his directive to form key apostolic leaders with a high degree of spiritual, intellectual and practical competence, he made a statement about their relation with the masses. "We must always have in view the masses, for nothing is accomplished without the masses . . . The masses have their own power, their own dynamism."

The Holy Father was speaking in the context of what he called "the scandal of the nineteenth century, the loss of the working classes to the Church." Students of the life of the Church today find that there is occurring an intensification of Christian life in a few along with a numerical diminution among the masses. Hence there naturally arises the crucial question: How well have elite leaders trained in small groups been able to obey the injunction so frequently repeated by Pius XI, "Go to the masses."? How many elite groups, for example, have succeeded in activating mass movements led by their own leaders? Or rather, how many leaders have they formed among the masses? For by the principle of "like to like" the masses will identify themselves with and follow only those who are of themselves and speak to them in the language of the masses.

Moreover, the relatively small membership of elite groups cannot possibly provide a fully effective exemplification of how mutual self-giving after the model of the Holy Trinity should be applied in human society. Men tend to regard such a small proportion of Catholics as not sufficiently representative to be convincing. For the Mystical Body to exert widely effective influence it must be seen involved as a whole, in all its members. Otherwise men are treated to the spectacle of relatively few Catholics, the elite, trying to build a new society, while other Catholics who are also members of Christ stand aside and do not see how they can take part. A student of political science in the United States recently wrote me: "Both political parties have organizers for every precinct; in many precincts there are contact persons in every block. If a political party can find thousands of eager workers in every large city, why can't parish priests find zealous and respected laymen as leaders of the Catholic masses in each parish block?"

Can it be that, in our pre-occupation with the functioning of the cell as such, too little thought has been given to the larger apostolic organs such as the parish? Have we overlooked the fact that a cell is formed also whenever a Catholic enters into apostolic contact with his neighbor, though it may not be a formally organized one? Perhaps some lay apostles may be practicing what David Riesman calls "groupism." In the group they achieve a certain psychological security, find a solution to certain personal problems, but at the cost of over-dependence on the group as such. One meets lay apostles, for example, who are faithful to some agreed group task but fail to see the opportunities to manifest Christ in the course of daily contacts. We may ask, therefore, if their formation has been in the context of contrived or theoretical situations rather than concrete ones? Karl Jaspers says somewhere that to grasp a concrete situation as one meets it is the first step in the direction of its mastery. To scrutinize it and to understand it arouses the will to modify its being.

The group formation of apostles in interpersonal relationships must always be directly related to the primary apostolic goal, the "end of charity" as St. Augustine called it. The crux of the matter lies in our proper understanding of just what is this goal. It is to convert the world, not simply in the sense of bringing men to know, love and serve God as individuals but as mutually self-giving members of the Mystical Body. As we have already seen, the true sense of converting the world is to share life with men in such a way that they will share it with others. A criticism heard about some is that they approach the apostolate almost as if to satisfy a need for self-assertion rather than to help others discover in themselves the image of God.

Recently I heard a wise spiritual guide express this idea: To help another grow in the charity of Christ is done by stimulating his spiritual activity. Our action cannot develop his supernatural personality for him we can only encourage him to use his own spiritual powers in cooperation with grace. Our chief task as apostles is to show that we recognize in his good will the reflection of God's goodness and to accept this good will as a gift of God to us through him. Then he himself can come to understand its source. In other words, the other person is not simply an apostolic "object" that we work *on*, but a person *with* whom we grow together in charity. That is the process by which the other is not only brought to God, but is himself also made an apostle.

Obviously, such a growth together in charity can take place outside the organized apostolate as well. For example, a person in confession accuses himself of an habitual sin arising out of his environment, which he cannot escape. If the priest simply urges him to give up the sin, the penitent will find the task most difficult, perhaps impossible. A bad habit cannot be simply suppressed; it must be dispossessed by a good habit through modifying the reaction patterns of the person. It will be very difficult for the individual, however, to do this alone. But the confessor says to him, "Will you invite someone once a week: "Come, let us do something good for God?" It might be to visit a sick friend or hospital patients who have no one; it might be to teach catechism. Extending the invitation is much easier than going alone to perform a work of mercy, and now the penitent has a partner in charity to support him. Instead of simply trying to change himself alone, he sets up a social cell which begins to change his environment and make it more conducive to a life of virtue.

B. Specialized Movements and the Community

The aim of Specialized Catholic Action movements is to train elite leaders within a specific *milieu* or social group according to the principle of "like to like" enunciated by Pope Pius XI. We have already remarked the need of all Catholics to experience community as Catholics as well as its necessity for the apostolate to the masses. Now the community is formed by the common life and action of those who compose it, but the specialized approach has not sufficiently shared with the Catholic masses its own experience of community. Nor is an "overflow of grace" from the specialized movement to other Catholics, as I have heard it expressed, sufficient here. For by no stretch of the imagination could such be taken as manifesting before the world the community of charity within the Mystical Body. It is the entire Christian community that must bring its liturgical community out into the daily relationships of society and there express it in terms of charity meaningful to the masses of mankind.

This problem of forming the Christian community as an apostolic force will not be solved by trying simply to enlarge the specialized movements. There would be danger of lowering their own formation level, as we saw in a previous chapter. In fact, the masses simply could not follow the specialized method. Now if the chief role proposed to the masses is to assist by prayer, then the apostolate of the Mystical Body would often be deprived of persons able to do some active apostolic work among those of their own environment whom members of elite groups would not reach. Moreover, an apostle is one "sent" to bring a message, and it would be misleading to give the impression that prayer without action fulfills this idea. Of course, the life of complete self-immolation led by those who devote themselves to prayer and contemplation withdrawn from the world, holds a deservedly high place in the Church. But the question here is of the layman's vocation in the world of external action in which he plays a daily part. It would seem a contradiction for an office worker, a housewife or any other layman called by God to live in society to be given the idea that they can fulfill by prayer alone their apostolic vocation to bear witness in charity among the many human contacts they have every day. Even one chained to a bed of invalidism can and should be an apostle of the Mystical Body community in the human community where he is—with doctors, nurses, fellow patients, perhaps also by letters as not a few have done.

If the function of ordinary Catholics as associate members

of elite groups is conceived, on the other hand, as doing certain amount of work as "helpers," there arises the difficulty that few persons can get up much enthusiasm as "second-class" members. Some specialized groups promote discussion meetings among non-members to help them understand the apostolate and with a view that some will become regular members. One difficulty here is that the apostolate as one's own action is not "sold" by discussion so much as by the personal invitation, "Come, let us do something together for God." Another difficulty is that those taking part in such discussion represent a relatively small proportion of the parish and are often of the type that seeks to know rather than to do, so one cannot see how a mass movement could result. Indeed, our present apostolic efforts are so piecemeal that, while a certain number in the parish are receiving some form or other of apostolic training, the great majority are actually being subjected to daily greater secularizing influences of their environment. The only antidote to that influence is to have the entire parish take some positive, if simple, part in counteracting these influences in their own life situation.

The transforming effect of such participation is illustrated by an anecdote which Father Leo Ward of Notre Dame relates in a book describing his visit to the Antigonish, Nova Scotia, cooperative movement. An ordinary farmer in the cooperative made a simple observation that epitomizes the whole concept of Christian community. "Heaven must be like this, everybody together and God in their midst." Now the Christian community is at once the chief aim of the apostolate and its primary means. Failure to gear the lay apostolate to bringing the mass of men into Christian community by the practice of Christian charity in daily life would be to miss the essential role that Pius XII ascribed to the apostolate, "to build up the Mystical Body." We can neither teach community like the catechism nor administer it like the sacraments. The community of charity is achieved in only one way, by being practiced together so that all may know how to practice it in their turn with others and so lead them into the Christian community itself. That is the kind of apostolic formation which Christ gave His Apostles and they passed on to the early Christians.

One endeavor to find a solution for these problems was described to me by Vincent Giese, when he was editorial director of Fides Publications. He had moved into a parish on the Chicago South side which had less than twenty members of the Young Christian Workers out of several hundred young people. The others called them "Holy Joes" and they had few mutual points of contact unless their jobs happened to bring them together. Vince promoted a Young Adults Club for young people over twenty-one, with its own officers and program. Here was something that the mass of young people could call "ours" and identify themselves with. The club began with 100 active, paying members and several hundred on the mailing list for special activities. Few even of the 100 had previously known one another except casually. The YCW youth became ordinary members of the club and now could make contacts with the others as fellow members to interest them in apostolic action. They accepted no offices, but willingly served on various committees and were able to get the club to promote some simple apostolic actions instead of remaining almost entirely recreational.

Four years later Vince wrote of the club, "While it is not designed as a leadership training ground, in the apostolic sense of the word leadership, we cannot deny that it, too, is a framework in which leadership can be exercised. We look upon the club itself as an organization whose spiritual sights we hope to raise. Certainly the dating forums and the day of recollection, to cite two examples, were well attended and well received when our Catholic Action teams sponsored them under the auspices of the Young Adults Club. They revealed a genuine interest on the part of these young people for something other than social, even though the primary goals of the club are social. The larger Young Adults Club also has become a place where we can exercise our latent talents of leadership—organizational abilities, committee work, planning—all those elements needed to develop an effective and comprehensive youth program in the parish.

"From the still somewhat meager experience at St. Francis de Paula, it would seem that a fully rounded youth program in a parish would include both a general membership club as well as a small, leadership training program. Both the large group and the small group are needed. Both have their functions: one to appeal (through social activities) to all the youth in the neighborhood and bring them into contact with the Church; and the other to train leaders, interest young people in apostolic work, and help develop a social awareness among them and a deeper identification with the missionary goals of the parish." (Cf. *Apostolic Perspectives,* Fall 1956.) We would add the following comments: 1) the two types of cooperating organizations are needed also for the adults of a parish as a common point of contact between apostles and masses; 2) the larger group gives the apostolic groups an immediate and sympathetic first field of action as well as a recruiting ground for new members; 3) the members of the larger group can provide for the apostles greatly multiplied means of contact with the masses outside and by that take the first step in becoming themselves apostles.

C. Elite Identification with Community Action

St. Paul gives us the key principle for elite leaders to work with the Catholic masses for the development of parish community in out-going charity as a social model. He writes: "Have this mind in you which was also in Christ Jesus, who though he was by nature God, did not consider being God as a thing to be clung to, but emptied himself, taking the nature of a servant and being made like unto men" (Philippians

2:5-7). In order to associate us with His own higher life, God first came down and became one of us, identified Himself with us so as to make it possible for us to identify ourselves with Him. So the apostolic elite trained at the higher level of the specialized movements, can activate the Catholic masses by associating themselves with larger movements of the Christian community. Their training has prepared them spiritually and psychologically to "empty" themselves and identify themselves with the life of the Catholic community. They would continue, of course, as active members of their own movements, but they would regard the chief function of those movements as to be apostles to make the masses apostolic in accordance with the directive of Pius XI. They would, of course, keep "first things first" and never get involved in secondary details, such as organizing merely social activities in the parish. They would be catalysts, activators, of the community apostolate.

Here are some simple examples of such cooperation by apostolic groups with more general Catholic ones. In the secular colleges and universities of the United States there are associations of the Catholic students commonly known as Newman Clubs. It was usually found difficult to promote apostolic work in the clubs because of the student environment. Then the Legion of Mary was set up within some of them and the zeal of its members inspired the others to greater interest in knowing and promoting their faith. The Legionnaires are not ordinarily known as such outside the Newman Clubs themselves. One advantage of the Legion in schools, including Catholic ones, is that the members go naturally into the parish Legion when they graduate, thus bridging over the gap that so often exists between the apostolate in the school and the parish. The association of elite and general groups has vast possibilities. In Accra, Ghana, the interest of young people was aroused by setting up the Catholic Youth Organization, then from within it were recruited members for the

Young Christian Workers and the Legion of Mary. The Young Christian Farmers can associate themselves with Catholic Rural Youth or the 4-H Clubs. Within the general student organization of Catholic schools can be set up groups of the Legion of Mary or the Young Christian Students. In mission schools these have made many converts. The same principle applies, of course, to the adult apostolate in the parish.

The specialized movements, with their training in personalized group relationships, have indeed been prepared to act in the vanguard for the renewal of Christian community, now endangered by so many depersonalizing influences. One of their primary responsibilities is to share with all the people of the parish the gift of what God has taught them in their groups about Christian community. But just as the specialized groups learn community only by practicing it, so also must the general body of Catholics learn it. The authentic method of the apostolate is to work "with" others, never "on" them as if from without. The elite apostles must take part in and help form the general Catholic community to make it a model and a magnet for the great human masses without. This points the way to an integrated parish apostolate of community consisting of specialized groups which identify themselves with more generalized groups that belong to all and with which all can identify themselves. It is particularly by participating in this integrated parish apostolate that elite apostles can best carry out their own understanding of the nature and practice of the apostolate of Christian community.

It is a general principle of mass organization that there must be trained *cadres* (squads)to help activate the great human potential towards achieving the common purpose. The members of specialized movements are particularly fitted by their formation to act as *cadres* in general movements, they are ready to take the apostolic initiative and to make the sacrifices required for difficult tasks. They should act as exemplars and catalysts of personalized relationships in order to make the parish a model of Mystical Body community in face of the modern tendency towards secularist individualism. Obviously, the parish community must be composed of the elite and masses together. This does not mean that the elite dominate the mass movement or act even as temporary officers. Though they may assist the officers if need be, they must never do anything that would weaken the general movement as belonging to all. Their role is precisely the subsidiary function of which Pope Pius XI told us in the encyclical, *Quadragesimo Anno,* that higher level social organs should aid and support those at lower levels to fulfill the role which is proper to them.

Zealous members of the specialized groups who associate themselves with various parish societies can give these a new orientation and a new sense of apostolic purpose. They have a special outlook which can inspire the others to raise their sights. The elite members, on the other hand, will also gain much. They will have their own view of the apostolate enlarged and enriched from seeing it in another perspective. They will come to understand far better the proper role and function of the apostolate at different levels, and any tendency to theorize about it will be checked against the concrete outlook of ordinary Catholics. Their own experience of community will be widened far beyond the horizons of their small groups and they will discover with astonished joy apostolic good will and potential co-workers where they had perhaps least expected. Their best method of activating potential at this level, however, will not be that used in their own group but rather the simple formula, "Come, let us do something good for God." Finally, they will be able to envisage a program of approach to the masses outside the Church. For it is only the Catholic masses who can effectively manifest the divine goodness to the other masses afflicted with loneliness and their chief instrument is the visible Catholic community of charity.

D. Combined Action to Leaven Society

When Pope Pius XI proposed Catholic Action as the duty of every Catholic, many thought that it should be set up as a single organization mandated by the bishop as official Catholic Action for his diocese. This is known as the "unitary plan" of Catholic Action and is usually divided into sections of men, of women, of young men and of young women. One difficulty with this plan is that it does not take into account differences in lay vocations and tends to reduce all members more or less to the same dead level of the apostolate. There is a present growing trend to regard Catholic Action as an apostolic principle exemplified in various organizations, not as an organization itself. In this view, any organization which conforms to the requirement laid down by Pope Pius XI as participating in the apostolate of the hierarchy may be approved by the bishop as Catholic Action. The bishops of the Philippines have approved fifteen organizations as Catholic Action. Mutual cooperation of the various organizations in the apostolate is insured through diocesan and parish federations representing the various organizations. Hence this is known as the "federation plan" of Catholic Action.

According to the federation plan, there would be even in small parishes of a few score families both special and general apostolic organizations working together for the parish community apostolate towards the community outside it. A missionary in Japan, for instance, with 100 Catholic families, had the following for the various types of apostolic needs and vocations in his parish: Legion of Mary, Young Christian Workers, Marian Sodality of young women, Newman Clubs, Altar and Rosary Society, St. Vincent de Paul, Parish Men's Society, Neighborhood Associations. Every month the Parish Federation of Catholic Action held a rally for all those organizations together. All Catholics and inquirers were invited to attend. A number of the unit leaders were selected to report in detail what they were doing at the action level, no general survey or theoretical plan was accepted. The priest stated that the rally helped even the smallest groups to feel part of the parish community apostolate and to see it as a whole. He said also that the best reports were usually those given by such groups as the Young Christian Workers and the Legion of Mary. These helped the others understand better the real nature of the apostolate and inspired them with greater zeal.

Recent popes have stressed the need to leaven the various areas of society by forming occupational groups: doctors, lawyers, teachers, businessmen, government officials, labor leaders and others. It is important to recognize, however, that their area of apostolic responsibility is not limited to their own occupational fields, for they are also members of the larger Christian community. They should study what various positive aspects of community they should promote in the many relationships they have outside their particular field as well as within it. They must be leaders fulfilling their Christian responsibility in, for example, civic affairs or their neighborhood and not simply in their own special field. Occupational groups are a form of specialized apostolate, but they should never remain isolated in outlook and action from the parish apostolate of the Catholic masses to the masses outside. For the Catholic masses need help to look at all mankind through the eyes of Christ in the Gospels so that they also may identify themselves with mankind as He did and develop a lively sense of responsibility to share with them the kingdom of God's people.

The cooperation of elite and masses must extend particularly to the apostolate of the marketplace, of social institutions, because they all participate there together. Moreover, the elite alone do not constitute the Christian community which must transform the larger community into itself. This apostolate is not so much a directly religious one as to demonstrate God's action in the world through His children acting as His delegates by word and action in all their relationships. This is of the utmost importance everywhere, not least in the mission field, because so often the relation between religion and social morality as distinguished from personal morality is not clearly seen. How frequently that is demonstrated by graft, favoritism, and "pork-barrel" or "log-rolling" tactics in government. In India I was told of a public conference sponsored by missionaries on the relation of religion to social morality in the modern state. A Catholic priest who stated our traditional position was contradicted by a Hindu speaker who said that business ethics, for example, was a strictly social matter with which religion had nothing to do. The other Hindus agreed with him. Later I heard of one government official arrested for large-scale graft who was said to devote three hours daily to contemplation.

In most mission area cultures, no matter how strong the traditional social solidarity may appear to be, the individual conceives it mainly in terms of clan loyalty and the sense of personal responsibility to the larger common good takes a weak second place. A simple example is the fact the stealing within the clan incurs serious punishment, while to steal from someone of another clan is punished only if the culprit is caught by the other clan. This is one reason for the widespread practice that a man takes only members of his family or clan into business with him. Governments of the newly emerging countries may be demoralized by failure of a certain number in responsible positions to distinguish between public and private good. Lack of concern about having professional competence, such as an official or school teacher, is another expression of this attitude. Our converts in mission lands may still harbor the idea that a government post is the golden opportunity for private gain, for they also spring from that background and are still part of a clan-centered society. It is important, therefore, that the missionary begin forming social consciences through developing their apostolic sense of responsibility towards others beyond their family and clan. He may begin with small groups or *cadres,* but they must in turn act as a leaven in the community by promoting parish and diocesan action in which they get other Catholics to participate.

In planning the apostolate, however, it is most important not to become so much concerned with "structures" as to overlook the fact that the essential note of the apostolate is welcome into the Christian community. Wherever the faith seems to be losing its hold, one will always find the Catholics as a whole lacking in the practice of this welcome. In one mission area of 100,000 "old Christians" too poor to have their own schools, I was told that half the boys lost their faith in the government high schools. The adults are most faithful in their practice, but are noted for a "ghetto" mentality. If young people form part of a Christian community that has a positive aim to win others, their own faith will be in little danger. Father Jean Daniélou, in *The Salvation of the Nations,* gives us the explanation: "Catholicism loses its hold on souls in the measure that it ceases to present, as an urgent task to be accomplished as soon as possible, the unity of all men in a *single* religion." Contrast this with the Communist marching cry, "Tomorrow the world will be ours."

Wherever there are Catholics, though only a handful, they must become the nuclear cell of apostolic openness to the larger community. Let us take two rather extreme cases: one a mission parish of perhaps 50 baptized or even an outmission with one or two families, the other a large homeland parish where only a very few attend Mass. The priest begins with those who do come; the fact that they are before him shows at least a minimum of good will. Every sermon, every instruction, every conversation, should show the priest's ardent desire to win men for Christ. He uses Canon Cardijn's personal approach method. He may tell them: "God loves us as our Father. Jesus loves us as our Brother. He comes to us here in the Mass, gives Himself to us in Holy Communion. He loves all men, all your relatives, your neighbors and acquaintances, but they do not know that He loves them. Will you remember five of them by name in this Mass? Will you be God's messenger to invite them to visit the church? You are their friend and they will pay attention to what you say. If you think some will not listen, you can open their hearts to God's grace by inviting them to help others. 'Come, let us do this good thing together for God.'"

Even the most simple, unlettered people are capable of being apostles among their own. In Indonesia I was told this story. Several years before World War II a Capuchin missionary baptized about 100 members of a tribe in Sumatra. Every Sunday he would speak of the great gift they have from God and how it should be shared. "If you share pigs, taro, rice with others you will have less, but if we share God's spiritual gifts with others then God gives us even more." After Mass he would sit with the people and his catechist and talk about their helping him to convert the tribe. He told the parable of the talents. "We must not bury God's gift of faith in a hidden place in our hearts as people bury valuables in the ground. God will ask us why we did not share the great gift He has bestowed on us with our brothers who have not yet received it." The war intervened and the priest was interned, leaving the people and catechist alone. When he returned after four years, five thousand converts had been instructed and baptized, twenty chapels built. The catechist had recorded the baptisms; all marriages had been properly witnessed and recorded.

As a practical summing up, the apostolate cannot depend only on what the members of a few groups can do with their own two hands, no matter how well trained they are. The whole Christian people must be brought to take part according to the capacity of each and at its own level of existence among the people around them. Trained *cadres* of elite can help them develop a greater social awareness and a deeper identification with the missionary goals of the Church. The *cadres* risk failure, however, if they do not carefully take into account that the apostolic action of the masses will be in many ways of a different type from their own. Both apostolates must combine in order that the welcome of the Christian community may be fully demonstrated, within as well as without. I once heard a diocesan leader in the Legion of Mary say that much of their work in bringing back the careless was without permanent fruit because the parish did not make them feel welcome and wanted. All our experience makes clear that the spirit of Christ-like welcome shown by the Christian community is the primary factor both in extending the kingdom of God and in maintaining its apostolic morale. It must be shown by Catholic with Catholic, adults with youth, as well as by Catholics towards those not of the Faith.

14. APOSTOLATE OF THE NEIGHBORHOOD COMMUNITY

At the Second International Congress of the Lay Apostolate in Rome, 1957, Pope Pius XII emphasized to the assembled delegates that the parish must form a "true community of all the baptized, mobilized in apostolic charity for the service of the Church." The prayer and liturgy of the Church alone are not enough, because they are for the baptized. Each Christian must so incarnate Christ visibly in his daily human relationships that all men may be able to recognize Christ in the human form of His members.

The Holy Father's words initiated a new concept of the part to be played in the Church's mission to men by all the laity without exception. If the lay apostolate is really to change the face of the world, said the Holy Father—particularly in the towns, which have a dominant influence in modern life—it is not enough for the parish to have a few dozen apostolic souls in certain movements. The apostolate needs not only specialists, it needs also a working force of many hands. Those with special training or higher education must encourage and assist ordinary Catholics to be apostles. By the principle of subsidiary function in the apostolate, those with superior gifts must put them at the common service of the Church's mission to mankind. Only the action of all working together can form the true Christian community adequate to the task assigned to it by Christ. The participation of all Catholics is necessary to make the multiple contacts at every level through which alone the Mystical Body may be clearly seen by all as the model of a new society.

In the apostolate of the parish community we may consider two chief fields of action. One field is the marketplace and the social institutions that belong to it. The other field is the neighborhood and its familial institutions. Both are interdependent and essential. The lay apostle in the marketplace takes man as he is, with his personality already formed, and tries to secure his cooperation for building social institutions according to the divine master-plan. The lay apostle in the neighborhood undertakes the fundamental work of forming the Christian person from childhood in the sense of Christian community so that he may better fulfill his role in the world as an adult Christian. The place of Catholic education in this fundamental preparation to implement the divine plan for social institutions has been discussed in a previous chapter. In the present one we shall deal with the neighborhood apostolate as such and in the next with the apostolate of the marketplace.

A. Community in Today's Neighborhood

The family is the basic cell from which are constituted both society and the Church. The family is itself a society, but an imperfect one which needs the help of other families in order to fulfill its part, in the Church as well as in society. This help was strong in the close-knit society of the past, and the parish community was built on a natural neighborhood community rich in human relationships and mutual interaction among the families. People did not feel lonely and isolated. A Catholic felt close to the other Catholics of the area because, if not relatives, they were neighbors who had grown up together. The parish was therefore itself a neighborhood composed of Catholic families who gave one another both religious and social support to live according to Christian ideals. The parish was homogenous because the area was, not of itself. Today the individual Catholic family may tend to lose the sense of religious security in the measure that it loses the sense of social security which it formerly had as part of a close-knit group of families. To restore this sense of social and religious security is one reason for today's emphasis on the neighborhood apostolate.

It is the young who are in the process of formation that suffer especially this twofold insecurity from the weakening of socially expressed agreement on good religious and moral values. Wherever a strong community spirit exists in all parts of a parish, the effect of its support for youth in desiring religious instruction and receiving the sacraments is clearly evident. Conversely, in an area where the Catholic community spirit is weak, youth tend to be little interested in learning about their Faith and careless in receiving the sacraments. Mixed and invalid marriages increase, becoming in many parishes the chief cause of leakage from the Church. In some parishes the rot permeates almost the whole body, in others it is chiefly evident in certain areas or among certain groups. The priest in the mission field may happily baptize large number of good people, only to see them grow lukewarm in the next generation. "Of course the Catholic religion is good," they will say, yet somehow the parish does not satisfy all their socio-religious needs. As Christians there are many community customs in which they can no longer take part, yet the parish has failed to develop Christian community activities. This occurs especially in the towns.

From the fact that social conditions exercise so great an influence on men's lives, the parish today tends to experience ever greater difficulty in fulfilling its function as a Christian community. Some have suggested that the geographical parish is out-moded, especially in industrial areas, and that Catholics should be grouped by occupation into some kind of "super-parishes." Though there is need of carrying on certain activities today at a super-parochial level, it appears that the suggestion of super-parishes runs counter to the conclusions of sociology.

The sociologists point out that modern civic planners envisage the city of the future as made up of small, self-contained communities, a conception of the town which corresponds perfectly with the Catholic concept of the parish. Canon Cardijn keeps repeating that the district where the young worker lives and the way he uses his leisure time count much more in his life than the place where he works and the hours spent at work. The Holy Father, in letters to Social Weeks in Canada and elsewhere, has also emphasized the irreplaceable role in the Church of the parish system.

Bishop De Smedt of Bruges, Belgium, draws attention to the fact that when the whistle blows in the evening every worker goes back to the district where he lives, even many miles away. The center of his life is his family and he spends his free time either at home or in the general neighborhood. The worker, above all, has few interests elsewhere. As we saw earlier with regard to the missions, he tends to spend his evenings with neighbors who are also workers. Bishop De Smedt holds that the parish can become a true center of community by forming sub-communities within itself which will serve as communities "of man's measure." Thus the neighborhoods on which parish community must be based will be restored on the higher level of the Mystical Body in place of their old natural level. The Bishop has established in his diocese of Bruges what is known as the STRADA Movement, by which a committee of family heads is formed in each district of the parish for all the more than 200 parishes of the diocese. The committee, says Bishop De Smedt "makes personal contact with everybody, shows interest in everything that concerns them, and charity is practiced in all its forms." He told his priests: "The Church, the diocese, the parish, are worth no more than the streets and the neighborhoods are worth." He sees the parish of the future as a "federation of neighborhoods in which the different socio-cultural milieu will be able to live a Christian life" *(Christ to the World,* 1961, No. 2).

One often hears Catholics say, "When our parish was small we were like one family; now that it is large we seem like strangers." It would be a mistake to think that the average parish can function "like one family" without any intermediate organs. The larger parish community must be built of smaller communities composed of families who are in direct relationship with one another socially as well as religiously. Some years ago I was present at a discussion in New York City where one of the participants held that the village parish represented the ideal form of Catholic life that could never be achieved in the city. A priest in the group replied, "There is no turning back the clock, and we need not try to do it in order to have parish community. A parish of 10,000 people, even a city of millions, can be broken down into the equivalent of villages. The method is to group them as neighborhood units where in Christ they again become persons to one another, mutually practicing cooperation. This practice of community as members of the Mystical Body would be at an even higher level than in a village where community was based chiefly on natural propinquity."

B. The Family in Neighborhood Community

Catholics today live almost everywhere in what is known as a "pluralist" society. It is a society in which there are not only many differences of religion but also different standards of conduct. This presents a particular problem in carrying out Christian family ideals. The practice of Catholic ideals requires training from early youth for the proper control and direction of natural drives. It requires also that Catholics belong to a social group that has the same ideals so that they will not be subjected to undue difficulties in living according to the ideals in which they have been trained. Now the conduct values of the society in which the average Catholic lives today so often fail to support his Christian values, with the result that he finds it hard to maintain his own values. The problem is particularly acute in the case of the young, who tend to follow the crowd and accept its values. The reality of this danger is pointed up by the increasing number of Catholic young people who grow careless about religion and who defend such ideas as contraception, divorce and marriage with divorced persons.

Father John L. Thomas, S.J., stated in *Social Order* (April, 1955), that in considering such problems the real significance of man's social nature is often ignored. "For all practical purposes," he writes, "the individual is regarded as a self-enclosed, relatively self-sufficient unit, rather than as a being immersed in society from womb to tomb. What is more important, little consideration is given to the profound effects which social relationships have upon the individual in forming his character and in carrying out his ideals. For example, the quality of the social environment plays a highly significant role in the control of the reproductive drive and in the realization of Christian family standards . . ." To understand the psychology of modern man, therefore, we need to know his cultural and sociological background. And for the individual Catholic to carry out his proper role in the world he needs social support in his family, neighborhood and parish, as well as in his educational, working and other environments. The spirit of community in the neighborhood and its extension, the parish, is essential to support Catholic family life. How can the Christian family keep its ideals otherwise, generation after generation.

It must not be lost sight of that Christian moral ideals were not set up by commandments of the Church which she can change or from which we are excused when they are seriously difficult to observe. Moral ideals are part of the "natural law," the law of man's nature which God gave him by creation and which can never be changed or excused. They are part of a Catholic outlook on life which flows from

God's plan for man's highest development. For example, the child must remain many years in the care of its parents because human development is the slow process of an unfolding. It is because the child develops gradually instead of being fixed by instinct like an animal that progress of the human race is possible. Now such trends outside the Church as today's social "pairing off" by young people of the opposite sex before they are sufficiently matured inhibits their natural development. There are well-defined stages in the child's growing up and each should be completed before entering the next. Too early emotional involvement between boys and girls "short-circuits" their natural unfolding. Such a situation not only involves moral dangers but the even more serious problem of arrested personality development due to over-preoccupation with each other so that they do not make real contact with the world of other people.

The prevalence today of "early dating" and "going steady" are due to several factors which are contrary to the Catholic view of human life. One factor is that many parents push their children too fast in a search for "status" or popularity through their children. In some cases the "steady" provides an emotional support that is lacking at home. Another factor is that not a few educators treat "growing up" as a goal rather than as a process. Psychologists and sociologists insist that, "When fathers and mothers think it is cute to see a couple of 12-year-old sweethearts acting like grown-ups, they are bringing great harm to our society. Children who begin to act like adults just out of infancy are bound to remain emotionally immature. The best friend of a young girl should be another young girl, not a 'miniature husband.'" Indeed, "petting" is at any age so exciting of the emotions that it becomes the main interest of dates and the slow growth of true affection is made impossible. One common result of precocious stimulation between the sexes is impulsive teen-age marriage, in which the divorce rate is three times that of adult marriages. More and more Catholic young people are thrown into contact with such youthful divorced persons, fall in love and marry them outside the Church.

It often happens that even Catholic parents who are opposed to such early emotional involvement give way to uncertainty when met with the cry: "But mom, you don't understand; everybody does it." That is the plea of the 12-year-old who wants to wear lipstick and of her teen-age brother who wishes to borrow his father's car, "Unless you have a car, you're nobody anymore." It is the protest of the 14-year-old who is not allowed a steady date and of the 16-year-old who is told to be in by midnight. The youngsters unanimously agree that they will be ostracized unless their parents give in. Their parents, they say, were "born old" and are really decades behind the times.

One Catholic mother who resisted the pressure of allowing her 13-year-old daughter to date, said, "Her schoolmates who go courting are not little girls, but little old ladies. I tell my daughter that when she's sixteen, she'll be the new girl in town. She will have unfolded naturally like a beautiful rose." Later her daughter went to college and wrote her mother, "How right you were. Now I am having fun in a natural way, while the girls who dated too young are fed up, full of conflicts, find pleasure only in emotional 'kicks.' " Catholic mothers often fear the danger of parent-child tensions if they take such a stand contrary to the social environment. Such tensions will not arise when the family is part of a neighborhood group that has agreed standards of discipline.

The modern individual household, the "nuclear family," offers many advantages for the greater fulfillment of husband and wife as equal co-partners. It may also have many serious disadvantages, particularly in a pluralist society, in the not infrequent case that one of the partners cannot or does not make his full contribution. If, for example, one of them dies or becomes an invalid, there is thrown upon the other a very heavy burden of child-rearing. The economic difficulties may be alleviated by insurance or by public welfare assistance, but that does not solve the psychological problem of the children lacking a father or mother. Then there is the still more common case of weakness on the part of one parent, or even of both. It may be drink, gambling or another vice; it may be neurosis or immaturity. The children of such parents tend to become like them unless they have close relationships with stronger adults in the community. Catholics have their full share of families that are "under-privileged" in this sense. In a close-knit Catholic neighborhood the other families of the "clan Christian" would come to their assistance.

In the "clan Christian" concept of neighborhood, the stronger families help the weaker, just as used to occur in the close-knit "extended family." Immature parents receive in such a neighborhood the best kind of counseling support by acceptance from the motive of charity into the sphere of mutual love and concern. There is no danger of seeming to interfere if one shows respect and love for the other as a person created in God's image, tries to discover and encourage the good qualities God gave him. Today even "normal" persons can easily become confused in face of social pluralism and pressures. I once heard a mother say, "Before I belonged to a group with the same ideals in the Christian Family Movement, it was very hard to go into the supermarket visibly pregnant when the previous child was not yet walking and see the raised eyebrows, hear the 'catty' remarks." The approval of contraception has become a cancer in our culture that spreads into Catholic homes. The selfish and calculating spirit so often behind this practice casts a shadow of ungenerosity over the lives of the children that are allowed to be born. Good religious vocations are rare from such a family environment.

Close-knit Catholic neighborhood groups promote good Christian family life in many practical ways. They provide an informal school where youth learn the true values of love and marriage and a training ground for Christian maturity in the atmosphere of mutual love and trust. The presence of those to whom one can go in confidence helps solve many personality problems that would interfere with happy marriage. Experts point out that modern society makes far greater demands than ever on the individual, yet provides him with fewer social supports. The groups may organize Maternity Clubs for helping families when a baby is born, perhaps contribute small amounts monthly to a fund from which parents may borrow at such a time. One group made inquiries and found that some doctor's fees for complete natal care were about half those of others. Some have promoted the La Leche League for information on breast feeding, the natural method of spacing babies designed by God Himself. When bottle feeding is used, the mother may be faced with a difficult problem of properly spaced births by the rhythm method, though now drugs to stabilize the menstrual cycle are being developed. It is said that when a baby is fed at the breast, the mother in 97 per cent of cases will usually not be fertile during the whole nursing period and for 4 to 6 weeks after the child is weaned.

Groups could even duplicate one psychologist's research project. A litter of six puppies was divided into three pairs. Two puppies suckled by the mother grew normally, their play was lively, their rest normal and they never attempted to suckle except at the mother's nipples. Two others were bottle-fed, with holes in the nipples that made the feeding period about five minutes. These puppies were much more restless and often tried to suckle other objects. The last two were fed from bottles with nipple holes large enough to be drained in two minutes though exactly the same amount as the others. They lost weight, were always restless, nervous and irritable, stayed close together and would often snarl and fight with the others. Lastly, they tried to suckle everything around them, including each other. There is good reason to believe that bottle feeding is harmful to the human infant's sense of security.

C. Family Meetings or Neighborhood Committees?

There are two chief ways to organize the neighborhood community, either by groups of families which meet regularly or by neighborhood committees. The committee method is often easier to organize and the leaders may afterwards promote family discussion groups, on either a permanent basis or for certain periods. A simple form of the first method is the Filipino Barangay of the Virgin. Another form is the "Neighborhood Association" widely used in Japan and Korea. This was first developed by Father Spae in Himeji, Japan, on the pattern of the traditional Japanese civil associations. The 1200 Catholics in Himeji, a city of 240,000, are divided into neighborhood units containing about thirty adults each. Father Spae says of them, "They feel that they are the Church, that our task is theirs, that we need them . . . Little churches dot the city; we seem to be everywhere." Beginning in 1948 with 150 Catholics, the parish grew by more than 100 converts a year owing to the work of these groups. The leaders of the groups meet once a month with the priest in a "pilot meeting" that is a preview of the one they will hold in their neighborhood. All members of other Catholic organizations also attend the neighborhood meeting held in a family home.

Some parishes report that they find it difficult to hold the interest of members at neighborhood meetings unless the priest also attends, but this takes too much time at small meetings which are not specifically for leader training. The necessity of the priest's presence would seem to show that he is in fact the real leader, in spite of there being lay leaders. Yet the civil associations of Japan are conducted entirely by the people themselves. Do their meetings perhaps respond better to the members' social and psychological needs? We speak of a meeting leader, but actually all must be leaders in the sense of their active participation. Hence the program must be such that they can participate and do so eagerly. The key lies in the pilot meeting itself. Do the leaders there show a real eagerness to take part, or do they enter into the discussion rather because they feel that is what the leader must do? Does the priest dominate every step of the pilot meeting or does he briefly present a theme and ask them to discuss from what aspects it would interest the members of their groups? Perhaps it should be presented differently? Note the ideas to which the leaders respond best; these are almost certainly the ones that will prove most interesting to the members as well.

The rather formal discussion methods used by specialized groups are clearly not suited to neighborhood meetings, since their membership is not selective. Keeping in mind that these are meetings of families, it seems that they might be built around the four elements which have been found essential for good family development because they respond to real needs. These elements are: religion, love, work, recreation. The meetings would not, of course, attempt to embody these elements fully, but would have in view to promote their practice in the neighborhood and its families. Community does not consist simply in the meetings, but in doing together the things that at once exemplify and promote community. The meetings would be conducted according to the "pedagogy of action," on the premise that Catholics already accept Christ's command to love their neighbor but need to learn "how" to love him in daily life. A person acquires this learning by discussing the practice of love towards others in "his" family, among "his" neighbors, at "his" work and recreation. By such learning he grows as a person, in self-awareness of his place in life, and this makes the meetings of deep interest to him.

Experience has shown that two common obstacles to member interest are: the monotony of always similar meetings and emphasis chiefly on individual action. While the same meeting plan may be kept, a variety of small projects for group action should be introduced. The rule for such group projects is that they do not require too much effort, at least in the beginning, that they will be completed within a relatively short time, and that they give every promise of being successful. The Communist practice is to promote a more difficult project on the wave of a previous very successful one. If a project fails, they immediately launch a short and simple one that is bound to succeed. Douglas Hyde says that people come to the Communist Party chiefly through getting involved in activity. They are attracted by its campaigns, that it is "doing something" to meet needs. This is the key to Communism's attraction for young people and would help get our youth interested in the neighborhood group. By being asked to take part in action they are made to feel valued, wanted. Catholic groups talk much about the Mystical Body and love of neighbor, but so often they fail to work out concrete group action that would make each one feel part of a going movement. Some projects should be undertaken by a number of groups at the same time.

A very good type of project for neighborhood groups are competitions of various kinds, for example, in some areas for the best-kept home and the one showing most improvement. To promote group morale the prize is given to the best among a number of groups. Prizes need be only ribbons or plaques with the citation and date. Children's competitions are always good, for example, an annual parish Catechism Day, preceded by local competitions. During Lent there could be a campaign of prayer, sacrifice and home meetings for instruction in preparation for Easter Communions. The practice of the works of mercy, also, can be much stimulated by the project method. For instance, before Christmas raise funds or make gifts to be laid before the Crib and given to needy families chosen by the group. The pilot meeting might sometimes vote a commendation for special efforts made by a group to care for a family with illness or other needs. Recreational activities between groups or units of several groups would be promoted. Neighborhood plays, even in the open air, are always popular and form an excellent youth activity. There should be an annual Parish Rally of all the neighborhood groups. Each project or campaign should be organized by its own committee. In group meetings a brief period would be given to discuss it, but the group itself never acts as a committee of the whole to plan a project or campaign.

The second method of promoting neighborhood community is by means of neighborhood committees rather than by home meetings of families. A very simple method is to choose leaders in each neighborhood, sometimes called "block captains and lieutenants," who visit the homes and meet with the priest once a month to make reports and plan action. The leaders should not be asked during those visits to collect money or ask information on marriages, which might make them unwelcome. The STRADA Movement in Bruges, Belgium, is a development of this method. A man or woman STRADA leader is chosen for each "street" or neighborhood of at most thirty families. In the case of two equally competent persons, the one who will receive most help from his family is selected. One very important responsibility of the leader is to encourage and coordinate action in his neighborhood by the various approved Catholic organizations each of which is responsible in its own field. In Bruges these are: League of the Sacred Heart, Confraternity of Christian Doctrine, Legion of Mary, St. Vincent de Paul, Lay Order of St. Paul working with fallen-aways and non-Catholics, a Communications and Public Opinion Organization. In areas where Catholic apostolic movements function well, the STRADA Movement avoids duplication in organization. Where they do not function well, it would help to develop and guide them.

Says Bishop De Smedt, "STRADA has the magnificent mission to give Christ a visible human form in its 'street.'" The parish priest appoints a STRADA head of the parish for a three-year term and with him chooses as parish committee two capable persons from among the leaders of each section embracing ten or so "streets." To the parish committee are added several specialists in various fields (such as housing, community development, education) and one top parish officer from each of the lay apostolate groups. The committee meets once a month before a Statue of the Sacred Heart enthroned between two candles. After a decade of the rosary and a Gospel reading by a layman, the priest presents briefly some point of doctrine and its relation to the family and neighborhood apostolate. The session continues with reports on action and plans for work. The two delegates on the committee from each section act as co-ordinators and meet at least once a month with the other STRADA leaders of their section. For the diocese, a small central secretariate of laymen aided by a diocesan chaplain is named by the bishop. The secretariate is advised by a diocesan council which meets several times a year. The council comprises, in addition to the members of the secretariate and diocesan chaplain, representatives of the parish clergy with parish representatives of STRADA and of the approved lay organizations taking part. In large dioceses, there may also be deanery councils working with representatives of the central secretariate. In a Santiago, Chile, parish of 70,000 people, I saw this plan being organized section by section with 400 leaders and lay apostles already at work within three years.

D. The Family as Apostolic Team

A priest friend wrote me a short time ago: "Every mature Christian family disposes very special missionary graces that no celibate has." First of all, the Christian family is a community, a human cell in the divine community of the Holy Trinity as extended to mankind through Christ. When this family community shares its love with others they experience an exchange of love that is not only modeled on that of the

Divine Persons for one another but truly shares in it by grace. The family apostolate, whether in its own neighborhood or going out to less fortunate neighborhoods, is irreplaceable. When we look at the roles of husband and wife in both family and society they are seen as definitely different, though complementing each other. Why not also in the apostolate? Our apostolic literature emphasizes the place of the husband as head of the family, but how much attention is given to his role as leader in the social community of families? We are told that the woman is heart of the home, but it is difficult to find mention of her as also the heart of the social community of families. Neither men nor women alone represent the human race. They must cooperate in all aspects of human development.

As we study the situation of the Church throughout the world, it is clear that not only the apostolate but the whole field of men's and women's approach to religion depends on their distinctive qualities and their conception of the life-work they have from God as men and as women. Why, for example, is it so often taken for granted that men are "less religious" than women? Do our spiritual writings and conferences take sufficiently into account that God has assigned men a certain role different from that of women and that therefore their approach to Him would understandably be different? The man is more directly involved in this dynamic world, for in God's plan he is its primary architect and builder. Yet how often is he told from the pulpit that he is God's delegate to build a good society? He is by nature aggressive in temperament, as befits one who must push himself mentally and physically to fulfill his role as the builder of social, economic and political structures. Woman is by nature more passive and patient, as befits the mother who must day by day nurture her child's unfolding. Her temperament is affective and her religious approach also. It often looks as if we consider that should be the man's approach as well.

Let us here take a brief glimpse of men around the world

in view of the Church's mission to them. In Korea I was told that seventy per cent of the adult converts are women. Can it be that the affective aspects of the Faith which appeal to women have been more stressed than that of man's social responsibility as co-creator? When a missionary comes to visit a district where interest has been shown in the Faith, the children gather with their mothers to see what he has brought. If he shows slides or films, the place is crowded and the dignified Korean men look in at the door, then walk away with the impression that this religion is for women and children. Why not a first conference for men by the catechist, without the priest present so as to avoid the crowd, to discuss what the Church teaches about man's place in God's plan?

The men of Japan are among the most active and enterprising in the world. Every man is ambitious to have a business of his own, even if only a cubbyhole shop tended by his wife while he works elsewhere. Japan has probably the highest percentage in the world of small enterprises employing less than ten men. How can these masculine qualities be tapped by the Church and given an outlet in the Christian life and apostolate? Perhaps we can find a suggestion in the fact that, like the men of Korea and China also, they have a strong sense of their position not only as heads of their families but also of the social community. Co-creators with God? It's an entirely new concept of their worth as men, gives a new idea of their religious nature.

The men of India seem less practical and aggressive in their social role, due probably to the strong mystic content of their religion. There is much emphasis on gaining personal merit by contemplation and certain kinds of good deeds. For example, a little rice may be put aside each day and given to beggars on certain festivals, yet it is difficult to interest men in the social conditions that produce beggars, which they ascribe to the inexorable turn of destiny. It is also considered meritorious to protect the lives of animals and even insects. The Indian farmer will not accept the use of insecticides and the protection of cattle as sacred results in great herds that deprive humans of food. Most Indian states permit the slaughter of beef only at ages running from 8 to 25 years. It is almost impossible to raise winter crops even where irrigation water is available because traditionally the cattle are allowed to roam about from after the autumn harvest until just before spring planting. The men of India are little concerned about having life well organized, for they look on it as a voyage on which one should not carry much baggage. They will put far more energy into an evening's discussion about a certain "holy man" than into plans for bettering the condition of those who suffer social evils. It would appear that Christian social action should be presented in India specifically as an expression of Christian holiness.

In Africa many men are polygamists, with each wife and her children having a separate hut in the one compound. The men and women in a family have clearly differentiated work and responsibilities, and during his early years the boy shares mostly in those of his mother. He sees his father chiefly as lord and master of all in the compound rather than as partner with his mother. He becomes early aware of competition among the wives as the husband's favorite. Unconsciously he absorbs the feminine outlook on life and is apparently little prepared for his social role outside this pattern. Most African young men seek to demonstrate their masculinity in chiefly a sexual way. They appear to come relatively late in life to a man's fuller sense of social responsibility. They probably acquire it rather by experience from association with other adults, having lacked its roots from earlier sharing the life of their father. It seemed to me that men in Africa need very much to take part in the neighborhood apostolate, with emphasis on social responsibility and on their role as family educators of their sons. The Cursillos would be of great assistance here to lay a foundation.

In Latin America I became convinced that the men's wholesale desertion of religious practice was related to the question of proper formation in their masculine role as Catholics. The very men who do not go to Mass will turn out to put a new roof on the church! It would appear that the message which should be preached to the men up and down Latin America is that they are God's co-creators to build a new world, in the family and in society. The early training of the Latin American boy is almost entirely in the hands of his mother, which in religion is an affective and devotional type. As he grows to manhood this no longer satisfies him, but not having experience of any other approach, he comes to look on religion as for women and children. The Cursillos give great promise in this matter, but as yet they have reached relatively few.

The Latin American man of the great masses remembers his home life as one with the father dominating the mother rather than cherishing her. Among the masses, 85 per cent baptized, no more than 50 per cent of the households represent stable unions and less than 30 per cent are valid marriages. The boy is thus usually entirely dependent on his mother. Lacking the guidance of a father as to a man's responsibility, he tends to grow up strongly individualistic. If a committee is formed, everyone thinks he should be chairman. A political party is usually a collection of the leader's personal followers; if he dies or loses, it falls apart. In Cuba, men who should be natural allies against Fidel Castro cannot cooperate because it would mean one having a higher place than the other. The Cursillos seem to offer the best solution also of this problem because they bring men together under the higher leadership of Christ. The strong strain of hero-worship in the Latin American operates here.

The apostolic task of the Christian family, therefore, is to show mankind how men and women should carry out their respective roles both in the family itself and in all areas of human life. The Christian head of a family must be a good husband and father, but he has also a special social task to promote in the world of business and politics God's plan that men build a good social structure where all families may live and grow as they were meant to do. The Christian homemaker must be a good wife and mother, but she must also bear witness in the world of families and in all that concerns families how God destined woman as the heart of humanity to form it according to the divine model of love. That is still the vocation of the woman who works in the marketplace, for, as Pope Pius XII tells us, "Every woman is born to be a mother." This refers to spiritual and social motherhood and not physical alone. Woman's approach to all spiritual and social problems should be dictated by a mother's outlook.

Husband and wife have, therefore, their own specific apostolic roles in the world, but directed towards a common goal and completing each other in the family team. It should be an apostolic family, including the children, so that the apostolate will be passed on as a family tradition. This kind of family apostolate needs to be developed in all the mission countries to help their people meet the great new spiritual and social challenges of our modern age. But families of the homeland need it no less, because they also must meet many new situations brought about by social change. One of the most serious arises from the fact that husband and wife are nowadays so little together as a team in the life of the family itself. The man works all day away from home and he may easily conceive his role as simply to provide a living for his family. The care of the family during the day devolves entirely on the mother, with the result that the father may tend to leave that to her even when he is at home. As an apostolic team concerned with human needs, however, they are much more likely to become aware that the family itself should be the first and basic team in both Church and Society.

15. THE LAY APOSTOLATE IN THE MARKETPLACE

Some students of the lay apostolate believe that there has been a tendency to one-sided emphasis on the lay mission among persons by the diffusion of ideas. They say that too little is being done among communities by the concrete testimony of action. In support of this position they point to the progressive secularization of modern social institutions in spite of many individual conversions to the Faith. Action in the community is the chief way by which man demonstrates the place of God in the world.

What exactly are social institutions? They are the ways in which people customarily carry on their many inter-relationships in the community and hence cover a range as wide as the innumerable activities of mankind. Some examples of more important social institutions are: marriage and family, education, social customs, business methods, management, labor, government, the law, religion. Each social institution has an accepted way of procedure for a certain activity or group of activities and a people's culture pattern is constituted by the intricate, unbroken web of their social institutions. We are faced today with the fact that social institutions are becoming progressively more secularized, more and more separated from a sense of relationship to the Creator. Higher institutions of learning in the United States which were once centers of strong Christian influence are now dominated by secularism. The world picture of our government is a secular one in spite of its having been founded on the concept that human rights are inalienable only because they come from God. Most newly independent countries adopt completely secular constitutions.

The kind of social change occurring today tends to modify our social institutions with great rapidity. As we know, human activities were formerly carried on chiefly within the local community, which gave solidarity and unity to the pattern of social institutions. Today, particularly in cities, people's place of residence, of work, leisure, education, are commonly separated and specialized. Where human life was once lived largely in a single "geographic dimension," it is now carried on in those different "functional dimensions," with each having its perhaps disparate influence on the personality and outlook of the individual.

Another aspect of city life which exerts a strong action on social institutions is its high degree of socialization, in the sense of man's increasing dependence on others. Man in the city not only lives in several human areas, but these become more and more mutually interdependent: government, commerce, industry, education, communications. This leads men to act increasingly as a mass, with consequent impoverishment of personal values. Hence the urgent need of penetrating today's social institutions with the spirit of Christ and His respect for the person.

A. My Apostolate Where I Am

It is quite clear that the Church, the society of the Mystical Body, has a mission to transform human society. She is present in human society, however, chiefly in her members. The common "functional dimension" or area of life which the Catholic shares with his fellow man at any moment of the day serves as a natural and easy point of contact. The key is to develop such contacts in a Christian way. Father Keller of the Christophers keeps emphasizing that the opportunities are all around us. In his book, *You Can Change the World,* he tells of an elderly woman who made her living sweeping in a department store after hours. She decided to work where she could be an apostle and changed to a similar job in the dormitory of a large women's college. She does not say much, but shows loving solicitude for the girls and few are not touched when she says to one of them, "I suppose a lot of folks will tell you there is no God, but I say there is! And He loves you—and I pray to Him every day for you at Mass."

In Christ to the World (1962, No. 3), Archbishop Guerry of Cambrai, France, describes the work of an organization known as Workers' Catholic Action. He states that it carries out the social apostolate first of all by its existence in the midst of the working classes, making Christ present in the working environment instead of leaving the field to Marx. It dispels the prejudice so long current there that one cannot be at the same time a real Christian and a real militant of the workers. Furthermore, Workers' Catholic Action acquaints all workers with the thought, the doctrine, the position of the Church with regard to economic and working life. Having thus penetrated the workers' environment, Workers' Catholic Action fulfills its apostolic mission by getting the majority of workers to perform acts of service, devotion and mutual assistance for their brother workers. By this means the whole workers' milieu is gradually freed from selfishness and led to the discovery of love and other Gospel virtues. Members of the working class thus participate in their own improvement as human beings and their own progress towards God.

What Archbishop Guerry says of Workers' Catholic Action makes clear that society and its institutions are transformed chiefly by groups or movements which themselves have a social nature. This gives them an "affinity" with social institutions. The single apostle in any area of human activity should seek to form around him a Christian "cell" or team, even if informal, because it has a social character as well as promise of growth and permanence that the individual lacks. It provides a much stronger focal point of welcome and acceptance to others than can an individual. The cell is better able than the individual to give others in this welcome a sense of personal value in a social setting that is so lacking today. The cell provides more joy in work by making it the occasion for human relations of value. In this way people are helped to overcome the selfish boredom that so devitalizes modern society and come to see that work itself has essential human values which are in turn related to still higher values. We have seen how Workers' Catholic Action demonstrates this.

In his address to the 1957 World Congress for the Lay Apostolate held at Rome, Pope Pius XII indicated some of today's great challenges to the Catholic laity in the social mission of the Church. "Since the climate of work by contact," he said, "is fatal to young men, the Catholic 'cell' must intervene in workshops, as well as on trains, buses, in the families and districts . . . Thus a Catholic foreman will be the first to take care of the new arrivals, help them find decent lodgings, establish desirable friendships, contact the local church life, and assist them in adapting easily to their new position in life." The same Pontiff had the year before written to the Catholic Day gathering of Germany: "You are committed to an important task, that of giving to the world of industry a Christian form and structure . . . To stamp it with the imprint of Christ." Only the Catholic masses who participate in the many different areas of modern life are in contact with the world's masses and "speak their language." Only they have the opportunity and the number to accomplish what the Holy Father directs.

Speaking to the same Lay Apostolate Congress in Rome about Latin America, the Pope noted that its population, ". . . from 92 millions in 1920 had more than doubled and there were hardly 35,000 priests instead of the 150,000 which is figured as the bare minimum necessary . . . Efforts must first of all be made, therefore, for the systematic formation of lay apostles who must be put to work in the giant parishes of 50,000 to

100,000 faithful, at least so long as there is a shortage of priests. Then one must introduce into the ranks of teachers, extending from elementary education to the university level, teachers and educators who are exemplary Catholic men and women. Thirdly, the lay apostolate must be introduced into the economic, social and political life . . . There is need for a thorough social formation and the action of a Catholic workers' elite which would patiently and persistently draw the workers' organizations away from the influence of Marxism."

Turning to Asia and Africa, the Holy Father said, "With the exception of the Philippines, among the peoples of Asia—and this also applies to the greater part of Africa—Catholics are in the minority. Therefore they should distinguish themselves all the more by the example they give! They should take more interest in public, economic, social and political life . . . but they must also enter public life after adequate preparation. The Catholic social doctrine is not sufficiently known in Asia. And the European and American universities should willingly help the Christians of Asia and Africa who wish to prepare themselves for public offices. One must train competent teachers to work in the schools of every grade . . . For Our part We would wish to see those people teaching religion give more care not to separate doctrine from life itself . . . In Africa, particularly, We witness with joy and gratitude the extraordinary dynamism of the young Catholic generations in the cultural, social and political fields. They should therefore cooperate with the Christian inspired trade union movements . . . and establish cooperatives of sale and consumption. They should take part in national representation and communal affairs; the Church not only inspires piety, but also answers all the questions of life" *(Apostolic Perspectives*, Fall-Winter, 1957).

Again and again I have met apostolic groups that were zealous in making contacts, on trains, buses, at work. But often they found the effort disappointing, chiefly because people tend to put up their guard against a direct approach. One way for groups to make contacts without this obstacle is to help people take advantage of the many public services which can aid them in difficulties. Those who have the greatest need often do not know how to apply or fear they would be disappointed. A group of boys at a Catholic college in England who were studying Catholic social doctrine began to visit the surrounding area, meeting the people and discussing their problems. They found that one village was being regularly flooded by a small river nearby because the stream had become blocked over the years. The boys went to the local officials who sent them to the county authority and were passed on from one to the other. Finally they discovered that the body ultimately responsible was in London, 110 miles away. The deputation they sent there obtained the solution of the flooding problem as well as assurance that the stream would be kept clear in the future. This kind of contact gains good will and opens the way to get people helping one another, "Come, let us do something good for God."

Care must be taken never to get absorbed in social action to the neglect of the person in his relationship to God. The Workers' Catholic Action described by Archbishop Guerry was not content to be merely present among the workers or even to explain the Church's social teaching. It undertook action which led the workers to discover mutual love and other Gospel virtues. In a *New York Times* article (December 5, 1961), the question was asked: "Why do so few Negro families buy homes in suburbs where by now public opinion, in these northern communities, is on their side? The climate has been altered in the last decade by the many fair-housing groups, the distribution of open-occupancy pledges, wholesale mailing of literature, public meetings, private persuasion, and the listing of homes available to Negroes." The answer is found in the case where a Negro family did move into a community where all those steps had been taken, but the most necessary step was not taken, to welcome them. "We've been living as the only Negro family on this suburban street for two years now, and no one ever speaks to us when we go out in the morning or come home at night." An apostolate of social structures which does not lead to closer relationships as persons must be considered a failure.

B. The Citizenship and Labor Areas

"Democracy is not simply one man, one vote," declared over and over again Msgr. Coady of Antigonish Co-ops fame, "but a social system in which the people share consciously in the social processes." Our present system of government has come, he said, to be one in which the people go to the polls for a few moments at certain intervals to vote for representatives who have all responsibility for managing the public business. As our social structure grows more and more complicated and the people are further removed from contact with their representatives, several serious questions arise. One is whether we can continue to carry the burden of rocketing costs that result from the constantly growing magnitude of government. Another problem is whether there is not danger of democracy becoming the victim of planning by real or fancied experts as they gather constantly more power into their hands. A third question is whether growing dependence on the day to day decisions of others at every level is not a grave threat to our human values as free and responsible citizens.

This last question involves the most fundamental problem of all, the ordinary citizen's self-image of his own value in society as a person—or as a ward of the government. Father Houtart, a Belgian sociologist, has pointed out what vast spiritual and moral decay takes place in a large urban center when it becomes simply an "agglomeration of individuals" who no longer take part in "a community of their measure." Msgr. Coady, not long before his death, told me his idea of how to provide that participation "in the social processes" so essential both to man's well-being and his development. "Every man," he said, "needs a vision, a consciousness of destiny, of being worth something, to make him a dedicated man. The masses react to a vision; that was the secret of success for Hitler, the Communists. You have to sell the common man a vision, a big picture of the future, but then you have to break it down to something small, local, practical, which he can tackle himself. Each man can participate in the social process on the level of his daily life. Social services are the lazy way out and not the ideal democratic solution. A truly democratic people should kick off the service with all their bureaucracy and do the job themselves."

"We must go back to the idea," continued Msgr. Coady, "that the development of the people will primarily be by building up their own democratic institutions. Now the participation of the people in civic life, in the social processes, must not be divorced from the economic, because it is the economic that touches man most closely. His basic desire is to provide for his family. Profit-sharing, industrial councils, do not give the real personal participation in economic responsibility that men need for their development. Men as workers, men as consumers, must build up at least some economic institutions of their own. The economic interest is basic and essential in adult education. It is responsibility in his own economic institutions that makes the average man think, stimulates his initiative and creative ability. Hence it provides a practical basis for beginning his social, cultural and spiritual adult education. It also provides a necessary goal for youth education. To give a man responsibility on the level of his economic position will help to offset the monotony of the machine and solve the problem of leisure resulting from machines."

Msgr. Coady devoted his life to promoting economic cooperatives as a means to make the common man "feel" himself a real part of dynamic society. In preceding chapters we have seen some of the immense human problems that arise when men feel like inanimate cogs in a machine, a subhuman force used for gain. It is the chief cause of social and moral decay in a society or part of a society. Delinquency, for example, begins in the society of the family from lack of a sense of belonging, being valued. Today's alarming increase in the crime rate indicates the degree to which among certain classes the sense of responsible sharing in "a community of their measure" has been lost. Many young people today, lacking experience of organic community in our society from the family onwards, feel themselves adrift on a sea of humanity with no purpose except to follow the impulse of the moment without regard to anyone else. We recall here the *anomie* which may cause youth to engage in purposeless or even destructive activities. Father Rosier pointed out how the depersonalized structure of modern work causes the worker to seek compensation in boasting and in explosions of revolt, or in alcohol and the satisfaction of the passions. Pius XII stated; "The climate of work by contract is fatal to young men."

These brief considerations indicate something of the magnitude and urgency of the task that faces today's Christian Social Apostolate. The 'welfare state' is not the answer. It alleviates symptoms temporarily, but deprives the citizen of participation in social responsibility at his level. It runs counter to the clear principle of social philosophy enunciated by Pope Pius XI in *Quadragesimo Anno,* that of subsidiary function by which the government should help the people undertake social responsibility at their own level. Indeed, unless we apply that principle to build an organic society composed of mutually related and supporting human communities, we are in danger of coming to live in something not far different from a patron-peon society. The welfare state produces a frightening increase of the "get something for nothing" mentality. Reports from England deplore the loss of incentive among young workers. "Why work?" they say. "Unemployment and health benefits take care of all our needs." It becomes clear that one of the primary duties of government is to promote such personal participation in the social processes at people's own level that they will develop a proud sense of social responsibility as men. If that sense is lost among a sufficient number, no police force can make our society safe from criminals of all kinds. We can see that already happening in certain areas of our cities.

The Holy Father has said frequently that it is necessary to reform social institutions, because it is they that largely control the attitudes and behavior of people in society. In modern urban America that means to reform the institutions, including government, which allow or even abet, sub-standard housing, juvenile delinquency, racial discrimination. Those institutions must be reformed which are responsible for citizens having little opportunity to share in a meaningful way in social and economic processes, are responsible for loss of hope and sense of personal value among the under-privileged. In its work of reforming social institutions, the method of the social apostolate will always be to set up ways in which people can engage in positive action and develop positive attitudes that will crowd out negative attitudes and negative action. It is the method par excellence of helping the under-privileged everywhere in the world. Here is a challenge to the increasing number of educated Catholics. An ordinary city parish, for example, often counts several hundred college graduates in its congregation. If they organized even ten such apostolic programs for education and development of the under-privileged by participation, what a social transformation it would produce.

Catholic citizens trained in sound social principles are much needed in the key areas of our society. One of these areas is the *foreign service* of the United States, where Catholics should be witnesses to the Church's viewpoint. Few can attend a school of foreign service, but wide-awake Catholics can accomplish much good in secretarial and similar positions. The United States Information Agency and our foreign aid programs also offer Catholics an excellent opportunity for social action. Students, research people and professors should take more advantage of the Fulbright program for study abroad. Another area in which Catholic principles are not sufficiently influential is the *political field* of local, state and national government. Too often the Church is represented in politics by the wrong kind of Catholics. Organizations like the League of Women voters also need the ideas that trained Catholic women can bring them. In one American city a Christian Family Movement group found that the City Council often held merely token meetings to satisfy the law. Then the wives of the group began attending meetings and city government showed immediate improvement.

The area of *organized labor* has particularly numerous and important apostolic possibilities for Catholic graduates. It is the number one target for Communist penetration. There is great need of labor lawyers, labor economists and labor specialists who are imbued with true social principles and deep respect for the person. Catholic workers themselves can contribute much by taking part in "labor schools" or forming ACTU (Association of Catholic Trade Unionists) type groups within the local labor movement. One aspect of labor that needs special attention is participation by the workers in the social processes. Our labor unions have so far tended to concentrate chiefly on increased wages and similar benefits with less attention to the worker's growth as a man. Let us not forget Msgr. Coady's stress on man's need of sharing in economic institutions such as cooperative societies suitable to their condition. There is a vast field for Catholics with special skills to promote these and to help train organizers, managers and accountants for them. Why should not workers live in cooperative housing, perhaps with some government help in long-term financing, rather than remain always tenants? Msgr. Coady would call government housing as a solution "the lazy way out."

C. Education and Communications Areas

There is a tendency among Catholics to have little interest in the area of public education because they have their own schools. This is completely unrealistic. The great majority of our fellow citizens, all God's children, are being formed there, as well as half the Catholic children of elementary age and a still larger proportion of those at the high school level. We pay taxes to support the government schools and have a responsibility as citizens to play our part in seeing that they do the best possible job. In St. Louis, Missouri, a Christian Family Movement group discussed this question and urged one of the men to seek election to the City Education Board, known to be graft-ridden. He won the post and obtained evidence that sent the Board's purchasing agent to prison. The President of the Board and another member resigned as a result of the disclosures. The whole city school system benefited from one social action taken by that group of Catholic parents.

An exceedingly serious problem is the concerted effort being carried on to make the schools centers of subversive attacks on human freedom. Children readily believe what they are told by teachers or read in textbooks. Father Keller, in *All God's Children,* tells how Communist-inspired teachers in a large city used to refer to the P.T.A. as the "paper and towels committee." The teachers got the parents to be concerned with incidentals while they were busy injecting subversive ideas into the children's minds. It is not enough merely to be "against" subversive groups. Catholics must work to counteract the ideas of Karl Marx which are being zealously promoted night and day. He said, "The democratic concept of man is false, because it is Christian. The democratic concept holds that . . . each man is a sovereign being. This is the illusion, dream, and postulate of Christianity" *(Das Kapital).* Father Keller urges that it is the responsibility of Catholic parents' groups to find out what is being taught in the schools of their area. We should encourage as many persons as possible to enter the teaching career and to strive as hard to preserve in the field of education the basic principle that our rights are God-given as others are working to destroy it.

Even more harm is being done, however, by teachers who are secularists and materialists than by outright Communists. Most products of teachers' colleges during the last 30 years have been influenced by the ideas of John Dewey, who did much to improve educational methods, but held a secularist philosophy. In the May-June 1933 issue of the *New Humanist* occurs this statement signed by him and others: "We regard the universe as self-existing and not created . . . We assert that modern science makes unacceptable any supernatural or cosmic guarantee of human values." Father Keller tells of a "modern" professor in a large Eastern university who told his class, "There is no power in democracy—bar none—greater than the majority." A student challenged him that then such evils as the murder of six million Jews by the Nazis would be right, but he replied that it had not been decided "by the democratic process." The student pointed out that, unless we believe people have their rights from a higher power, how is the democratic process to be guaranteed? The majority could be simply a mob stirred up by a demagogue like Hitler. As the class murmured agreement, the professor changed the subject.

Once Father Keller pointed out to a young man how those who wrote our Declaration of Independence made it clear that every man, even the most forgotten, gets certain rights from his Creator and not from the state. The only purpose of the state is to protect and promote the rights of all. The young man answered: "Here I am finishing college and no one ever told me that!" Father Keller found that school instruction on the Declaration of Independence is required in only eight states—California, Illinois, Minnesota, New Jersey, New Mexico, Pennsylvania, Virginia and Wisconsin. He states that every American citizen has the right and obligation to demand explicit teaching in all schools on this subject so fundamental for the preservation of our freedom. He suggests: "Persuade every organization that you know (labor unions, veterans' groups, fraternal organizations, women's clubs, parent-teacher associations, youth movements, etc.) to concentrate on having the Declaration of Independence, the Constitution and the Bill of Rights taught in the schools so as to infuse their living spirit into every segment of private and public life in America."

One very serious educational problem which Catholics should lead in solving is the high rate of chronic unemployment among the insufficiently educated. Catholics can promote practical action by the community, by industry and government. They can teach classes for dropouts and deprived youngsters. A third of the unemployed cannot read a want ad or look up a name in the telephone directory. They can be taught to read from a newspaper, perhaps the sports' page, arithmetic in terms of personal buying, the principles of freedom from the story of our country. The tutor of a group acts as a "resource person" to stimulate their self-activity and their mutual sharing as persons, for they need more than simple vocational preparation. The self-image of defeatism ground into them since infancy must be replaced by a sense of their own value through the respect shown them by the tutor and the group. If a few of them are activated to be apostles among their own for a better life it can set off a chain-reaction. Then delinquency, dope-pushing, promiscuity will be crowded out by new positive values. No one can do those things for them or make them good citizens, but they themselves will act if we help them acquire a belief in themselves.

Another area in which Communists are extremely active is that of the communications media which influence public opinion. One trick is to offer themselves as book reviewers so they can promote the works of authors who follow the Communist line. They also seek key positions as writers, directors and reviewers in the cinema industry. A field which is crying for Catholics is that of newspaper columnist. A good columnist may be syndicated countrywide and has an unusual opportunity to speak of true democracy and freedom in his comments on the daily scene. Perhaps in no area are the American people more subject to being misled than in reporting news from abroad. We were told, for example, that the Chinese Communists were "agrarian reformers," that Fidel Castro in Cuba was worthy of our support, that Buddhist political agitators in South Vietnam were suffering a religious persecution. Of course, Catholic journalists and free-lance writers who reported the real "news behind the news" would doubtless find the going hard, but the apostolate of Christ is not easy anywhere.

D. Training for the Social Apostolate

It is quite obvious that the unrelated efforts up to now of a few individuals and groups will not go far in covering this vast field of the modern social apostolate. Nor can the laity be expected to take large-scale concerted action outside the machinery of the Church organization. The Communists have a deep envy for the Church's system of dioceses and parishes so admirably suited for promoting ideas and action. The first impulse to the social apostolate should be setting up a survey committee to gather information on needs in various social areas. There might be sub-committees to secure data on government, business, labor, education, communications, cooperatives, neighborhoods and the help of experts would be sought. The results of the survey would be arranged according to the various social areas and their problems, with some suggestions as to action that could be taken by individuals or organizations. The diocese and parish federations of the lay apostolate would then have all the essential elements for promoting a comprehensive and successful program. More fortunate parishes should assist those with greater needs.

An important item in local planning is to make a list of the people that count in the various areas, including religious leaders, newspaper editors, radio directors, cinema managers and natural neighborhood leaders. Then sort them out into categories according to their attitude towards Catholic ideas, as friends, opponents, neutrals. Consider how to make friends of the neutrals by friendly contacts, perhaps asking them to take part in some effort for the common good of all. Endeavor also to win the good will of those who oppose us, or at least render their opinions neutral. There are said to be few people in the world whose attitudes cannot be changed by appropriate and persevering effort, at least, in their external expression. One may begin, for example, by showing a real interest in the ideas of even those opposed to us, for everyone has hold of some values of truth. Do not, on the other hand, take the friendly persons for granted. If people do us a favor, if newspapers or radio give good publicity to Catholic matters, we should get a number of people to express appreciation. One Catholic group that had free radio time on the local station failed to say "thank you" and found itself cut off when the schedule was changed.

For general civic affairs there should be a community council composed of public-spirited people from the various walks of life. The community council would represent a number of neighborhood councils, these composed in turn of block clubs whose officers form their neighborhood council committee. The need of strong community councils in the modern city is constantly being demonstrated by the progressive decay of order and morality in one neighborhood after another because singly they cannot make their voices heard by the police and the city government. The community council is also needed in various "urban renewal" plans to represent the people in such matters as re-location, small businesses, rent levels. Planning must be for people first, for profits and political prestige second. In one large Eastern city, a civic committee to draw up a new zoning ordinance that involved great changes consisted only of politicians and financial interests, with not one representative of the common public or one authority on social planning. When officials in some cities do hold public hearings they often turn out to be so arranged that all real discussion is neatly dodged. They bring to mind the Supreme Soviets' hand-clapping approval of five-year plans already decided.

At the parish level, why should there not be in each of the world's 200,000 parishes a social guild to train Catholic leaders for the social apostolate? We must first of all abandon any conception that only those with a certain level of schooling are capable of being trained. In East Africa I saw a social guild in a country parish where the school system did not go beyond the second primary grade. The guild included several teachers, two catechists and two Legion of Mary members who could not read. There are natural leaders at every social level, and the purpose of the guild is to discover and activate them as social apostles at their own level. No matter how poor or ignorant our people may appear to be, we must help them fulfill better the responsibilities of their own small world and at the same time show them wider horizons. The very people who are ignorant, who suffer most from bad social and economic conditions, are those who turn towards Communism precisely because it gives expression to their needs and makes them aware that their situation can be improved.

When Pope Pius XI declared, "This is the age of the common man," he had in view the apostolate of the common man to other common men. Only by including the common man can apostles be sufficiently multiplied. The chief thing the social guild tries to do is instill in ordinary people a sense of social responsibility as Catholics. It would be a grave mistake to present Catholic social action as a sort of neutral program with little if any relationship to God as the author of human society. The training method should be eminently concrete, for the common man's view of the factors that make up human life, including religious factors, is eminently concrete. If, for example, the social guild discussions take up abstract religious concepts as motives for the social apostolate, few parishioners will take part. But their interest is aroused and held if religion is presented from the viewpoint of its relation to the personal and social problems that arise in the concrete situations of daily life.

An excellent point at which to begin the social guild formation is with Christian family life, the essential basis not only for family happiness but also for the development of Church and Society. St. Augustine summarized society as—home, city and world. This practical approach will interest the most ignorant and at the same time relate the social apostolate directly to their own experience. Some aspects of family life that might be discussed are: the father's part as head of the family, harmony in the home, proper training of children, family prayer, health and home management, responsibility to neighbors and in the community, cooperation of families for the good of all and many other topics in an ascending scale. Eventually the group will bring up obstacles to good family life in their own environment. Discussion on such problems is much more effective if introduced by the members, an indication that they are beginning to apply the lessons already learned.

The moderator will often find it useful with beginners in the social guild to include in his brief opening presentation of a subject two or three points as topics for discussion, perhaps written on a blackboard in question form. The conclusions of the group should answer these questions. If someone raises another subject, a brief discussion on it is permitted but then the group is brought back to the topic at hand with some such statement as: "This is a very interesting question that needs more time for discussion." Of course, everyone is encouraged to bring up matters of his own experience connected with the subject at hand, for it is thus that members relate it to their own lives. They acquire from the discussions a better understanding than their neighbors have of certain social problems and an easier facility to speak about them. This will make them regarded as leaders so that others turn to them not only for information but also for guidance. Those regarded as leaders in one line tend to be followed in others as well.

At the beginning of each meeting there should be a brief Gospel discussion in relation to life in the family and in society. There is nothing more valuable for Catholics than to discover the social meaning of the Gospels and draw appropriate lessons for social action based on religion. So many have a tendency to think of our relations to Christ and of religious activity in terms of interior action by the individual. For example, to increase family or neighborhood unity many will at first suggest prayer, probably individual, rarely expressions of thoughtfulness or kind words and deeds. Chapters 5, 6, 7 and 25 of St. Matthew should be gradually committed to memory, also Chapters 13, 14, 15, 16, and 17 of St. John. Even those unable to read can do it by repeating a phrase or verse at a time after someone else. People make far more effective use of Gospel passages they know by heart.

The first manual of Catholic social doctrine should be the encyclical, *Mater et Magistra,* of Pope John XXIII. A good way to use it is to propose concrete situations, actual or hypothetical, then discuss how the Pope's teaching should apply. For example, the worker has a right to a just wage. This wage is just when it equals the worker's creative contribution to the thing produced or the work accomplished. But he cannot always be given that much, because a part of what is due him may have to be used for maintenance and modernization of the enterprise. The answer is found in paragraphs 75 and 77 of the encyclical. The portion of the worker's labor that has been reinvested in the plant should be credited to him in the form of shares in the company which has increased in value. Thus the principle of a just wage is concretized in a general way. It does not establish what would be just wages for the worker in a particular plant, in a particular country at this particular moment. That must be worked out, the Holy Father states in paragraph 71, according to the norms of social equity as well as social justice. This encyclical is distinctive in its practical approach to social problems. They must be considered on three levels—of unchangeable principles, concrete general norms, individual application.

Every guild meeting should decide on some kind of field work for the members to carry out, usually in teams of two. This may sometimes be to gather information on a certain subject, sometimes social action. The work need not always arise directly from the discussion of the meeting but may be part of a continuing program. In the early stages, social action should relate directly to the good of families: help in sickness or other needs, whitewash houses, provide safe water, give religious or literacy instruction, combat mosquitoes, arrange for inoculation against polio or other disease, make latrines. As the group develops, non-members may also be invited to assist with various forms of voluntary community action that will suggest themselves. An important action will be to get young people cooperating, make them feel useful and needed by others, appreciated by adults. Young people can teach children, direct their recreation, act as volunteer helpers for sick mothers, the aged and hospital patients, organize athletic activities.

The parish social guild might have a senior group under the direct guidance of the priest. They would act as 'tutors' in junior groups or adult discussion groups. They could give talks in schools and elsewhere on Catholic social teachings, but always based on the family as the key social unit. I am very doubtful about the real value of Catholic social training which fails to put its students through an apprenticeship in the social apostolate as related to the family. One of the best ways for the social guild to present an idea before a public gathering is by the method of "role-playing" in the form of a short skit which features both "pro" and "con." Young people do especially well at this. From time to time the guild would invite men to address them who hold responsible positions in government, education, business, agriculture, nutrition, sanitation, community development, credit unions and cooperatives. They would be careful not to attack the views presented but the talks would be discussed at subsequent guild meetings as to the principles involved and how well the speaker applied them. This gives members valuable formation in picking out the key points of talks and evaluating the statements made by those in positions of public responsibility.

16. ALL THESE ARE MY OWN BROTHERS

Today, for the first time in history, the forces opposing Christ form a relentless, worldwide community, which has a highly developed program to dominate the earth and concentrates all its resources to that purpose. This community, in spite of its ruthless methods, finds support in the minds and hearts of the millions who feel cheated of their right to a more human life. So long as we seem by our indifference to deny this right, no political or military efforts we make can stem that community's advance.

Dom Bede Griffiths, O.S.B., in the *Catholic Herald* (Calcutta, March 28, 1958), explained the 1957 election of a communist government in the strongly Catholic state of Kerala, South India. Actually, the Communists were before long ousted by the central Indian government, but only because they had killed a number of people protesting the take-over of their schools. Dom Griffiths wrote, "There are many reasons for the rise of Communism here, but one of the principal is this: there is a large group, said by some to be nearly one-third of the whole population, which has been for centuries an 'outcast' community. They were apparently not originally Hindus and were regarded as 'untouchables.' They had little or no religion, lived in extreme poverty, did all the heaviest and most menial work, and were despised by both Christians and Hindus . . . Can anyone be surprised that they went over to the Communists in a body and that they identify the Church with the rich and powerful who have been their oppressors?"

Father Griffiths could have added that a generation ago this whole group, the Ezhavas, expressed a desire to embrace the Church, but nothing was done.

"How un-christian of the Kerala Catholics," we may exclaim, but it is an excellent example of how old attitudes tend to endure unless proper emphasis be laid on social as well as individual religious duties. We in the West have many such family skeletons. Father Rosier found that the working classes of Europe gave up religion and turned to Communism because they identified the Church with the "practicing" Catholic capitalists who exploited them as an impersonal "work force" to be used for gain. The United States, proud "home of democracy," presents to the world a shameful spectacle of race prejudice which treats 20 million Negro and Mexican fellow citizens as inferiors, with little or no reaction against it from a large proportion of Catholics. How many comfortable middle-class American Catholics are giving a part of their time to remedy the frustration and denigration of the person suffered by some twenty per cent of our fellow citizens who need those who "care" to help them rise from the ranks of the underprivileged?

A. Man's Search for God's Justice

A long-time student of today's new world has been Father Louis Lebret, O.P., a trained sociologist and economist who directs the study center, *Economics and Humanism,* in Lyons, France. At a symposium in Rome some years ago he gave a paper, "Modern Man's Search for God," which we quote from *Apostolic Perspectives* (Spring, 1958). "In former ages," said Father Lebret, "man's needs were satiable. He who had what was necessary to eat, to clothe and house himself was satisfied and could then give attention to his appetite for spiritual values. In a technological age the demands of comfort can never be satisfied. There is an 'always more' to be acquired.

The insatiability of expanding needs has become a major characteristic of contemporary society.

"Yet large sectors of the population in certain well developed countries and the immense majority of the population in underdeveloped countries live in misery . . . As a result of education, these masses evolve quickly from passivity to reactivity, and from reactivity to aggressiveness. It is easy in such a disturbed evolution to yield to an ideology of revolt and of liberation from misery by collectivism.

"In face of the communist ideology, the common western ideology offers little more than an ideal of comfort in which the privileged classes and those of some financial means will be the only ones to benefit. The spiritual erosion of western civilization pervaded with practical materialism leaves the field open to dogmatic materialism. A further misfortune is that western civilization contaminates the countries it tries to influence . . . There is in effect a contradiction between the Christian ideal and the eroticism of the western films, between the ideal of satisfaction by obtaining what is necessary and the level of pleasure that is projected upon the screen.

"In many countries the elite, and sometimes those who call themselves Christians . . . are concerned primarily with safeguarding their privileges. In their insensitivity to the misery of their brothers, they fall under the energetic admonitions of the Fathers of the Church to the greedy. By using land in a ridiculous way . . . the increase of agricultural products does not keep pace with population growth. The private capital of underdeveloped countries, when it is not invested abroad, is largely employed in speculative investments in real estate . . . Capital, instead of being invested in the interests of a balanced economy, is deployed only in those areas of greatest profit and security.

"In general, the capital of rich countries is invested in poorer countries only in very small quantities. Rich countries continue to exploit the resources of the world greedily and to increase their wealth and their comfort without concern for the harmonized and integral development of the countries where they set up their business. Instead of furnishing multilateral financial and technical assistance to underdeveloped countries, they limit themselves to a bilateral form of assistance which soon provokes hatred.

"And while we can observe a leveling of class differences in the developed countries, the same is not true of the underdeveloped countries. The average salary difference per person, in the poorer countries as compared with the richer countries, is widening at a frightening rate. Now estimated at a 1 to 40 ratio, it will be more than 1 to 100 at the end of the century if the present trend continues. In a world thus structured, the growing spirit of hatred cannot guarantee either the conditions of peace or of spiritual growth.

"And in the countries that are both developed and egoistic (including Christian countries), the scandal of such hypocrisy that is so oblivious to the aspirations of other people will take on unimagined proportions . . . The underdeveloped world is in reaction against the richer nations less as a result of their misery than from the fact that they are not loved. The world awaits a manifestation of authentic and intelligent charity." Father Lebret states the problem facing us today with a clarity that I have not found surpassed anywhere.

The bishops of the United States at their 1959 annual meeting issued a statement, "Peace with Freedom." We quote: "Ultimately the problem of Communism as a threat to peace and freedom will be met only when we exemplify the principles that we proclaim as Christian members of a nation dedicated to God's law . . . Instead of proclaiming freedom under God as we did in a more robust time in our history, we have emphasized the material fruits of our freedom, we have so praised a program of supplying machines and calories and pleasure that these fruits of freedom and peace are made its substitutes. Today throughout the world, too often it is thought that when we speak of the American way of life we are speaking only of a high standard of living.

"We have often acted in our international relations as if the products of industry and methods of production were our only contribution to the welfare of our neighbors. We have given them the impression that material progress is our sovereign if not our exclusive concern. In particular, we have fostered industrialism and education as the ends and not the means of elevating nations. In so far as we have done this, we have tacitly accepted the materialist philosophy of Communism as our way of life. We have aimed our efforts at satisfying the body, and, paradoxically, have allowed the Communists to capture the minds of men. We must convince the world that . . . our motive in gladly pouring out our resources is not simply as a natural pity for the misery of our fellow man or as a damper to conflict, but recognition of his dignity as an equal son of God endowed with freedom."

Bishop Fulton Sheen, in *Communism and the Conscience of the West* (Bobbs-Merrill, 1948), has shown how Communist materialism is a natural result of our own materialism. Indeed, it is the people who feel exploited turning our own weapons of exploitation against us in self-defense.

B. Grave Situation in Latin America

Perhaps nowhere in the world is the situation as described by Father Lebret more clearly illustrated in all its aspects than in Latin America. Father Roger Vekemans, S.J., of the Bellarmine Center in Chile, writes in *Ave Maria,* "Social conditions in Latin America are the worst in the world." He declares that the greatest threat, far more serious than Protestantism, comes from a weak, uninstructed Catholicism confronted with modern technology. The population, which in 1930 was 100 millions, is now double that and will double again to 400 millions by the year 2000. The most urgent need is more food, but there are two obstacles, unjust distribution of the land

and its wrong use in a basically agricultural economy. Half of all Latin American farm land is in *latifundios* of over 15,000 acres where the owners grow "cash crops" such as coffee and sugar rather than staple foods. The situation cannot be met by industrialization alone because the predominantly farm population lacks the purchasing power to support much industry.

A recent study by the Inter-American Secretariat of Catholic Action states, "There is not a single country that does not suffer the consequences of hunger." The report estimates that there are 30 million farm families in Latin America, constituting 75 per cent of the population, but 80 per cent of them are "agricultural proletarians" without land who work on the *latifundios* and have an income that rarely rises above the bare subsistence level. In the United States, by contrast, only a little more than 10 per cent of the people are farmers, yet they consistently produce far more than enough food for the whole population. Unfortunately, the cost of shipping and distribution would make it impracticable to share the surplus with Latin America. The needs of a country in staple foods should be met by increased production where the people are. In Bolivia and Ecuador the land has been largely redistributed, but the new farmers are slow to produce more than for the needs of their own families.

In the days of Spanish and Portuguese colonialism huge land grants were made to families from Europe which developed into the typical "plantation economy" of Latin America with two classes of people, the "patron" or owner and the "peons" or slaves. In Brazil, which has almost half the Latin American population, less than 1 per cent of the families control 60 per cent of the arable land. Of this 60 per cent they cultivate only 4 per cent because they get along very well with the profits from that. In Colombia, only 5 farm workers out of 1000 own land! In Guatemala, about 2 per cent of the people own more than 70 per cent of the land and produce mostly crops for export, such as coffee and bananas, rather than food for the people. In Chile, the rich lands of the plain between the Andes and the Pacific belong to a few families and are planted mostly to vineyards, while much of the wheat for bread, staple food of the people, must be imported.

Living conditions in 80 per cent of the rural homes are, states the study, "inhuman," and the animals on the estates are often better housed than the workers. In some areas, a man's wealth is counted less by his land acreage than by the number of peons he has, who are kept enslaved by debt. For these workers there is no other alternative so that they have a saying, "A man without a patron has not even a place to die." The pressure of population increase drives many into the rapidly growing cities, where their only refuge is the mushrooming slums, 'shantytowns' without streets, lacking light, water and sewers. In the past ten years a million people have moved from rural areas to Buenos Aires, 400 thousand to Santiago, Chile, and proportionate numbers to Lima and Caracas and to the great cities of Brazil. Sao Paulo in Brazil is the fastest growing city in the world. In Caracas I was told that 65 per cent of the people live in slums. "The districts," observes the study, "are the destroyers of family values and human dignity, as they are equally destroyers of social organization and community living. They become centers of vice, agitation and violence. The political stability of the continent is thus endangered." The industrial development planned for the next 15 years can absorb less than half the new workers that will be seeking jobs.

The Y.C.W. in one country of South America some years ago made a survey of conditions among young workers in the cities. Each year nearly 400,000 children of 14 years and under start to work. Here are some typical reports: In a fish-canning factory, juveniles worked with their hands in salt and their fingers were completely raw. The excuse of the manager was "They are used to it." In a footwear factory, young girls take along not only food but their dolls to play with during the lunch hour. In a fireworks factory explosion two girls were killed and all the 28 youngsters (mostly girls) injured and their faces burned. None received compensation, though the factory was at once rebuilt. In many cities, juvenile bus collectors work 13 hours a day. One company has 10 buses and 20 collectors, the ones that come first get work. Some arrive at 2 a.m. and sleep in the buses. A young girl became ill and went to the factory doctor who said there was no point in giving her a prescription because she could not buy the medicines. Antonio leaves for work at 3:30 a.m. and arrives back home at 11 p.m. He has been doing this for 10 years. Great numbers of workers spend six hours daily going back and forth to work.

What of the future, the next 5, 10 or 20 years that most agree will decide the fate of Latin America? These countries will not be saved by our urging them to set up democratic governments because they simply lack the bases for such in our sense. In the West the experience of democratic responsibility has been slowly growing over a long period, from the time of the Magna Charta in 1215 which listed the rights of the common people. We have only to look at the history of Spain and Portugal to see that the lands settled by them would have rather a tradition of the divine rights of kings and governments. Father Vekemanns and other Catholic social thinkers in Latin America say that the beginnings of democracy there must be made with organizations of the common people like labor unions and cooperatives that would have well-defined roles in the socio-economic pattern as a means of adult education in the democratic processes. Farmers' cooperatives would help slow the great migration to the cities. These organizations, while temporal in character must be Christian and democratic in inspiration, for there is no alternative between Christianity and Marxism. It is a mistake of the West's, say these men, to offer Latin America as models certain types of associations which, good as they are, have a neutral outlook in what is not simply a struggle to banish destitution but an ideological battle for men's minds.

Many times during my stay in Latin America I was told by foreign observers, even those not Catholics, that the Church is becoming the strongest social democratic force among the people. Though older bishops had tended to favor the "right," already in the 1930's Catholic thinkers were beginning to analyze the situation and warn of the coming crisis that might leave the Church little place in the future Latin America. By 1945 the warning was having its effect, and some bishops were calling for a change in position. Today the Church in most of Latin America is in favor of basic socio-economic change as a necessary prelude and concomitant of religious revival. Concrete action in this sense is daily more evident. The bishops of the Dominican Republic were hounded by dictator Trujillo for issuing a joint pastoral on human rights. In Chile, the foundations of a social program have been laid, Christian labor unions and rural syndicates formed. The Cardinal of Santiago, by his pronouncements, his cooperatives and division of Church lands has become a symbol in all Chile that the Church stands with the people. In Brazil, Catholic priests have been denounced by landowners as Communists because they preached land reform.

Careful note must be taken, however, that this movement of the Church away from its traditional alliance with the upper classes is to an identification with the masses, not with the middle class as in the U.S. and in other countries. This difference and its reasons must be taken into account in all our thinking about Latin America. The middle class in most of Latin America does not exceed 5-10 per cent, so that it would be very difficult to establish stable middle-class democracy in the western sense. One man told me, "The political power here will be in the hands of the numerically far superior masses from the moment they discover their strength. To avoid the danger of mob rule on the Peron model we must aim to develop a large and stable "lower middle class" of small farmers united in cooperatives and organizations of workers who have a share in the enterprise where they are employed. Social planning would not be entirely in the hands of only a few people at the government level. The findings and recommendations of government experts would be reviewed by the people's organizations in whatever concerns the common welfare, so as to establish broad democratic bases for a program to benefit all."

The people's involvement would result in a mobilization not only of vast human resources but also of much unsuspected wealth. As an example, economists had deplored unanimously the social and economic situation of the Inca Indian descendants living in Peru around Lake Titicaca at an altitude of 12-15 thousand feet. In 1955, Father Daniel McLellan of Maryknoll began a credit union here with 23 members and deposits equal to U.S. $24, just about what the experts expected. Then suddenly the "hidden" wealth began to appear. Within six years there were 4000 members, of which 80 per cent were Indians, and the deposits averaged U.S. $90 per family. Peru, which is 60 per cent Indian speaking, now has over 200 credit unions. In the mountains from Mexico and Guatemala to Peru, Bolivia, Paraguay and Chile, live some 6,000,000 Indian families. If each brought out an equivalent amount of this unused wealth, it would total $540 million! Put into credit unions, it would establish a "credit standing" by which up to three times more could be borrowed from foreign sources at 6 per cent interest and loaned to the credit union members at 1 per cent a month for community development. Certainly, the hidden wealth of Latin America's 40 million families, including jewelry, must reach a considerable amount. A continuing source of credit union funds is the income that passes through the people's hands each year, say U.S. $100 per family. Given an incentive, perhaps 5 per cent could be deposited in the credit unions for a total of $200 million annually! The chief problems are mutual confidence and social organization.

In *World Justice* (Louvain, September, 1963), Ramon V. Carrasco points out that parallel with the people's organizations there must be certain public or semi-public ones to provide them with the technical, administrative, financial, social and educational assistance they need. Otherwise the popular movements themselves cannot develop and fulfill their functions, or will even fail, resulting in a frustration which can only play into the hands of the Communists. He gives examples that show the importance of such assistance. For instance, the agricultural cooperatives of Haiti needed deep wells against long months of drought, but required help in trained personnel and to finance the cost of drilling. In Chile, home-building co-ops have been very successful over the last ten years, due to services furnished by the Chile Chamber of Building and the Catholic Caritas Housing Institute. The *Centros de Madre* in Santiago have a flourishing clothing producers' cooperative because of help given them in administration, while a tailors' cooperative in Caracas failed utterly for lack of business management. To set up such supporting organizations for the people's movements would be an excellent work for groups of educated Catholics.

C. Giving Ammunition to the Enemy

A young priest of Uraguay who had studied in the United States wrote me recently. He had taken back with him a number of books in English. One day a teenager caught sight of them in his bookcase and spat out: "Yankee imperialism." The priest told me that newsreels showing North American scenes are often hissed or booed. I had read, of course, how Vice-president Nixon was attacked in Caracas and threatened in Lima, but put it down to Communist agitators as did most Americans. But my friend in Uruguay assured me that the feeling goes deeper and is very widespread. The people are becoming more and more aware of how much their economy depends on the prices we pay for the wool, copper, sugar, coffee, bananas, cocoa, Brazil nuts produced by Latin America. During the last 20 years, coffee prices to the producer have gone from a high of 80 cents per pound to a low of 39 cents, and in the period 1955-1959 alone the purchasing power of Latin Americans is said to have fallen 20 per cent. The Latin American economy thus loses in some years many times the amount received from us in aid!

Economic experts confirm the findings of Father Lebret which we have quoted, saying that we are now in a 50-year period of inordinate profits by industrial nations which have the financial power to dominate the markets of the world. They say that the only solution would be an international profit-sharing agreement, such as some advanced countries now have within national boundaries. An alternative would be for an International Bank or World Trade Body to take the necessary action. The present very unfavorable position of the underdeveloped countries in the world market provides ammunition for the Communists to attack us as economic imperialists.

More light is thrown on the anti-Yankee feeling in Latin America by an article in *Sign* magazine (January, 1964), entitled, "The Ugly American Is a Catholic, Too." The author, David Finley, states that most Latin American countries have many North American plantation owners totalling some "three thousand American overlords." One of them, a well-dressed, middle-aged American Catholic, showed Mr. Finley his hacienda and coffee plantation. "Look! I employ five hundred Indians here. They are completely dependent on me for everything. I feed them all the beans they need and I lend them space on which to build a shack. Why should I want to educate them? It would just mean trouble. Once they learn to read, they'll want more money and land. They'll be ungrateful for all I've given them in the past twenty-five years." Another burst out indignantly, "Don't any of you newcomers with your left-wing ideas try to tell us how to handle the natives. We know what to do when they step out of line: whip them to the ground." Mr. Finley saw another Catholic one Sunday after Mass fire his foreman because he had accepted a labor union's invitation to speak to their social club. What excellent ammunition these Americans, even Catholics, are giving the Communists!

In *Christ to the World* (1960, No. 3), Father Leo-Paul Bourassa describes the concentrated mass campaign launched in Latin America by the 21st General Congress of the Communist Party at its Moscow meeting in late 1959 and early 1960. The Congress gave the local communist parties precise orders to join with other parties in opposition to the government in power and to focus all efforts on "the struggle against North American imperialism." They were instructed to enroll in this "fight for liberation," workers in the towns and in rural areas, the lower middle classes, intellectuals and university students, as well as those already communist sympathizers. The basic appeal would be to touch national sensibilities, showing that the miserable social conditions were due to nothing but the economic and political hold of the "Colossus of the North." They should blame the *Yanquis* for the fall in price of export commodities.

A very concrete plan of campaign was laid down: 1) To demand "agricultural reform," but concentrating on North American owned or rented coffee plantations, fruit orchards, forest concessions, without touching the locally owned estates. 2) To demand the nationalization of big foreign industries, especially North American mining and petroleum companies. 3) To get control of the trade unions, especially of ports, railways and other means of communication so as to be able to overthrow or intimidate governments by demonstrations, disorders, strikes. Thousands of young Latin Americans are sent every year to Moscow for training as propagandists. A special school in Budapest trains workers to capture the labor unions as instruments of political, even military power, as happened in Cuba. At the convention of the Cuba Confederation of Labor in November, 1959, the Communists allowed non-communist officers to be chosen. Then when the delegates relaxed and began to leave they pushed through a resolution authorizing a workers' militia. Castro armed them and provided officers for training. Then within two months most of the non-communist officers of the Federation were purged. The Sugar Workers alone counted 55,000 armed men and it was chiefly the workers' militia that was credited with defeating the free forces at the Bay of Pigs.

Mr. Gary MacEoin summarizes in the *Sign* (May, 1961), today's situation: "Urgency is added by the new awareness that people live better elsewhere. This does not result from living in full view of wealth. The extremes were always visible in Latin America. Rather it is the fruit of modern communication and propaganda. At least in a vague and often distorted way, it is now a part of the dream in each man's heart, even the most remote and uninstructed. Urgency further stems from the catalytic effect of Fidel Castro. I think this is a fact of history. No matter what may be his fate, no matter how much further his reputation may decline among Latin Americans, he has sounded the knell of the old order. Change must come quickly in the power structure. If it does not come by evolution, it will surely come by revolution."

What can be done to help the Latin American make come true the dream in his heart of a more human life? In a town of perhaps 6,000 people deep in the interior of Northeast Brazil I met a young man from Boston who was teaching English in a Catholic high school. "Sometimes," he said, "I wonder if it is worth while, so many of our graduates become Communists. The average man of the community, if he thinks about it at all, pities them that they have no work, no future. But the Communist says to them, 'You have nothing to do? Come, let us study how to solve the problem and you can go tell others.' As an individual I can be friendly and generous, but they simply say, 'You are different!' It does little to solve the real problem."

D. Our Brother Calls to Us

Dr. Tom Dooley wrote in *World Campus* (February, 1960), "Get beyond your campus and your continent. Listen to the voices calling you from all around the world . . . Listen to the voices of Asia; to the voices of Africa. Listen to the voices of new nations, old nations. Look at the civilizations that have been torn apart. Look at the shattering new ideas that have come into your life and into my life. Look at the destinies that you and I have got to control, to handle and to mould. Expose yourself to these ideas, and never forget that most of the world, through ignorance, hate you. Know why they hate you. Understand this hate; do not fear it. Realize that it can best be fought by the weapons of love. You are fortunate if you invest some of your humanity to take care of the least of His. Aim for this. Decide early in your training that you want to do this for a part of your life. It is not enough to blather and bleat about the brotherhood of man, but we must go out and act upon our belief. We must give action to our words." A year later Dr. Dooley was dead of cancer.

Almost daily we read in the news about the thousands of communist "technicians" who go to the underdeveloped countries of the world. They are laymen, every one. From the United States scarcely a hundred Catholic laymen a year go to serve their brothers abroad, and many of these simply replace others, so that the expansion of their work is very slow. Latin America alone needs ten thousand a year for the next ten years. They should be supported by their home parishes and other sending groups. The Holy Father's asking the United States for 10 per cent of its apostolic force, priests, religious and laymen, is no exaggeration. Only truly massive help can save the situation. The challenge is to mount a Christian revolution against the Communist one that is already well advanced. One of the first acts of Pope Paul VI in his pontificate was to issue a solemn warning not to delay taking the necessary steps even at the cost of much sacrifice. The hour is already late, how close to midnight, to the zero-hour of explosion, no one knows. The spiritual stake defies the imagination, one-third the Catholics of the whole world, and nothing less than a real mobilization of the other two-thirds can suffice. Politically, our own national existence is in danger. We can prevent the mounting of hostile missiles on a relatively small island like Cuba, but it would be impossible to do that on the South American mainland.

The lay missionary vocation covers all the areas of service by which we express concern for our brother, such as doctors, teachers, experts in every field. The primary need, however, is to help him make his dream of a good life come true, to give him a clearer vision of it and show him how to make it work. If the lay missionary can help the emerging peoples tap their vast undeveloped human resources, then they themselves can build a new world. Clearly, we cannot build it for them; we must always put them in the forefront. Lay missionaries should live some distance away from the church to make it easier for them to enter into the life of the people. Each group should assure the continuity of its work, perhaps by having only one member of a team changed in any one year. The ideal would be something like a Secular Institute that would provide a permanent nucleus of persons dedicated to the work. The formation of local people to undertake their religious and social responsibility can hardly be assured by those whose term of service is scarcely long enough to acquire a reasonable knowledge of the language and of the people.

Some of the social problems facing the lay missionary in Latin America have already been discussed. For an example of the religious problem we quote from an article, "The Laity in the Church Today," by Father John P. Considine, M.M., in *Apostolic Perspectives* (March-April, 1960). In the summer of

1957, Bishop Santos of Valdivia in southern Chile sent a team of fourteen university students from Santiago into a cluster of industrial towns in his diocese that for two generations had been practically without the services of a priest. In a sampling of 500 families, abortion was favored by 60 per cent of the men queried and disapproved by 40 per cent. The dominant concept of the family among the workers was of the wife as a sort of servant to her husband. She seldom ate with the husband or went out with him. In a good number of cases, the union was entered into only for practical reasons and with no love element evident. Some instances of family religious guidance were noted such as the teaching of prayers, but the great majority remained indifferent on the subject.

As to religious beliefs, 75 per cent believed in God, 17 per cent had a formed belief in God the Father; 74 per cent recognized our Lord as true God and true Man. On baptism: 94 per cent baptized; their children baptized, 85 per cent. Mass attendance: never, 49 per cent; funerals only, 18 per cent; certain feasts, 30 per cent; regularly when possible, 6 per cent. On the Catholic priesthood: in one or other way opposed or critical towards priests, 77 per cent; favorable and understanding towards the priesthood, 23 per cent. One member of the team reported: "For the present-day worker the Church is its priests. The worker has no inclination to participate in this organization which he regards as being managed completely by people alien to his milieu, managed by the rich." Another stated: "The Church and those who represent it, the hierarchy and the priests, are completely absent from working circles. The workers assume no position of open hostility towards the Church, but, far more serious, rather one of omitting it completely from any practical considerations."

The social and religious situations in Latin America indicate quite clearly the main lines along which lay missionaries should work. 1) Make themselves really "present" among the people, accepting them as persons beloved of God without the least note of criticism or condemnation. 2) Explain the social as well as spiritual dignity for which God created them. When speaking of religion we must speak also of the social justice and social equity that God wishes for all and speaking of social justice we must also speak of its source in God. 3) Set up on-the-job formation programs for lay apostles, volunteer catechizers, neighborhood leaders, based on what are man's two fundamental interests of religion and family even if imperfectly lived. 4) Organize social guilds for training Catholics and sympathetic non-Catholics through discussion of concrete questions to make them devoted and capable leaders in social, economic, labor, educational and government fields. To arouse the widest interest, these four lines should be followed concurrently. Use the Gospels to provide motivation in social charity. To get people showing responsibility towards others in the lay apostolate from religious motives is the best foundation on which to build a leader training program. It is the best preparation for honest zeal in credit unions, cooperatives and other forms of community development. The fact that the majority of even the neglected Catholics are baptized, believe in God and in our Lord is a natural opening for discovering with them the true brotherhood of the Gospels.

The lay missionary should first acquire in his homeland a formation in the apostolate and a working knowledge of the language he will use. He should learn how to activate people as cell leaders while himself remaining in the background, how to apply the principle of multiplied contacts by apostles so as to reach the maximum number of people. He needs experience in home meetings, the discussion method of teaching, the on-the-job plan for training volunteer teachers and action leaders. He should acquire some basic notions of cultural sociology and of economics, from field work as well as books, based on the theme of God's socio-religious plan for mankind. From study of his own culture he becomes better able to observe another culture. He would participate in Gospel discussions with the aim "to find concrete answers for concrete human problems," and should become familiar with the New Testament in the language he will use. Formation after reaching the field would be particularly in "area studies": the history, geography and culture, the economic, social and religious conditions of the area. Such preparation will enable him to identify himself with the people.

The candidate for lay missionary work should also make a Cursillo and learn all he can about the movement. I have seen nothing so well able to rouse people out of spiritual and social lethargy to become truly zealous for Christ. One exceedingly critical aspect of the Latin American situation is that the Church is already almost entirely crowded out of the institutions for social formation, such as the government schools. Of 30,000 school teachers in Peru, for example, 4000 are Communist Party members. A large proportion of the teachers are women, and it is therefore very important to have women's Cursillos. They are needed also for office workers and career women, as well as the wives of men Cursillistas. If Peru had enough Cursillos centers for 5 per cent of the teachers each year to make a Cursillo, along with a proportionate number of people from labor, business, the professions, farmers, not only the critical areas of education and labor but the whole social pattern would begin to change within five years. The Cursillistas would form cells to penetrate all walks of life. The teachers would give religious instruction in all schools! If priest and lay volunteers would concentrate on this work and on the formation of national priests as Cursillistas guides, their two or three years there would mean leaving behind them apostles really able to renew the Church.

The lay missionary apostolate in a diocese or region should profit from the help of experts in various social and economic fields. For example, the drought-ridden northeastern Brazil, with one-third the country's population in one-sixth its area, raises sugar cane on the better watered land and has not enough food for its people. By better land use methods, the same amount of cane could be grown on half the acreage and an adequate food supply on the other half. One of the chief elements in malnutrition among the underdeveloped peoples is protein deficiency, yet they all produce large quantities of oil-bearing seeds which have a high protein content (peanuts, soybeans, coconuts, cottonseed, Brazil nuts). At present the 50 per cent protein residue left after extracting the oil for cooking is fed to animals instead of being prepared for human use. An agency which puts free expert advice in community development at the service of the missions by mail is DATA International, 437 California Avenue, Palo Alto, California.

Lay missionaries must be above all life-bearers, not simply spiritual parents but grandparents, forming the people of the place to themselves communicate life. This is particularly important when the missionary, priest or layman, works in a land not his own, is not a product of the country and the race. In Mexico City, for example, a missionary inspired a family of the Mexican Christian Family Movement to spend one year in a miserable jungle area. They set up a Credit Union, two CFM groups, small home industries, several volunteer catechetical centers, Cursillos and Jornados (apostolic days for adults and youth), trained several men as leaders at Mass. The work is guaranteed continuity by the CFM, which sends and supports a family in that area. In fact, the 9000 Mexican CFM families now support 6 full-time lay apostles in various parts of Mexico. This is in addition to 15 volunteer "Ecclesial Teams" of nearly 300 persons (doctors, nurses, social workers, engineers, parents, children, priests and religious), who go out to conduct the Christmas and Easter liturgy in neglected villages. Only the missionary who makes his adopted people themselves actively missionary is really establishing or restoring the Church.